AGE OF CONCRETE

NEW AFRICAN HISTORIES

SERIES EDITORS: JEAN ALLMAN, ALLEN ISAACMAN,
AND DEREK R. PETERSON

David William Cohen and E. S. Atieno Odhiambo, *The Risks of Knowledge*

Belinda Bozzoli, *Theatres of Struggle and the End of Apartheid*

Gary Kynoch, *We Are Fighting the World*

Stephanie Newell, *The Forger's Tale*

Jacob A. Tropp, *Natures of Colonial Change*

Jan Bender Shetler, *Imagining Serengeti*

Cheikh Anta Babou, *Fighting the Greater Jihad*

Marc Epprecht, *Heterosexual Africa?*

Marissa J. Moorman, *Intonations*

Karen E. Flint, *Healing Traditions*

Derek R. Peterson and Giacomo Macola, editors, *Recasting the Past*

Moses E. Ochonu, *Colonial Meltdown*

Emily S. Burrill, Richard L. Roberts, and Elizabeth Thornberry, editors, *Domestic Violence and the Law in Colonial and Postcolonial Africa*

Daniel R. Magaziner, *The Law and the Prophets*

Emily Lynn Osborn, *Our New Husbands Are Here*

Robert Trent Vinson, *The Americans Are Coming!*

James R. Brennan, *Taifa*

Benjamin N. Lawrance and Richard L. Roberts, editors, *Trafficking in Slavery's Wake*

David M. Gordon, *Invisible Agents*

Allen F. Isaacman and Barbara S. Isaacman, *Dams, Displacement, and the Delusion of Development*

Stephanie Newell, *The Power to Name*

Gibril R. Cole, *The Krio of West Africa*

Matthew M. Heaton, *Black Skin, White Coats*

Meredith Terretta, *Nation of Outlaws, State of Violence*

Paolo Israel, *In Step with the Times*

Michelle R. Moyd, *Violent Intermediaries*

Abosede A. George, *Making Modern Girls*

Alicia C. Decker, *In Idi Amin's Shadow*

Rachel Jean-Baptiste, *Conjugal Rights*

Shobana Shankar, *Who Shall Enter Paradise?*

Emily S. Burrill, *States of Marriage*

Todd Cleveland, *Diamonds in the Rough*

Carina E. Ray, *Crossing the Color Line*

Sarah Van Beurden, *Authentically African*

Giacomo Macola, *The Gun in Central Africa*

Lynn Schler, *Nation on Board*

Julie MacArthur, *Cartography and the Political Imagination*

Abou B. Bamba, *African Miracle, African Mirage*

Daniel Magaziner, *The Art of Life in South Africa*

Paul Ocobock, *An Uncertain Age*

Keren Weitzberg, *We Do Not Have Borders*

Nuno Domingos, *Football and Colonialism*

Jeffrey S. Ahlman, *Living with Nkrumahism*

Bianca Murillo, *Market Encounters*

Laura Fair, *Reel Pleasures*

Thomas F. McDow, *Buying Time*

Jon Soske, *Internal Frontiers*

Elizabeth W. Giorgis, *Modernist Art in Ethiopia*

Matthew V. Bender, *Water Brings No Harm*

David Morton, *Age of Concrete*

Marissa J. Moorman, *Powerful Frequencies*

DAVID MORTON

AGE OF CONCRETE

HOUSING

AND THE SHAPE

OF ASPIRATION

IN THE CAPITAL OF

MOZAMBIQUE

OHIO UNIVERSITY PRESS   ATHENS

Ohio University Press, Athens, Ohio 45701
ohioswallow.com
© 2019 by Ohio University Press
All rights reserved

To obtain permission to quote, reprint, or otherwise reproduce or distribute
material from Ohio University Press publications, please contact our rights and
permissions department at
(740) 593-1154 or (740) 593-4536 (fax).

Printed in the United States of America
Ohio University Press books are printed on acid-free paper ⊗ ™

29 28 27 26 25 24 23 22 21 20 19   5 4 3 2 1

Library of Congress Cataloging-in-Publication Data
Names: Morton, David, 1975- author.
Title: Age of concrete : housing and the shape of aspiration in the capital
  of Mozambique / David Morton.
Other titles: New African histories series.
Description: Athens, Ohio : Ohio University Press, 2019. | Series: New
  African histories | Includes bibliographical references and index.
Identifiers: LCCN 2019018753| ISBN 9780821423677 (hbk : alk. paper) | ISBN
  9780821423684 (pbk : alk. paper) | ISBN 9780821446751 (pdf)
Subjects: LCSH: Housing--Mozambique--Maputo--History. | Maputo
  (Mozambique)--Economic conditions. | Maputo (Mozambique)--Social
  conditions.
Classification: LCC HD7374.A3 M37 2019 | DDC 363.5096791--dc23
LC record available at https://lccn.loc.gov/2019018753

CONTENTS

ILLUSTRATIONS

ILLUSTRATIONS

x

ACKNOWLEDGMENTS

Even if I were gifted with perfect recall, the following would remain an abridged account of all those who have helped produce this book. A list of the people I interviewed, who generously shared their stories, their personal archives, and their mornings with me, appears at the beginning of the Sources section. If academic conventions were other than what they are, that list would appear right here.

This project would not have been possible without the support of the University of British Columbia's Department of History, the UBC Hampton Fund, the Fundação Calouste Gulbenkian, the Fundação Luso-Americana, the University of Minnesota Office of International Programs, a Mellon Scholar Fellowship administered by the University of Minnesota's Interdisciplinary Center for the Study of Global Change, and a Fulbright Program grant sponsored by the Bureau of Educational and Cultural Affairs of the US Department of State. A predoctoral fellowship at the Carter G. Woodson Institute for African-American and African Studies at the University of Virginia, led by Deborah McDowell, allowed me two years to write an earlier iteration of this book in excellent company.

I have been in excellent company throughout, actually: in Chamanculo and among colleagues at the University of British Columbia, the University of Minnesota, the Center for African Studies at the Universidade Eduardo Mondlane (led by Carlos Arnaldo), and the Centre for Humanities Research at the University of the Western Cape (led by Premesh Lalu). In Mozambique, Padre Humberto Kuijpers of the Igreja de São Joaquim da Munhuana and Bento Sitoe of the Universidade Eduardo Mondlane kindly put me in touch with several of the people I interviewed. In xii

Portugal, Miguel Vaz of the Fundação Luso-Americana and Paulo Batista of the Associação Cultural e Recreativa dos Naturais e Ex-residentes de Moçambique connected me with Portuguese who had lived in Mozambique before and after independence. It was a great pleasure to explore Chamanculo's history with Januário "Hytho" Chitombe, my research assistant for most of this project. I am also grateful to Andrade Filipe Muhale and Gil Chirindza, research assistants in early 2011, for their help in getting the interviewing project off the ground. Manuel Macandza facilitated and took part in conversations I had in 2008 with residents of Hulene B and Xipamanine. Chapane Mutiua and Hélio Maúngue transcribed many of the interviews. Ernesto Dimande and Crisófia Langa translated several interviews from the original Changana and Ronga, as well as several articles from the Ronga-language pages of *O Brado Africano*. Jake Harms and Eusébio Xerinda provided additional research help. Michael Taber compiled the index. Thank you all.

Due to a lack of available information, I unfortunately could not identify the photographers of all the archival images I used in this book, but if I learn more I will provide more complete attributions on the book's Ohio University Press web page.

Alejandra Bronfman, Noëleen Murray, Jeanne Penvenne, Betty Banks, Ben Machava, Colin Darch, Paul Jenkins, and Anne Pitcher offered sharp commentary on some or all of the final manuscript. I have been bouncing my findings off Zachary Kagan Guthrie almost since I started finding them. Jason Cherkis, with his keen storytelling skills, worked hard to help me invigorate the prose, and I also received key editing help from Glenn Dixon, Cody Rocko, and Paul Morton. Cody Rocko put all the images into beautiful shape, revealing many hidden things in the process. The manuscript's anonymous reviewers and the editors and production staff at Ohio University Press, led by Gillian Berchowitz, Nancy Basmajian, and Beth Pratt, have helped make the material sing. Allen Isaacman and Helena Pohlandt-McCormick supervised the thesis that became the book; I am tremendously indebted to them for the guidance they have offered me over the years. It has been my great privilege to explore Mozambique's past with Allen, *il miglior storico*.

Um abraço enorme for Luciana Justiniani Hees, a unique creative talent, for being an important part of many aspects of this project and for helping me understand what I was seeing.

In Vancouver, Álejandra Bronfman, Bill French, Heidi Tworek, John Chistopoulos, Eagle Glassheim, Tina Loo, Michael Lanthier, Nicolas Kenny, Tatiana van Riemsdijk, Brad Miller, and especially Roxanne Panchasi have been vital sources of personal and intellectual support. Nikolai Brandes, Gabriella Carolini, Euclides Gonçalves, Silje Sollien, Katie McKeown, Elliot James, Sian Butcher, Vanessa Díaz, Sílvia Jorge, Vanessa Melo, Emily Witt, Alicia Lazzarini, Marcia Schenck, Todd Cleveland, and Rowan Moore Gerety were some of my fellow researchers in Portugal or southern Africa or both at the time when most of the research for this book was conducted, with all the nourishing mutuality that entails. Nikolai led me to the library and archive at MITADER, site of many treasures. I am very grateful for the help and guidance offered by the staffs of all the archives I worked in, in Mozambique and in Portugal, with special thanks to Joel das Neves Tembe, director of the Arquivo Histórico de Moçambique (AHM), António Sopa (AHM), Maria Isabel de Jesus Mahutsane (CDFF), and Sérgio Mucavele (MITADER).

I also benefited greatly from conversations with or comments from Fernando Arenas, Patricia Lorcin, Maria de Lurdes Torcato, Joaquim Salvador, Marissa Moorman, Todd Cleveland, Claudia Gastrow, Euclides Gonçalves, Décio Muianga, Teresa Cruz e Silva, António Botelho de Melo, Eric Sheppard, Michael Goldman, Rachel Schurman, Karen Brown, Gary Minkley, Chico Carneiro, Nicole Ridgway, Joe Miller, Kathie Sheldon, Patricia Hayes, Ciraj Rassool, Eléusio Filipe, Carlos Fernandes, Ernesto Capello, José Teixeira, Geoffrey Traugh, Tucker Sharon, Cláudia Castelo, Nate Holdren, James Coplin, Aïssatou Mbodj-Pouye, João Sousa Morais, Alan Mabin, Carol d'Essen, Miguel Santiago, José Manuel Fernandes, Clara Mendes, Isabel Raposo, Cristina Henriques, Bento Sitoe, José Luís Cabaço, Tiago Castela, Sandra Roque, Richard Roberts, Samuli Schielke and other participants in the 2013 "Still in Search of Europe?" workshop at the Zentrum Moderner Orient in Berlin, Morten Nielsen, Anna Mazzolini, Flora Botelho, Carla Mirella de Oliveira Cortês, Jonathan Howard, Idalina Baptista, Lucy Earle, Luís Lage, the late António Rita-Ferreira, Manuel G. Mendes de Araújo, Yussuf Adam, Ivo Imparato, Ivan Laranjeira, M. J. Maynes, Ann Waltner, Judith Byfield, Deborah McDowell, Maurice Wallace, Cynthia Hoehler-Fatton, Nicole Burrowes, Celeste Day Moore, Katherine Wiley, Laura Helton, Ellen Tani, La TaSha Levy, Kwame Edwin Otu, Tammy Owens, Ava Purkiss, Taneisha Means, Jon Forney,

Erin Nourse, Zakiyyah Jackson, George Mentore, Ellen Bassett, Adria LaViolette, Louis Nelson, Sheila Crane, and Robert Fatton. Eléusio and I traveled together to Luís Cabral and to Ricatla, Rui Gonçalves gave me an architect's perspective of Maxaquene, and Ana Magaia lent some of her charm and star power to a day of interviews in Chamanculo. Otilia Aquino and Raquel de Aquino Vedor gave me the space (their Akino café) to air ideas. Of course, I am responsible for the directions taken in the book, and I would not want to suggest that the appearance of people's names here means that they would approve of what lies in the pages ahead. I will also point out that Jeanne Penvenne has been extremely helpful in her suggestions over the years, and beyond that, her decades of rich scholarship have given anyone aspiring to write a history of Maputo a strong foundation on which to build.

In Mozambique, South Africa, Portugal, Minnesota, and Sweden, I enjoyed the gracious hospitality and friendship of Juliana Soares Linn, Castigo Guambe, Hawa Guambe, Rosa Maniça, Chico Carneiro, Roberta Pegoraro, Ivan Laranjeira, Amália Mepatia, Juliet Lyon Edwards, Scott Edwards, Nils Mueller, Mindy Hernandez, Lucas Bonanno, Gabriel Borges, Thais Ferreira, Richard Jordan, Katie McKeown, Marcel Du Toit, Robynne Hansmann, Joe Dawson, Luisa Casal, Margarida Casal, James Coplin, Heidi Coplin, and Anita Ullerstam.

And a wink and a smile for Cody Rocko; my aunt and uncle, Trudi and Allen Small; my brother and best friend, Paul; and most of all, my mother and chief strategist, Joan Morton.

AGE OF CONCRETE

Figure I.1 Polana Caniço, 1987. (CDFF)

INTRODUCTION

You, mother!
Transforming the reeds into zinc
and the zinc into stone
in the wearying battle against time

—Calane da Silva, from "Incomplete
Poem to My Mother" (1972)[1]

IN 2010, about two dozen architecture students at Maputo's main university were sent into the *subúrbios* in search of the last of the city's reed houses. There are many ways to describe the low-lying neighborhoods where most residents of Mozambique's capital city live, but any frank depiction must underline the fact that, historically, life in the subúrbios has been conditioned by a lack of basic urban infrastructure. For most of the twentieth century, flooding was frequent, and the absence of sewage and drainage lines left neighborhoods vulnerable to cholera outbreaks. To dispose of trash, people had to bury it in their yards or burn it. Very few residents had ready access to running water or electricity. By the second decade of the twenty-first century, however, Mozambique's nearly double-digit economic growth was changing the picture. The threat of flooding remained, but the water and energy grids were rapidly expanding into suburban households. Many latrines now had concrete septic tanks. Most people were building their houses out of concrete blocks.

A majority of people in the subúrbios once lived in houses built from the reeds that grow beside waterways throughout rural southern Mozambique.

The fences of their yards were usually made of reeds as well. But now, even in the neighborhood called Polana Caniço—*Polana* was a chief's name, *caniço* means "reed" in Portuguese—reed house construction, which had been declining for decades, was very rare. The architecture students went to Polana Caniço to record specimens of the elusive suburban reed house before the use of concrete pushed it to extinction. When they found one, they took its measurements and documented it with photographs and architectural renderings, and they interviewed residents about their experiences building with reeds.[2]

Despite the rustic appearance of the suburban reed house—some might call it a shack—its construction is actually highly standardized.[3] Reeds, wood stays, and all the other building materials are purchased at local markets. The basic unit, a low-slung, two-room rectangular structure, is smaller than a one-car garage. The shade of a tree makes the outdoors more comfortable and more sociable than indoors, so daily life—preparing meals, washing clothes, conversing with friends—takes place outside, in the yard. At one end of the yard are a pit latrine and a bathing area, each screened with reeds. As with so many urban housing types, the roof of the reed house is corrugated, galvanized (zinc-coated) iron or steel sheeting. For residents of the subúrbios, the sound of rainfall is a hard, metallic rattle.

To the curious architecture students, the reed houses connected present-day Maputo to a long vernacular building tradition on the city's margins. "We were trying to learn how they were built so we don't lose this knowledge," Maputo architect Rui Gonçalves, who was one of the student researchers, later told me.[4] "How can we learn from what we did here, from our own culture, from our own history?" The part of the neighborhood where their professor sent them was a sandy area adjacent to the bay shore and its polluted but popular beach. Gonçalves and the two other students on his research team spent hours looking for reed houses but had no luck. "We started getting desperate. We asked people, 'Where can we find houses of caniço?' Most people couldn't help us. We walked and we walked, until we got to what you could say was the end of the line: a swamp. We felt let down." But then they decided to walk around the edge of the swamp, and they found an isolated reed house here, another there. Occasionally, there would be two next to each other. The inhabitants of these houses were among the most impoverished people in the subúrbios, living on land where no one else would build. Water lay just below the surface.

When the students asked residents questions, they were happy to answer, but they had trouble finding anything good to say about their houses. Reeds rotted quickly, they said, and the material was expensive to replace. Bare reed walls were no better than a sieve against blustery winds and chilly fog. Living in reeds was almost like dressing in rags. Many residents were already stockpiling concrete blocks. "No one is proud of living in a reed house," said Gonçalves. Residents were bemused that the students thought they possessed anything of value, let alone a house that they themselves thought so little of. It turned out that only a small number of them had built their own houses; most had paid someone else to do the work. Some had recently migrated from parts of Mozambique where houses were built from different materials. In Maputo, local knowledge of reed construction was once nearly universal. Now, only a relative handful of builders were keeping those methods alive—and only because their customers could afford no better.

Well before the architecture students came calling, the reed house had its admirers. In the 1960s and 1970s, Pancho Guedes, the noted Portuguese architect, would circulate in the subúrbios and photograph the colorful patterns painted on the wood doors and window frames that distinguished some reed houses. Other outsiders who ventured into the subúrbios at the time spoke approvingly of reeds as if they were freely available—as free as the reeds used in houses in the countryside—and good for air ventilation. But the subúrbios were not simply villages transposed to the edges of a city. In dense conditions, where one person's bedroom might be a few feet from another's latrine, reeds offered little privacy or protection. Reeds were once so closely identified with the precarious life of the subúrbios that all these neighborhoods were also known, collectively, as "the caniço."

People of greater means in the subúrbios might use reeds for their fences, but not for their houses. Until the 1970s, they built wood-framed houses clad entirely in galvanized metal panels, and some were quite regal, with lots of rooms, a veranda, and a many-gabled roof.[5] Many landlords also built wood-and-zinc compounds, in which tiny units were rented out to the very poor. Wood-and-zinc construction predominated in the oldest parts of the subúrbios so that well into the twentieth century, these districts bore a resemblance to nineteenth-century mining camps. Wood-and-zinc houses stood firmer than reed houses, and the larger models were a mark of status.

Figure I.2 A path in the caniço, late 1970s. (Eva Sävfors)

But this construction method posed its own problems. Termites fed on the wood, and depending on the weather, the house could be unbearably cold or intolerably hot.

On the eve of Mozambique's independence from Portugal in 1975, the subúrbios were home to more than three hundred thousand people, about three-quarters of the population of Lourenço Marques, as Maputo was then called.[6] The remaining quarter lived in the central part of town colloquially called the City of Cement—or simply, "the city"— which was then predominantly European (Figure I.3). In local languages, this area continues to be called Xilunguíne, which means "place of the whites," even though the vast majority of the European population left Mozambique around the time of independence.[7] The apartment blocks and high-rises of the City of Cement are not primarily made of cement, per se, but of concrete. Concrete is the more durable substance that results from mixing cement together with water, sand, and gravel or other crushed stone aggregate and then allowing it to cure.[8] To be even more precise, the City of Cement is mostly of steel-reinforced, concrete-frame construction with blocks of either concrete or clay used as infill. The name City of Cement has by and large fallen out of use for the same reason that the subúrbios are no longer called the caniço. Since masonry architecture, sometimes just referred to as stone, is the norm in the subúrbios, it no longer distinguishes the haves from the have-nots. Most people now have it.

There was nothing inevitable about the hardening of the caniço into stone. The decades-long transformation of tens of thousands of houses from reeds and wood-and-zinc construction into structures of more resilient materials was a drawn-out but often high-stakes drama and not exactly linear. For a long time and from an official standpoint, everything about the subúrbios was supposed to be temporary, including most people. During the colonial era, the vast majority of Africans in Lourenço Marques not living as domestics in the homes of their employers lived in the subúrbios.[9] And until the 1960s, most of them required an official pass for the privilege of living even there. They needed to be formally employed to keep the pass, and many went without one, hoping not to be caught. Few had title to land. Many rented units in cramped compounds. Many others paid a ground rent to a private landowner for a small plot with ill-defined boundaries on which to build. But the rental receipts

7

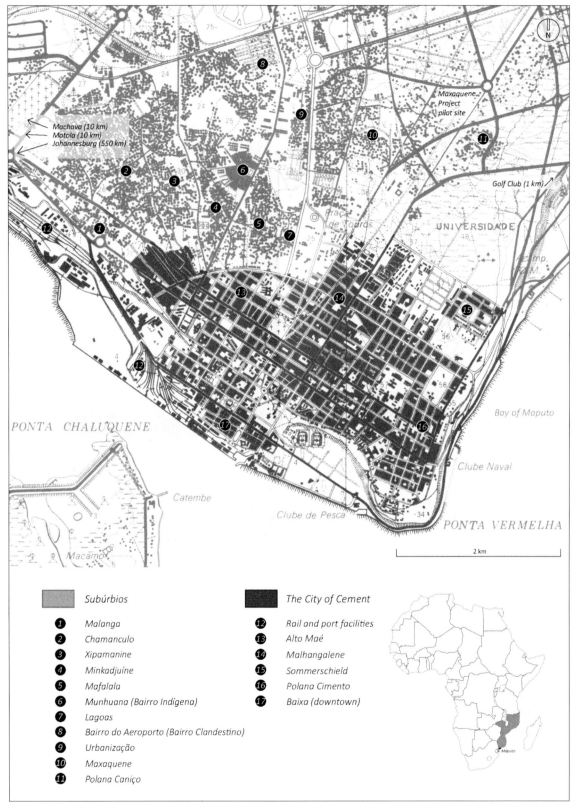

Figure I.3 Maputo in the late 1970s. (Map illustrations by Sarah Baxendale, based on an undated map located at MITADER)

people stored in suitcases under their beds hardly amounted to anything like secure tenure. In the 1960s and early 1970s, land values spiked, and so did the fear of displacement.

Housing in the subúrbios was not quite legal, at least not categorically. It was tolerated. The municipality allowed reed and wood-and-zinc construction, but it prohibited anything that might hinder future upgrading plans. Thus, with few exceptions, one could not build in concrete even if one could afford to. Beginning in the 1960s, though, many more had enough money to build in concrete, and during the last decade or so of Portuguese rule, several thousand people in these neighborhoods, including a number of lower-income whites, overcame their fears of displacement and ventured to build houses (albeit often rudimentary ones) out of some combination of concrete and clay blocks. In doing so, they risked stiff penalties and possible demolition. I will not be the first to point out the importance to people of building lasting homes on tenuous ground.[10] Beyond comfort and beyond status, a permanent house "stakes a claim to belonging" in places that work against it.[11] Masonry construction was a political act—a break with expectations that Africans should be satisfied with perpetual impermanence—though it would be many years before most people in the subúrbios felt they could even consider it. The colonial regime, for its part, grasped the power of concrete in uncertain times. The rising skyline of the City of Cement in the 1960s announced to whomever saw it that, despite the wave of decolonization across Africa, Portugal belonged in Mozambique—or, as Lisbon put it, that Mozambique was part of Portugal.[12]

This book foregrounds what historians usually render as background: neighborhoods of the kind often thought of as undifferentiated, ahistorical slums.[13] Each neighborhood in Maputo and each yard is a specific place with a specific past. Taken together, the countless gambles, disputes, impositions, half measures, achievements, and failures inscribed on the landscape constitute an enormous, open-air archive. The book spans the period from the 1940s to the present, but it concentrates on the roughly three decades straddling Mozambique's independence. It offers a different kind of story about decolonization than the ones that are often told. Strikes, rallies, nationalist appeals, boycotts, armed rebellions—these were the conventional signposts on the way to independence during the twilight of colonial rule in Africa. Epic-scale development schemes and efforts to

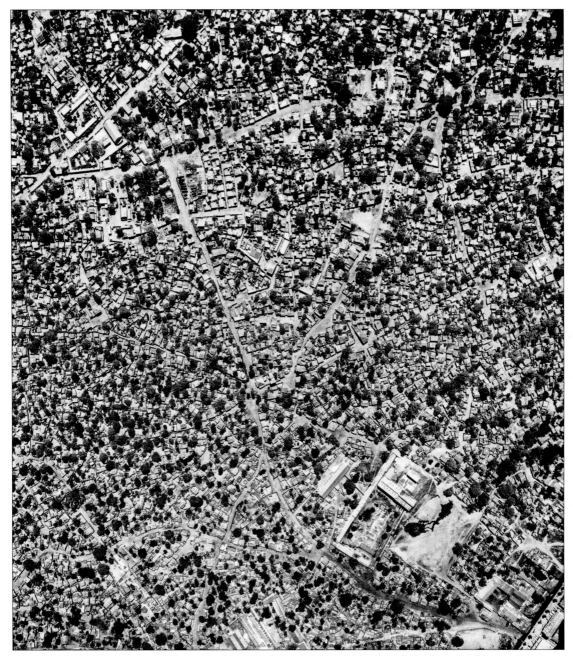

Figure I.4 Chamanculo, one of the oldest neighborhoods in the subúrbios, 1969. (MITADER)

Figure I.5 The City of Cement, 1974. (AHM, c-2-4762)

mold new national identities tend to frame the discussion of how people after independence attempted to uproot colonial-era legacies. And yet, in cities throughout Africa, there were many people who, whether or not they were caught up in politics of a more explicit sort, were engaged in a politics around housing and infrastructure that did not always call itself politics. In this volume, I argue that the house builders and home dwellers of the subúrbios of Mozambique's capital helped give substance to what governance was and what governance should do. This is especially remarkable when we consider the authoritarian nature of rule under the right-wing Portuguese dictatorship and then the Marxist-Leninist dictatorship that eventually succeeded it. At stake was not just a vision of what a "modern" city should be but also a vision of what a modern society was and what it meant to belong to one.[14]

Clandestine masonry home builders were a small, if growing, contingent in late colonial Lourenço Marques, but they were emblematic of a longer struggle to improve living conditions in the subúrbios. Both before and after independence, people attempted to integrate the city's center and periphery, in part by pushing authorities to acknowledge their neighborhoods and to take responsibility for them. Responsibility, in turn, meant "urbanizing" neighborhoods with infrastructure and adjudicating the many disputes that arose there over tenancy. There are dangers in treating the subúrbios only as a pathology—as problems to be solved—as many policy makers have done; we risk turning these places into mere abstractions and dehumanizing the people who live there. But it is also true that, historically, people living in Maputo's subúrbios have recognized the conditions in which they live as a problem. They have sought answers, alternatives to the brute-force solution to so-called slums that governing authorities everywhere have reflexively resorted to: clearance.

This book departs from much of the historical scholarship on the built environment in urban Africa in that it further shifts the emphasis from laws to practices; from the architect's drafting table to the building site; from housing officials and professional planners to landlords, tenants, and home builders; and from government-led projects to places better characterized by official neglect. Yet as a political history, it is not a history from below as that approach is frequently understood. The shape of the city is neither imposed from above nor orchestrated from below.[15] It results from the friction of many interests colliding in tight confines.

Scholars often describe the kinds of ground-level interactions that happen in cities as the politics of the everyday because the jostling among neighbors and the tangled dynamic between individual residents and municipal agencies or state authorities do not fit the typical image of what a political contest looks like. In Maputo, the episodes in which these everyday politics were revealed did not feel ordinary to the people who experienced them. Between 1950 and 1990, the population of the capital grew at least tenfold, and there are many people alive today who, depending on their age, have witnessed the population of Maputo and its satellite city Matola increase between thirty and fifty times over, to almost 3 million people.[16] This kind of dizzying growth rate since the midcentury is not uncommon for African cities, but it is a fact worth emphasizing for readers who have not themselves lived through a similar hyperexpansion from town to metropolis. We can imagine what such growth meant for those hoping to manage it or for those making a home amid what was a fierce competition for space. Into this same span of time, the people of Maputo compressed the experiences of forced labor, independence, and then civil war, as well as the traumatic results of efforts to impose first colonial capitalism, then a socialist command economy, and then the policies of structural adjustment. One way to look at these episodes is to see how they were reflected in the city's built environment. But this approach makes it seem as if changes in the cityscape were a sideshow to the real action. Another approach, the one taken in this work, is to see how the making of the built environment shaped people's expectations and aspirations and how people understood historical change.[17] When older residents of the city speak of the more distant past, they are careful to clarify that the city they are talking about is Lourenço Marques, not Maputo. Although the main reason is to delimit the era of Portuguese rule, another motive for the distinction is that, in memory, the neighborhoods where they grew up were, by comparison to today, *mato*—or "bush." When some were children, trees and other plants still marked off the boundaries of their yards, if they were marked off at all. The thought is astonishing to people as they recall it today, within a landscape of concrete. Without having moved anywhere, they occupy a different place.

THE UNPLANNED

Frantz Fanon described the typical colonial city as divided brutally in two. One part, the "white folks' sector," was "built to last, all stone and steel." The other part, "the 'native' quarters, the shanty town, the Medina, the reservation," was a place "that crouches and cowers, a sector on its knees, a sector that is prostrate."[18] Writing in 1961, he was justifying violent revolution. But historians of the African built environment limit themselves when they address only how cities were split unequally between colonizer and colonized and, relatedly, the role of European administrators and professional architects and planners in doing the dividing.[19] European officials often put great faith in city plans. Some cities were clearly intended as demonstration models of the ruling ideology, with each race in the civilizational hierarchy slotted into its proper place on the urban map. Racial zoning, triumphal boulevards, ostentatious institutional architecture, and housing designed

13

for African workers certainly reveal a lot about what colonial officials and design professionals thought of Europe's place in Africa. But when scholars continually dwell on a relative handful of government officials and functionaries, it is as if everyone else in the city was a passive bystander. A dream in blueprint is assumed to have created the desired reality on the ground. Projects that impressed their designers are assumed to have impressed their African audiences. Segregation is assumed to have been complete. As Laurent Fourchard argues, if we see cities only from the commanding heights, the history of colonial cities, including South Africa's apartheid variant, becomes little more than an uncomplicated tale of the colonizer controlling the colonized. The emphasis on schemes imposed from above, particularly on spatial planning based on race, "omits the agency of African societies, their capacity to overcome such divisions, to ignore them or even to imagine them differently."[20] Home builders in the various "native" quarters of the continent were not, as Fanon put it, prostrate. Lourenço Marques was a starkly segregated city, but it was not *only* segregated.

An important departure from the top-down trend is the work of Garth Myers, who, though concerned with official planning schemes in Zanzibar, also takes care to elaborate how these schemes failed over much of a century because of the continual pushback from Zanzibaris.[21] Planners never appreciated people's deep attachment to long-standing local practices of land tenure and house construction, he argues, with all the meanings for patronage and status these practices conveyed. Myers calls the Zanzibaris' stubborn resistance "speaking with space."[22] In a similar vein, though in a very different context, Anne-Maria Makhulu calls living in the informal settlements on the outskirts of 1970s and 1980s Cape Town "activism by other means."[23] Squatters may not have been openly fighting apartheid as militants from the African National Congress (ANC) were, but they were challenging apartheid's premise that their proper place was in a barren rural Bantustan.[24] James Brennan's work on Dar es Salaam addresses another way that politics was mediated through housing: how fraught landlord-tenant relations fed into anti–South Asian prejudice.[25] These tensions helped give form, after independence, to a racialized idea of who could belong to the new Tanzanian nation. Each of these scholars reveals the overlapping strata of power cutting through urban societies. Each traces continuities between life under regimes of minority rule and under the regimes that followed. And each explores how the making of urban space constitutes a kind of multilateral politics that has not always announced itself as politics—or even in words. These are also some of the animating concerns of this book. My points of emphasis are different because Maputo's history was different—peculiar even, owing to some of the peculiarities of Portuguese rule. Still, in the city's subúrbios, some themes relevant to the histories of many African cities are made more salient.

In African cities, things usually did not go according to plan, but Maputo reminds us that often enough there was no operative plan to begin with—at least not the kind produced by professional urban planners. Once we move past the dispossession and displacement that gave birth to the subúrbios, we find that the suburban landscape is better understood for what authorities did not or could not do there than for the ways authorities imposed themselves. Given this history of official indifference and feck-lessness, why begin with government initiatives, when the initiatives of so many households were on such obvious display? People built their own houses not only as a means of survival but also to realize their highest ambitions. And at key moments during the colonial era and since, many people in the subúrbios, rather than cowering in submission before an oppressive state, actually tried to bring government and sometimes even planners into their lives.

The subúrbios of Lourenço Marques exploded in size in the 1960s, just as unplanned settlement was booming across much of Africa and for similar reasons. Like the regimes of newly independent countries, Lisbon loosened urban influx controls in its African territories, and the appeal of cities was strong, even if in many cases this was less because of what the city offered and more because of what the countryside did not. Scholars of urbanization in Africa continue to puzzle over "informality," a concept intended to grasp all the economic activity outside the gaze of policy makers. As a description of how people in the subúrbios actually lived their lives, the concept helps us very little; in fact, it obscures all the unwritten rules that oriented how neighbors dealt with each other.[26] But the distinction made between the formal and the informal does capture a real and long-standing desire for a connection: not just by governing authorities hoping to intervene where they have yet to do so but also among ordinary people hoping that they will. Governance clearly exists at many scales and in many guises, but here I am referring to the kind that only states and municipalities, with their resources and stamp of universal legitimacy, can provide. People in the subúrbios have often yearned for this kind of governance because there is too much that they cannot do on their own or build on their own. When government is absent, it is a felt absence, not freedom. Residents have felt it when there is no active authority either willing or able to provide drinkable water, illuminate dark streets, or guarantee that people can occupy tomorrow the land they intend to build upon today. National authorities, during the colonial era and since, have felt it when, looking upon the living conditions of most residents of their capital city, they sense the emptiness of their own pretensions to leading a modernizing state. Mozambicans have had more reason than most to flee oppressive state power or to resist it.[27] But much of the urban politics set in and around the capital from the 1960s through the 1980s cannot be easily described as protest or resistance or opposition to state power. Those who would govern and those who would be governed also reached desperately for one another—usually without success.

This book emphasizes episodes in which people called out for intervention, doing what they could to make their neighborhoods visible to authorities who would not see them or who convinced themselves that the subúrbios were, for the time being, beyond help. In the 1960s, one of the only public debates that managed to emerge in Lourenço Marques, despite heavy censorship, involved black residents of the caniço talking about their living conditions to a daily newspaper with a mostly white readership. Shortly afterward, African nurses at the city's central hospital developed their own housing scheme for the subúrbios and put it before the municipality. Secret police were locking up people where there was only a whiff of dissent, and yet during a government survey of conditions at the Munhuana housing project, residents had the courage to openly and harshly criticize housing authorities. (All these episodes are addressed in chapter 2.) Even the clandestine masonry builders of the 1960s (discussed in chapter 3), though certainly eager to escape police attention, were in their own quiet way insisting that they were not temporary sojourners but integrated into city life, participants in what they considered a modernizing world.[28]

Scholars refer to appeals like these, in which people do things or say things that assert a right to be in the city and enjoy the benefits that permanence should entail, as acts of urban citizenship.[29] There is some awkwardness in applying the term to late colonial Lourenço Marques. Most people at that time were dubious that being a Portuguese citizen afforded them much of anything. For that matter, we should be cautious in using the word *state*, as if there were some kind of clearly realized apparatus of functioning institutions to which people could direct their appeals. John Comaroff has said of the typical colonial state that it was "an aspiration, a work-in-progress, an intention, a phantasm-to-be-made-real. Rarely was it ever a fully actualized accomplishment."[30] In some ways, Portuguese authorities in late colonial Mozambique could make themselves felt quite sharply, but in others ways, they were barely there. The same could be said for Mozambique after independence. The Frelimo state was, in many respects, an almost fictive entity needing people to fill it with content and meaning.[31]

In the years under discussion here, the connections between would-be citizen and would-be state were so faint and there was so little mutual understanding of rights and responsibilities that the effort of seeking government action required a great deal of imaginative heavy lifting. After independence, for instance, as people in the subúrbios attempted to give substance to being new citizens of a new state, they did so in part by acting as if the government were intervening in their lives—executing housing policy and urbanizing neighborhoods—even as the attention of authorities was absorbed elsewhere. This notion may seem abstract for now, but the latter part of the book will develop the idea further. Chapter 4 discusses the 1976 nationalizations of the City of Cement, which triggered the spontaneous nationalizations of suburban properties. Chapter 5 explores official urban planning in suburban neighborhoods during the first decade of independence—or, rather, what looked like official planning. During the early years of Frelimo rule, what appeared to be state-led initiatives in the subúrbios were sometimes carried out by people who were simply behaving as if the state were leading them.[32]

Some of this fits the picture of decolonization in its narrower sense—the story of a country becoming politically independent—but all of it was part of the process of decolonization in its broadest sense—how people tried to dismantle structures of inequality, both before and after independence. For residents of Mozambique's capital, the built environment was a medium through which this politics happened because the urban landscape was ever present and unavoidable.[33] The material qualities of buildings, houses, and streets—their tangibility, their visibility, their relative fixedness—made construction a necessarily public act. The book demonstrates this dynamic

17

at every opportunity, beginning in the first chapter with a tour of Lourenço Marques, where the density of urban space brought many different sorts of people so physically close together: Africans from around Mozambique, Europeans and South Asians from different social backgrounds, and authorities and those they attempted to govern. Lourenço Marques was defined not just by its divisions, racial and otherwise, but also by the proximities that persisted despite the divisions. The subúrbios, for example, came right up against the City of Cement. After independence, people who occupied abandoned apartments inhabited one of colonialism's most durable legacies. And the new regime was not just a voice blaring on the radio. The new regime was many people's landlord.

"Concrete tells us what it means to be modern," writes architectural historian Adrian Forty. "It is not just that the lives of people in the twentieth century were transformed by, amongst other things, concrete—as they undeniably were—but that how they saw those changes was, in part, the outcome of the way they were represented in concrete."[34] When historians describe societies they know little about, usually because the societies are ancient or not European, they often resort to terms from material culture. They speak of the Stone Age, the Bronze Age, and the Iron Age, and they often struggle with a very clouded view of the choices their historical actors were capable of making. In researching this book, I had the benefit of greater personal familiarity with many of the people I would write about, and yet I was still struck by just how much a single material shaped their expectations and conditioned their possibilities. As this book intends to make clear, it was and continues to be an Age of Concrete.

CHAMANCULO UP CLOSE

Subúrbios does not carry the same meaning that suburbs does in English. In Maputo, the subúrbios have been understood as places previously beyond the reach of urban infrastructure and still largely wanting. Some might object to defining places by what they lack. But this is one of the ways that many people in Maputo understand where they live, and they call these areas what they were called by the Portuguese officials who drew the municipal boundaries more than a century ago and put the subúrbios on the far side of those boundaries. Each neighborhood, or bairro, has its own name and its own history. Because of the low-lying topography of much of the subúrbios, many neighborhood names reflect a waterlogged past. Before drainage canals were built in the 1980s, flooding and disease outbreaks were more regularly recurring calamities in the area once called Xitala Mali—meaning, in Ronga, "place of the abundant waters."[35] Munhuana means "the salty place" in Ronga, and it is so called because of the marshy land there. Lagoas, in Portuguese, means "lagoons." The neighborhood that features most prominently in this book is Chamanculo, one of the oldest and most populous bairros in Maputo.[36] It means, in Ronga, "place where the great ones bathe." The great ones are the ancestor spirits believed to frequent a creek that once passed through the area. (The creek now only makes an appearance, never a welcome one, during heavy rains.) People have lived in Chamanculo in some numbers as long as there has been a city by the Bay of Maputo. Many of the older men who live in the neighborhood were once employed at the docks and rail facilities down the hill. The railway links Maputo to South Africa's Rand, the economic hub of southern Africa—a connection that initially provided this port city on the Indian Ocean with much of its reason for being.

In 2011, the municipality started paving Chamanculo's central artery, revealing some of the bairro's deeper history to those who were unfamiliar with it. The road, named in the colonial era for a Portuguese physician, had been paved for the first time, hastily, almost a half century before, and by the 1980s, it had crumbled to dust. The new road was to be a more deliberate affair, laid with paving blocks rather than asphalt. Even before it was completed, the road was renamed for Marcelino dos Santos, Mozambique's independence-era vice president, whose mother, over one hundred years old, still lived in a house in nearby Malanga. Because the road had to be widened from its existing footprint, a few feet or so of space had to be carved out of the houses and yards that hemmed it in on either side. As high concrete perimeter walls were peeled away, one gained a better glimpse into the larger yards where successive generations had built houses adjacent to those of their parents and grandparents. In some instances, one could see, in the cross section of a severed house partition, the rough impression left in plaster of old reed walls that had rotted away behind concrete-block walls, a kind of fossil of the not-so-distant past, before masonry construction was the norm. Homeowners affected by the new road had been indemnified for their troubles (though many said what they received was hardly enough), and at least one family's house had to be demolished altogether, its residents resettled on a plot on the distant out-skirts of the city.[37] There was no compensating, however, for the loss of two towering fig trees that were felled to make way for the road improvements. The oldest residents of Chamanculo could not remember a time when the trees were not there. They easily could have been a century old or more, their trunks had twisted together, and they gave permanent shade to what had long been one of Chamanculo's principal crossroads. Residents call the part of the neighborhood in the vicinity of the fallen trees Beira-Mar, after the long-defunct African football club once headquartered nearby. The team's wood-and-zinc clubhouse still functions as a bar, but the adjacent practice grounds disappeared in the 1980s when refugees from the country's civil war were settled there, ostensibly temporarily.

It is testament to the neighborhood's antiquity and to the long legacy of many families there that Ronga, the language indigenous to the Maputo area, is still the mother tongue of a significant number of residents. According to self-described purists, though, many of the younger people in Chamanculo who think they speak Ronga actually speak a blend of Ronga and Changana, a very similar language that, due to continual immigration from rural areas not far to the north, has predominated in the city since at least the 1960s. People who arrived in the neighborhood from the country-side in the 1950s and 1960s are still considered newcomers by residents who trace their local lineage back still further. Within a five-minute walking radius of where the fig trees used to be are some of Maputo's most estab-lished families. Eneas Comiche is a former finance minister, and in 2018 he once again became president of the Maputo City Council (essentially the mayor), a decade after serving his first term in that office. Some years ago, he worked with members of his family to restore the wood-and-zinc house they grew up in, though all that can be seen of it from the street is its handsome double-pitched roof. It was the house where, in late 1960, the family received Janet Mondlane, the American wife of Eduardo Mond-lane, the Mozambican academic who less than two years later assumed the helm of Frelimo, a newly formed movement for independence. The trip was Janet's introduction to her husband's land of birth. She wrote to Eduardo of the Comiche house and what she thought it revealed about their friend Eneas. About eleven people lived in only three rooms, she noted. "But the house is as well-kept and clean as a pin," she wrote. "The children are well-groomed . . . and suddenly I remembered the boy in

Lisbon, well-dressed and elegant in his dark blue suit, studying economics. It was here that they grew up, where there wouldn't be anything without a mother's love and affection."[38]

Ana Laura Cumba, who died in 2012, had lived in a house built by her late father, Frederico de Almeida Cumba, the man who, as the Portuguese-appointed traditional leader (called a *régulo*), was once perhaps the most feared and reviled African man in Chamanculo.[39] As régulo from 1945 until 1974, he made himself relatively wealthy, in part by extracting bribes, and had long before converted a portion of the house from wood and zinc into concrete block. Sometime after his death, Ana Laura rented out much of the house to tenants, keeping one bedroom for herself and another for her traditional healing practice.

Margarida Ferreira, the daughter of one of the régulo's counselors, lost her house when her husband died; her in-laws simply took it from her.[40] But her daughter Graça, who sold clothing, helped her lay the foundations and build partial walls for a new house. Ferreira's sons also helped. Following the fall of the Berlin Wall, they returned from East Germany where, like thousands of other Mozambicans in the 1980s, they had been factory workers.[41] They carried back with them a number of domestic appliances purchased in West Berlin. The appliances were assets. The brothers sold them in Maputo, and the proceeds were used to finish their mother's walls and install a roof.

Castigo Guambe was living in a wood-and-zinc house, palatial by Chamanculo standards, that his father, a hunter, had built in the 1930s.[42] The elder Guambe, who first arrived in Lourenço Marques in the early 1900s, never worked for anyone other than himself, and by the time he died, in the 1960s, he had managed to build a small real estate empire in Chamanculo. About a decade later, shortly after independence, more than two dozen Guambe properties were nationalized by the new Frelimo government, leaving only the original homestead for Castigo and his brother. In the 1990s, Castigo built new rental units and a bar in his yard.

These houses are not mere antiquities. They are not vestiges of a deep past that arrived in the present as the same structures they were when originally built, worn down by the corrosive effects of a process we oversimplify as "time." The houses and the spaces around them bear the marks of decades of historical change. More to the point, the houses *are* the change — or at least they constitute a significant part of the story of what change has meant for the residents of Chamanculo over the past century. Each of the houses I have mentioned is an ongoing project; each has never ceased to be a work in progress for the people who have lived in it. *Self-built* is something of a misnomer, as people have long hired professional carpenters and stonemasons to build their houses. If not self-built in the narrower sense, however, the houses have nonetheless been custom-made to the owners' specifications. For people on meager salaries or those simply making a little here and a little there, the costs of housing have added up over the years to a massive investment of resources, energies, and anxiety. People hope that their houses will serve as their largest bequests to the generations that follow.[43]

Buildings and spaces may seem to "say" a great deal on their own behalf, but they do not, of course, actually speak for themselves. A good deal of this book is based on interviews: with residents of Maputo, including a number of stonemasons and carpenters; with current and former Mozambican officials of various ranks, from neighborhood block leaders to cabinet ministers; with several former Portuguese-era officials, including those now living in Portugal and those who are now Mozambican citizens; and with several foreign architects who were attached to Mozambique's housing and planning agency in the late 1970s and 1980s. Much of the book is based as well on the stories that sons and daughters told me about their mothers and fathers. The interviews were conducted from 2008 to 2016, though they were concentrated during my longest stay in Maputo, from 2011 to 2013. In Chamanculo, I was usually accompanied by one of several research assistants, each of whom was a resident of the neighborhood. They would introduce me to people and translate from the Ronga or Changana on those occasions when Portuguese was not suitable, and they usually were as much a part of the conversation as I or the interviewee was. The interviews were deliberately conversational, wide-ranging, and generally long. I recorded more than 150 conversations, but many of these were with people I kept returning to again and again, and inevitably, many conversations were not recorded at all, including those with the people I stayed with in Chamanculo for several weeks at a time.

The question of housing did not always come up in interviews. In lieu of more substantial historical work on the granular texture of everyday life in Lourenço Marques and Maputo, one must read a number of social-realistic novels, newspaper chronicles, and published memoirs, as I have done my best to do—all part of an effort to grab from the past everything that one can.[44] There is no substitute, in any case, for listening to people talk about the past and how they regard their place in it. To ask them solely about housing would have been to foreground housing perhaps artificially. On several occasions, I video-recorded people giving me a tour of their houses. Digital copies of all interview recordings (both voice and video) and transcripts of the interviews will be deposited with the Arquivo Histórico de Moçambique as well as with the architecture and planning faculty of the Universidade Eduardo Mondlane, both in Maputo.

The interviews were a group enterprise of people convened by an American researcher with his own interests; his own priorities; and his own presumptions about house, home, household, and property—presumptions shaped by his own individual experience of the commodified US real estate industry and the marketing of the American "dream house."[45] I have tried not to impose such idealizations on the struggle for shelter in Maputo, such as by highlighting cases only because they conform to prior expectations of what aspiration looks like. For instance, the reader will not encounter a great deal of discussion about architectural distinction—as might attract the attention of an architectural historian—because architectural distinction is not, historically, what most people have aspired to in the subúrbios of Maputo. Rather, they have sought dignified conformity. Additionally, stories people told of making houses in Maputo often silenced the role of women. Women tended to put forward their husbands as the sole spokespersons for the history of their houses. And in the accounts men gave, they tended to exclude the role of women, often a primary role, in the financing of construction—as the significant participation of single women in the colonial-era rental industry helps to make evident. This is to say nothing of the general silencing of the role of women in the construction process itself, as well as in the ongoing maintenance of a house.

This book is mostly about the relationship of a household to its neighborhood, to the rest of the city, and to a state-in-formation. And though I attempt when possible to reveal the internal dynamics of households—much as the best urban ethnographic work does—this is not my emphasis. As anthropologist Karen Tranberg Hansen writes, the intimate spaces of houses are sites of conflict, and a house that for one member of a household signals a great achievement may be for other members of the household the product of their exploitation or unrewarded sacrifices.[46] Nor was

23

I able to explore as deeply as I had hoped to the living arrangements to which stigma was attached. A number of compounds in the colonial era, for example, were largely inhabited by women who relied on sex work, in whole or in part, for their income—and decades later, women were hesitant to even acknowledge that they once lived in a compound, whether or not they engaged in sex work. Furthermore, that many of the cases discussed in this book involve a married man and woman ought not lead the reader to assume that this was the composition of most households.

The consequences of not fully examining household dynamics for a project that attempts to explore the politics of housing are steep, since such dynamics are ultimately inseparable from such politics. At the same time, although this book argues that the spaces of the city are more than just the background to other dramas, it must be acknowledged that often and, in fact, usually in the course of daily life, they *are* mere background. Moreover, the background for many extends well beyond Maputo. People in the city have long maintained ties to rural homesteads, and many women in Maputo (and not a few men) travel to fields (*machambas*) not far from the city. This fact would be more significant, however, for a work that examines labor and livelihoods, which this book does only minimally. Nor can the book escape the choice of the neighborhood where most research took place. Because Chamanculo is one of the oldest neighborhoods in Maputo, with some of the city's longest-rooted families, its dynamics are quite different from those in neighborhoods to the north of the city, where very few people lived before the 1960s. People in Maputo's oldest neighborhoods have had a markedly different experience of colonial rule and independence than, say, people who arrived in the city as refugees of the civil war in the 1980s. And Chamanculo, where Presbyterians associated with the Swiss Mission had a significant presence, developed somewhat different types of social networks than, for instance, the nearby neighborhood of Mafalala, with its significant Muslim presence.

Though the chapters are organized in rough chronological order, each is thematically distinct, leading to significant chronological overlap. I have tried to avoid forcing a master narrative upon life in Mozambique's capital;

instead, I make use of many smaller narratives, an approach that might be dismissed as storytelling in some quarters. The object here is to reveal the palette of options available to people in history and the invisible frame of constraint—not to establish what the norms and possibilities definitively were (as if this were even doable) but rather to feel for their contours. To relate the histories of individuals with the details of their lives left in is not for the purposes of making dry history more "accessible." The stories are the evidence.

Figure 1.1 The archbishop of Lourenço Marques surveys the Bairro Indígena after a tropical storm, 1966. (Paróquia São Joaquim da Munhuana)

Chapter 1

THE SPACES OF
LOURENÇO MARQUES

IN THE months before and after the arrival of independence in June 1975, many of the people living in Lourenço Marques's City of Cement packed up what belongings they could and left Mozambique for Portugal, South Africa, and Rhodesia. Once-busy avenues were now quiet, and many apartment towers stood nearly empty; they stayed that way until early 1976, when Frelimo nationalized abandoned housing and rental units in cities of cement throughout the country. President Samora Machel announced the new policy on February 3, the first Heroes Day celebrated in independent Mozambique, at a plaza at the edge of the subúrbios. Lourenço Marques had "died" at 9:35 that morning, he declared at the beginning of his speech, and the city had been renamed Maputo.[1] Its City of Cement—or at least most of it—now belonged to the Mozambicans whose labor had been exploited to finance and build it, and the president led his listeners, rhetorically, on a tour of the people's new possession.

He first walked them from the subúrbios up the slope of Alto Maé. This was a neighborhood just inside the City of Cement and home to many people he called the intermediaries of colonialism, by which he meant people of mixed racial backgrounds. Then, he pointed out how, as one got closer to the city's poshest neighborhoods, they got progressively whiter. If one headed in a different direction from Alto Maé, one encountered the blocks where Indians lived, where Pakistanis lived, and where the small Chinese community lived. Even absent much of its preindependence European population, Maputo remained Lourenço Marques in its bones. "It is a form of apartheid," Machel said, "like in South Africa." He elaborated: "We have to face the reality of our country. It was colonialism that created all of this . . . our lives reflect at the present moment the structures of colonialism."[2]

Many in the crowd knew the route well. Each morning, they trudged up to the City of Cement for work, and each evening, they went back down the slope to home, to the cantina, or to prayer. Young Naftal, the protagonist of Lília Momplé's short story "Caniço," written in the 1980s about Lourenço Marques in the 1940s, rushes up the slope from the caniço to work as a domestic servant in a Portuguese household.[3] Momplé, who once was a social worker in the subúrbios, portrays Naftal's neighborhood as a place of garbage heaps, swarming flies, and children whose faces are swollen from malnutrition. On his walk to town, houses of reeds give way to the modest wood-and-zinc houses of Indians and *mestiços* (people of mixed race), with some concrete-block houses mixed in. Farther on, the wood-and-zinc houses thin out, and the streetscape is all concrete and greenery where "the pleasant scent of the gardens and acacia trees in flower replaces the stink of misery."[4] The passage through the city strikes Naftal as a forward progress through time. He gloomily reflects that the caniço is sinking further into the past.

During the independence era, it was tempting to characterize Lourenço Marques as an apartheid city, as Machel did. The colonial regime, a Mozambique-based Portuguese architect told a reporter in late 1974, sought to "maintain the population divided by economic 'apartheid,'" but it had gone about it with more cunning than the regime in South Africa had; the Portuguese had been "less overt and thus less scandalous."[5] All urban policy, the architect continued, had been geared toward housing a "colonial bourgeoisie" in the towers of the City of Cement and keeping everyone else in the caniço, "where in deplorable living conditions the great mass of workers is heaped." Comparing the Mozambican capital to South African cities targeted what had been a mainstay of Portuguese propaganda. For decades, Portugal insisted that its laws were color-blind. In the 1950s and 1960s, at a time when other European colonial powers were withdrawing from Africa, Lisbon held fast, arguing that during half a millennium as colonizers, the Portuguese had established they were historically exceptional, unique in their aptitude for absorbing other peoples into European civilization.[6] Johannesburg served as a convenient foil. Roughly 300 miles away, the apartheid metropolis, shaped by a proudly unbending racism, was an example of what Lourenço Marques was not. In revised histories of the Portuguese era that emerged once that era was ending, Johannesburg typified what Lourenço Marques, essentially, always had been.[7]

Mozambique's capital in the decades after World War II was, in many respects, a dual city. The paved street grid, energy grid, sewage lines, municipal trash disposal, and piped water all more or less ended at the curve of Avenida Caldas Xavier, and beyond it sprawled predominantly African neighborhoods of twisting dust lanes (Figure 1.2). At night, the difference assumed other dimensions. Crossing the narrow threshold from one side of the curve to the other, wrote journalist and poet José Craveirinha in 1955, one departed a visible world, lit by street lamps, and entered a darkness where sounds replaced sight: "Loose sand creaks underfoot, and feet gain the supernatural intuition of the blind, and guiding one through the roads are the chirps of bats, the trilling of crickets, and the ruffling of anonymous wings."[8] Authorities essentially prevented foreign researchers from working in the subúrbios and censored images of African neighborhoods because they acknowledged, if only to each other, that the caniço undercut Portugal's claims to being a racial paradise.[9] The subúrbios were what they were because of policies and practices throughout the colonial era that suppressed African wages, combined with a generalized neglect of African welfare.[10] Until 1961, nearly all black Mozambican men were subject to a brutal system of forced labor that dated from the late nineteenth century. Yet according to Portuguese propagandists, it was not discrimination and wage suppression and government neglect that kept Africans in poor conditions but rather primitive job skills: given time and the proper tutelage, Africans, too, would evolve and learn to take an equal part in the economy. As he visited Mozambique in 1956, the president of Portugal, a figurehead of the Salazar regime, told a French reporter that the Portuguese did not have

29

a "racial problem."[11] "No distinctions whatsoever are made between whites and blacks," he said, "except in respect to the degree of civilization reached by Africans, and in this area we give them all the encouragement possible for them to elevate themselves." Even in the 1960s, when the forced-labor regime had been officially abolished and the job prospects for many in the subúrbios significantly improved, most Africans could not afford to live in the City of Cement, and landlords tended to refuse the black Mozambicans who could.[12] Meanwhile, with the explosive growth of the subúrbios, conditions there in many ways got worse.

Although white supremacy structured the economy and how and where people lived in Lourenço Marques, the state did not make residential segregation by race a primary objective. Unlike in South Africa, Rhodesia, and colonial Kenya, there were no wide "buffer zones" to maintain great distances between predominantly African neighborhoods and predominantly European neighborhoods. The relative compactness of the city is evident in Momplé's story and even in Machel's words on Heroes Day. People in Lourenço Marques walked. There had been streetcars since the first decade of the twentieth century, and later, there were bus lines on the few roads that passed through the subúrbios. At least until the middle to late 1960s, however, the most common means of travel was on foot. One reason was that for many years, bus drivers refused to let people board without shoes, a restriction that barred many women.[13] Another was the relative proximity of homes, workplaces, markets, and churches and mosques, which meant a bus fare was often an unnecessary extravagance. Less than 3 miles separated the most populous neighborhoods of the subúrbios from the most exclusive neighborhoods of the City of Cement, and most of the city lay somewhere in between. The heart of Chamanculo, Lourenço Marques's largest African neighborhood, was situated a mile or so above the port and its rail facilities, the city's largest employers, and just past the rail station was the downtown commercial district, the *baixa*. Sailors on shore leave often walked up the hill from the port to the compounds where sex workers lived in the dense bairros of Malanga, Mafalala, and Lagoas—and beyond Lagoas, one reached sparsely populated areas that were just barely considered Lourenço Marques.

Given the various proximities, the South African urban planner probably would have found Lourenço Marques as exotic as the South African tourist did.[14] Unlike in South Africa, the displacement of Africans in

Figure 1.2 The curve where city meets subúrbios, 1969. (MITADER)

Mozambique's capital occurred as the City of Cement expanded, rather than to realize theories of racial "separate development." People in the subúrbios were more or less on their own, and the limited number of housing units built for Africans in Mozambique by the government or by religious charities during the entire period of colonial rule probably amounted to less than a single neighborhood in Soweto.[15] In the 1950s, several thousand poor and working-class whites lived in the Lourenço Marques subúrbios, often side by side with African neighbors and often with African companions. The cities of Portuguese Africa can certainly be understood as variations on an apartheid theme, but we could just as easily consider the personal intimacies that persisted despite segregation, as well as the separations maintained in tight quarters.

This chapter demonstrates the place of the built environment in people's lives during the decades after World War II, materially and symbolically: how urban space, at its many scales, did not simply reflect relations among city dwellers but also conditioned them. Perhaps all too typical of histories of the colonial era, the first part of the narrative emphasizes Portuguese initiatives and how Africans were compelled to respond to them. Even while attempting to center the subúrbios in the story of mid-twentieth-century Lourenço Marques, one cannot help but see them as the outcome of the colonial conquests of an earlier period. The tour hastens through previous centuries before lingering in the 1950s. Much of what is said here also applies to the 1960s and early 1970s, but the specificities of urban life during the last fifteen years of Portuguese rule are discussed in chapters that follow.

INSIDERS AND OUTSIDERS

The Portuguese were not the only Europeans to show interest in what they later called the Bay of Lourenço Marques, but they were the first (in the early 1500s) and the most persistent.[16] The bay and the estuary that fed into it gave access to sources of ivory, gold, and slaves in the southeast African interior; the name given to the bay derived from a Portuguese ivory trader, allegedly the first European to exploit the area.[17] For centuries, the Portuguese at Lourenço Marques never numbered more than a few dozen, and malaria tended to reduce the settlement to a handful until more troops could be ordered to repopulate the small garrison and more civilians could be compelled to join them.[18] From the late eighteenth century onward, the Portuguese military post and its adjoining settlement were located on the north shore of the estuary where it opened onto the bay, on a sandy spit of land described by historian Alfredo Pereira de Lima as less than a mile long and a quarter mile wide and "almost drowned by pestilential swamp."[19] The construction in the mid-nineteenth century of a stone-and-lime wall along the north side of the settlement helped stave off raids from that direction, but it did nothing to protect against mosquitoes. Beyond the marsh and on slightly higher ground were the scattered homesteads of people loyal to the Mpfumu chief, and on the south side of the estuary was the closely linked

Tembe clan.[20] The longtime inhabitants of the areas around the bay spoke Ronga, and they called the Portuguese settlement Xilunguíne, meaning "place of the white men." Throughout the nineteenth century, the vast majority of Xilunguíne's residents were not whites but rather Asians, African traders and slaves, and people who claimed diverse origins.[21]

Beset by disease, the settlement was, for most of its early history, a precarious place to be for virtually everyone who lived there. Considering the unsanitary conditions and the tumbledown state of most housing, it is no exaggeration to say that the first slum of Lourenço Marques was the settlement itself. Signs of vigor resulted from the growth of Boer settlement in South Africa's interior from the 1830s onward, together with the spike in the overall European population of the hinterland following the discovery of diamonds at Kimberley in the 1860s. Lourenço Marques was the closest seaport to Pretoria, and for the Boers it had the added advantage of being controlled by a power other than Britain. In 1876, shortly after Portugal successfully fended off a British attempt to claim part of the bay, the military post was elevated to the status of a town. One year later, a team of engineers arrived from Portugal to begin draining the swamps that surrounded the settlement on most sides, and they were celebrated as conquering heroes. These two linked developments—the resolution of Portugal's sovereignty over the bay and the infrastructural upgrades—allowed Lourenço Marques to expand in pace with growth in South Africa.

The rooting of the Portuguese settlement also coincided with the abolition of slavery in Mozambique in the 1870s, after which the town would become a showcase for how labor could continue to be exploited under different guises. Forced African labor dug the earth and hauled the rocks to fill the swamps surrounding Lourenço Marques. But according to Jeanne Penvenne, the public works projects that made the vicinity of the fort more tolerable for habitation simultaneously made life less tolerable farther afield.[22] The dirt for fill was excavated from nearby areas of established African settlement, thus displacing homesteads, and after the work was done, the empty pits became ponds of stagnant water and breeding grounds for malarial mosquitoes. In other words, infrastructural improvements displaced disease conditions from the growing town to the areas that were now on the town's outskirts. Just as significant to the future of African life in Lourenço Marques was a fire that swept through the Portuguese settlement in 1875. The fire was the latest in a series, and because it had been fed by reed-walled, thatched-roof structures, construction in reed and straw was prohibited. In turn, that presumably pushed much of the African population beyond the bounds of the town's perimeter wall.

With the opening of the goldfields in the Transvaal in the 1880s, the town came more fully under the glare of global capitalism. In 1887, the year the town was elevated to a city, the colony's chief engineer gave Lourenço Marques its first significant urban plan—essentially, a Cartesian grid imposed on a non-Cartesian landscape.[23] As Valdemir Zamparoni observes, it might have been easier to simply move the settlement to a more salubrious spot as some advocated, but the impulse to force nature to submit before man and technology overwhelmed pragmatism.[24] Surveyors marked out the straight lines of future growth, and street signs appeared for streets that did not yet exist. Over the next decade, Portugal's relationship to Mozambique and to the people who lived there changed rapidly and radically, as did the relationship of Lourenço Marques to the rest of the colony. What was known as Portuguese East Africa had been limited mostly to trading outposts on the coast and to posts and plantations along the Zambezi River; only in 1891 were Mozambique's borders with British Africa agreed upon. Now, by the terms of the Berlin Conference, Portugal sought "effective occupation."[25] In 1895, the Transvaal railway was completed, and in recognition of the city's centrality to Mozambique's economic prospects, the colony's capital was soon moved to Lourenço Marques from the Island of Mozambique, the sleepy former slaving port off the colony's north coast.[26] By 1897, Portuguese forces and their local allies had destroyed southern Mozambique's Gaza state, consolidating Portugal's control over the territory. Much of Mozambique was then parceled up and leased to concessionaires to administer and exploit, but the region south of the Save River, including Lourenço Marques, fell under Portugal's direct governance.

For administrative purposes, two concentric arcs were drawn on the chart of Lourenço Marques, relative to a point near its port.[27] The outer arc, with a radius of 7 kilometers, defined the *concelho* within it—that is, the principal administrative unit governing everyday life in the Portuguese settlement and its near vicinity. The inner arc, with a tight radius of approximately 2 kilometers, defined much of the northerly limit of the municipality, which would administer specifically urban services such as transit, trash removal, road construction, and building permits.[28] At some point (it is unclear exactly when), barbed wire was installed along the municipal boundary.[29] This line later became the route of the Ring Road, and sometime thereafter, the main segment of it was renamed Avenida Caldas Xavier. The area inside this curve was initially known as the ringed area. Beyond the curve, most of the responsibility of municipal authorities ended and the subúrbios began.

The full significance of the term *subúrbio* in the Portuguese planning tradition remains vague. In nineteenth-century Portugal, it was used colloquially to refer to new industrial areas surrounding Lisbon and to describe outer housing districts, some of them wealthy, some of them poor—just as the various derivations of the word were used in other parts of Europe and in North America.[30] There are some indications that the designation acquired a more precise meaning in Portugal's colonies, perhaps for the first time in Lourenço Marques in 1903 when areas between the arc of the municipality and the arc of the concelho were specifically identified, in a legal decree, as "subúrbios."[31] Doing so was part of an ongoing attempt to discipline the sell-off of land there, which for decades had been marked by landgrabs, giveaways, and corruption.[32] In Europe and North America, suburbs were unanticipated expansions of established cities. In many cases, they were seen negatively, as outside the reach of governmental authority and prejudicial to the development of the city itself. In Lourenço Marques, however, the making of a place called the subúrbios followed closely upon the making of a place called the city, in anticipation of the city's eventual expansion.[33] These areas were not urbanized yet—nor, for that matter, was most of the municipality itself—but they would be, eventually.

Crystallizing Portugal's renewed efforts at empire was the *indigenato*.[34] Instituted in 1899, with many revisions thereafter, this was the legal apparatus upon which rested Mozambique's system of forced labor. Basically, all "native" (*indígena*) men not engaged in formal employment had a "moral and legal obligation" to labor for the government or for a private designee of the government for up to six months at a time. Since farming one's own fields did not count as a formal job, most Mozambican men were vulnerable to impressment—and when authorities felt moved to, women, children, and the elderly were forced to labor, too. *Chibalo*, as this kind of labor was called in southern Mozambique, paid meager wages (if any at all) and often lasted more than the statutory six months. It could also be levied as punishment for not paying hut taxes or for the most trivial offenses, real or imagined. Beyond that, it imposed hardships not just on the men who

35

were forced into backbreaking, sometimes fatal work but also on the families they left behind. Chibalo was one of cruelest facts of Mozambican life, along with forced crop cultivation, which was instituted in the 1930s.[35] Both were legally abolished in the early 1960s, though various forms of coerced labor nonetheless persisted in many parts of Mozambique.[36]

Many scholars have plumbed the depths of chibalo, and the subject of forced labor will not be expanded upon here. Penvenne produced the authoritative account of how the indigenato functioned in Lourenço Marques, where chibalo labor built nearly all of the city's public works projects, including the cathedral that was erected in the 1940s by crews of men who were chained together as they worked.[37] A few aspects of the indigenato, however, deserve to be highlighted here.

The indigenato redefined citizenship within Mozambique, creating a legal distinction between so-called natives and nonnatives. Europeans, Asians, and many people of mixed race were considered nonnatives, or "civilized," and were conferred the rights of Portuguese citizenship at birth. But black Mozambicans—the vast majority of the population—were deemed natives unless they could prove themselves sufficiently "evolved" to be considered Portuguese. Those hoping to shed their native status had to read and write in Portuguese, earn a reasonable wage in a formal job, dress the way a Portuguese was expected to dress, eat what a Portuguese did, and eat it with a knife and fork. He or she had to speak Portuguese in the house, and the house at the very least had to be of wood-and-zinc construction, rather than reeds. The rules could be vague and were revised many times over the years, and the application of the law was particularly murky when it came to women and to the mixed-race children of "civilized" fathers who did not acknowledge parentage.[38] At some point after one successfully applied for citizenship, an inspector would visit one's household to verify that standards were being upheld. Over the decades, the African press frequently decried the double standard that did not require the many illiterate whites in Mozambique to pass a test to obtain citizenship. The deliberately rudimentary education provided to black Mozambicans ensured there was only a tiny pool of potential applicants. For black Mozambicans,

Figure 1.3 (*opposite top*) The subúrbios, 1978–79. (Barry Pinsky)

Figure 1.4 (*opposite bottom*) Mavalane, 1980s. (CDFF)

Figure 1.5 Pushing a truck through suburban roads, 1971. (*Notícias* archive)

becoming assimilated (*assimilado*) was usually necessary for pursuing more advanced educational opportunities and climbing higher up the job ladder.[39] Nonetheless, having to discard as inferior one's African identity was a humiliating experience for many, and some who met the requirements for assimilation refused to go through with it.[40]

Much like France and the *évolués* (evolved ones) of its empire, Portugal trumpeted the existence of assimilados to show its critics that its native policies were not racist, since they demonstrated that anyone, no matter the color of their skin, could become Portuguese.[41] Yet the number of assimilados was alone sufficient to refute that claim: by the abolition of the system in the early 1960s, there were perhaps only five thousand people with assimilado status in the entire territory, considerably less than 1 percent of the total African population.[42] Still, however miniscule the number of people classified as assimilado may have been in Mozambique during the reign of the indigenato, they were nonetheless a recognizable segment of the population of Lourenço Marques. Following the abolition of the

Figure 1.6 A water fountain in the subúrbios, undated. (AHM, icon 4621)

indigenato, the word *assimilado* continued to refer in common parlance to any black Mozambican who had acquired a certain level of formal education and secured a modestly paying job, such as clerk, office assistant, schoolteacher, bookkeeper, interpreter, or nurse—the highest positions to which a black Mozambican could realistically aspire during the colonial era.[43] In the years after independence, to have been assimilado carried with it the unjust stigma of having purportedly approximated oneself too closely to the *colono* (the Portuguese settler) and benefited from the impoverishment of one's Mozambican brothers and sisters.[44]

As Penvenne has illustrated, there had always been a number of more privileged Africans in the city during the nineteenth and early twentieth centuries, not a few of them highly visible figures in local affairs.[45] They were traders, elephant hunters, labor recruiters, journalists, and intellectuals, many with some combination of African, European, and Asian parentage. Their cultural and linguistic fluency—the ability to make connections between different groups of people and different spheres of urban and rural life—was a point of pride and often a source of profit. On paper, however, the indigenato pigeonholed more-privileged blacks into the single, distinct category *assimilado*, while hiving off those Africans with a more diverse racial background (called *mestiços*, *mulatos*, or *mistos*) as if they were a separate and identifiable community. The law flattened, conceptually, the myriad interests that collided daily in a place that still retained many of the characteristics of an unruly frontier town. The assimilado, the black Mozambican who had supposedly abandoned an African self in exchange for European status, was, in more than one sense, a Portuguese invention.[46]

The indigenato altered the lives even of those not directly taken for chibalo. The system institutionalized the debasement of all African labor so that it was cheap and more easily controlled. Natives who were engaged in waged labor and even Africans who held citizenship saw their roles diminished at the port, the railway, and the municipality—the city's largest employers. At the low end of the wage spectrum, African earning power was undermined by chibalo; the threat of it sent men to the city looking for any formal work they could find. And the earnings of those in better positions were eroded by the fitful though continual growth of the Portuguese population, as whites benefited from job preferences.[47]

Until the 1960s, natives carried a pass that showed they had been granted an administrator's permission to be in Lourenço Marques, and this permission was tied to the securing of a job. People in the subúrbios lived in fear of police raids. Those caught without a pass were subjected to vicious whippings or chibalo or both, and women, for whom formal work was much harder to come by, tended to live a particularly fugitive existence.[48] Assimilados, too, were stopped and ordered to produce documentation; they had to show they were not natives.[49] The right of all black Mozambicans, whether citizens or not, to simply walk the streets of Lourenço Marques or even the dirt tracks of the subúrbios was made contingent. One did not belong unless one proved otherwise.

The logic of the subúrbios and the logic of the indigenato, though initially articulated at roughly the same time, were not perfectly synced. The subúrbios were where the promise of municipal infrastructure ended; the boundary line that marked the frontier was drawn with a vision in mind of the European metropolis that some hoped would soon emerge within the curve's embrace. Ill-defined parts of the subúrbios were called native reserves, but in practice, these were not like the native reserves of South Africa and neighboring British colonies, that is, areas where all black Africans not residing at their places of employment had to live and where only Africans could live. As natives, most people living in the sub-úrbios were subject to the ostensibly customary authority of a Portuguese-appointed hereditary leader, or régulo (discussed in the following chapter), just as they would be in the countryside. But the word subúrbio in itself conveyed no precise legal implications relative to either race or citizenship. Officially speaking, one did not have to be native or black to live in the subúrbios, and one did not have to be white to live within the curve of the ringed area.

Thoroughgoing segregation was achieved nonetheless, testament to the power of racialized labor exploitation and restrictive ownership laws, as well as ever-more exacting building codes that excluded most Africans from a city being remade in concrete.[50] In the early twentieth century, natives who already claimed property within Lourenço Marques proper were allowed to keep it so long as they could establish proof of possession, but few could assemble the paperwork demanded by the municipal bureaucracy to do so. Those who could were limited to 400 square meters (less than one-tenth of an acre), enough space for a house and a small yard.[51] Also in the first decade of the century, municipal authorities indulged in what became a recurring compulsion to modernize the face of the city, and such initiatives usually resulted in the demolition of houses that did not belong to whites. As nearly everywhere in the colonial world, fear of the plague had justified the destruction of a number of houses belonging to Africans and Asians, in the city and the subúrbios; the rules exempted white-owned homes from health standards.[52] One health official described the capital in 1910 as having the "mean aspect of a city of tin," referring to a shantytown, and that year, citing sanitation concerns, the municipality decreed that all new construction within city limits had to be built in masonry.[53] The order confined to the subúrbios the new builders who could afford no more than wood and zinc. In 1932, costly bureaucratic procedures that were imposed on those who wanted to expand, renovate, or simply paint their existing houses made maintaining one of the aging wood-and-zinc homes in the city that much more onerous. Houses constructed of wood and zinc within the ringed area, furthermore, were assessed a building tax at a higher rate than those made of concrete block.[54] Because of the suppression of African

The Spaces of Lourenço Marques

wages by the indigenato and the inflow of whites from the metropole, Africans could not maintain a hold within the city.

In 1938, the governor-general marked out native reserves at some distance from the city, in which all natives had to reside unless they were living in an employer's compound or home.[55] Those houses remaining in newly designated native-free areas of the subúrbios would be destroyed. The draconian law would have been of a piece with South African–style segregation if it had been implemented. According to Penvenne, Portugal's colonial minister scuttled the plan, arguing that it violated the principles of nonracialism.[56] By then, there were very few black Mozambicans within the city proper who were not also living with their employers as domestic servants. Most had long since been pushed to the subúrbios. Those who were from Lourenço Marques and belonged to the original Ronga-speaking clans had already been squeezed off their land by arbitrary removals and stricter building codes.[57]

The displacement of Africans from the area where most whites lived had proceeded incrementally, though nonetheless inexorably. By 1960, the subúrbios were also home to two-thirds of the mixed-race population, somewhat more than one thousand people of Asian (mostly South Asian) background, and more than nine thousand whites—almost a quarter of the city's European population at the time.[58] Many of these suburban whites lived in concrete neighborhoods that had eaten into the subúrbios, displacing the people who had lived there, so even though their title deeds said "subúrbio," the neighborhood often had some degree of urban infrastructure. But other whites, mostly men, lived in the *cantinas*—general stores that doubled as bars—that they ran in the heart of the subúrbios or in wood-and-zinc houses just at the edge of the city proper, often with African partners. There were also white men who kept two households—one with an African companion and one with a white and legally recognized spouse in town or in Portugal. Alto Maé, a neighborhood just inside the curve, was somewhat comparable in its demographics to the suburban neighborhoods just outside the curve, though more prosperous relatively speaking. In the meantime, the curve itself had become a nexus for prostitution in a port city notorious for it. The borderlands where city met subúrbio represented the real diversity, in all respects, of the Portuguese Empire, though it was not the kind of racial pluralism that Lisbon image-makers were eager to promote.

In the 1950s, pushed by hut taxes, forced crop cultivation, chibalo, and land dispossession and pulled by Lourenço Marques's economic growth, more and more people from the countryside went to the capital seeking employment. At the same time, the immigration of Portuguese to the city, many themselves fleeing destitution in Portugal, was climbing apace. Between 1940 and 1960, the total population of both city and subúrbios almost tripled, to about 178,500 people, with the African population consistently accounting for about two-thirds of the population (though Africans were likely undercounted).[59] The influx of Portuguese immigrants in the 1950s and 1960s brought city development flush against the caniço.

This is when the ringed area truly became the City of Cement—more completely concrete and nearly universally thought of as "the white city" despite the enduring diversity of some neighborhoods.[60] Mestiço men and well-dressed black men (that is, assimilados) could be seen in restaurants, bars, the cinema, and shops. But most establishments in the City of Cement did not welcome black Mozambicans, most of whom could not afford to shop there in any case.[61] When residents of the subúrbios went to the City of Cement, it was to work, and when they clocked out, they were subject to a 9:00 p.m. curfew.[62] In any encounter or near encounter with whites, one was expected to show what was considered proper deference. Failure to step off the sidewalk to make way, to humbly lower one's gaze, or to stand up and remove one's cap in the presence of a police officer could result in a beating. Employers could request that police punish their employees for absences and perceived misdeeds. Until the early 1960s, labor relations throughout Mozambique were based on a credible threat of violence. In the City of Cement, it could often seem just around the corner.

THE REED HOUSE

For Mozambicans, the reed house was long the mark of poverty and squalor, as well as the precariousness of urban life in general, and it still is. This had less to do with the material itself than with where it was put to use. In the countryside of southern Mozambique, for instance, a reed house was nothing to be ashamed of. A rural house was circular in plan and walled either with wattle and daub or with caniço, a tall, fairly rigid reed that grew in relative abundance by the region's waterways.[63] Adequately sized tree branches were freely available to serve as pillars and stays. Sources of

43

Figure 1.7 Polana Caniço, 1988. (Carlos Cardoso / CDFF)

Figure 1.8 Polana Caniço, 1987. (CDFF)

Figure 1.9 (*opposite*) Cement mix was often used to plaster reed houses. Maxaquene, late 1970s. (Eva Sävfors)

clay were available, too, and often pillaged from anthills; the material was used to coat the inside and outside of reed walls, insulating huts against wind, insects, and rot. Houses were reasonably well ventilated. Fabrication of the roof was a communal affair. Neighbors joined in to bundle the straw tightly together and affix it to a conical roof structure; then, the cone was lifted onto their heads and conveyed to the hut, to be followed by a celebration.[64] A hut was customarily destroyed when its resident died, but the roof structure was preserved and used to shelter a succession of new huts. In the 1940s, years before he became Frelimo's founding president, Eduardo Mondlane provided descriptions of his childhood in rural southern Mozambique to his former teacher, Swiss missionary André-Daniel Clerc. In the resulting novel, *Chitlangou, Son of a Chief* (1950), the young protagonist recalls lying on the floor of his hut and looking up with admiration not at the stars but at the spiraling interior structure of the roof, a "venerable smoke-blackened cone" that had sheltered several generations of his family.[65] He remarks, "I have often marveled at the skill of the men of my people: from a bundle of sticks, a heap of branches, they have fashioned this covering, in a single piece, which faces all horizons and resists the four winds of heaven." In Chitlangou's meditation on roof structure, Mondlane and Clerc were perhaps offering a subtle interpretation of the Mozambican character: "These supple interlaced twigs form a cable which, in its patient itinerary, unites the center to the circumference."

Holes were dug in the ground by hand for the placing of pillars. Parallel stays were fixed horizontally to the pillars at two or three points on both the interior and exterior of the pillars, and they were tied in place with plant fibers. Reeds were then slipped into the gap between the parallel stays. Men—when there were men around to volunteer their labor—tended to do much of the construction work, but not exclusively. Most people knew how to build such a house, and most of them contributed at some point or another to the construction of one. The only significant cost to the home dweller in the countryside, other than the time spent locating materials, was in the preparation of brew for the party that followed the placing of the roof.

By the 1950s, however, the immediate surrounds of the Bay of Lourenço Marques had been stripped of much of their naturally occurring supplies of building materials, and so, unlike in the countryside, building a reed house in Lourenço Marques was a costly affair.[66] Contrary to the popular image of patchwork shantytowns improvised from scavenged waste, the materials for the typical reed house were paid for in cash at markets throughout the suburbios. Reed bundles and tree branches were trucked in from the countryside or arrived by rail from the Incomati valley to the north, where there were even caniço plantations.[67] (In the 1960s, materials for reed construction may have been the principal cargo of trains on the Manhiça line.)[68] Horizontal wood stays were either rough-edged scrap from the lumberyard and cheap or machine-cut, slightly more elegant, and pricey. For fasteners, wire and nails substituted for plant fibers. Corrugated metal panels were imported from Europe or South Africa until sometime after World War II, when local factories entered into production of some materials as well. The hardy, practical corrugated metal panel, called a *chapa* in Portuguese, could last for decades, and it changed construction patterns utterly: by the 1950s, most houses in the suburbios were built rectangular in plan to accommodate the panel dimensions.[69] (There is a further discussion of the chapa later in this chapter.) The houses varied in size, but many were about 260 square feet, twice as long as they were wide, and sheltered two rooms.[70] The width of the house was slightly more narrow than the width of the metal panel, to allow for a slight roof incline and eave.

In 1968, Alfredo Pereira de Lima authored a brief history of the progress of the city's European settlement by chronicling its changing building types. In the early nineteenth century, he wrote, the lack of good quality wood compelled the handful of pioneers who lived outside the fort's walls to build "African cabanas (of the hut type) covered in straw, subjecting themselves to the greatest discomforts."[71] Examples of that type of hut, he continued, were still in evidence, "almost without alterations," in the suburbios of Lourenço Marques. At the time Pereira de Lima was writing, there were indeed huts in the suburbios of the kind one found in the countryside—but not many. An aerial survey in the mid-1960s estimated that fewer than 7 percent of the structures in the suburbios had a circular plan, versus 88 percent of structures that were rectangular and also possessed a zinc-paneled roof.[72] One is left to speculate how many of the circular huts were residences and how many were instead the consulting offices of healers (*curandeiros*); even today, curandeiros build conical-roofed huts in their yards, beside their houses, where they meet their patients and store their medicines. By rendering the "traditional hut" historically immutable, the historian also failed to recognize how much the changed economics of construction in the suburbios altered the meaning of the house for the

47

people who lived in it. In any case, a durable, zinc-paneled roof was considered by most people a more practical alternative to straw. In Lourenço Marques, the spare time and neighborly cooperation required to build a sturdy conical roof of the kind Mondlane described may have been, like reeds themselves, in shorter supply than they were in the countryside. One suspects that the fading use of conical roofs also diminished neighborly cooperation.[73]

The 1969 master plan for Lourenço Marques included a study of home construction in the subúrbios. The author, a Portuguese architect, praised reeds as an urban building material. Reeds, he speculated, filtered out dust and noise but allowed air and speech to pass through, regulating the relationship between intimate home life and outdoor public life without strictly separating them. Perhaps the group feeling typical of African culture owed something to the permeability of reed walls, he continued. Concrete walls, by contrast, would impose European-type individualism and were liable to stifle African conviviality "as coercive obstacles, as exoticisms that modify people's psychological characteristics."[74]

It is unclear whether the architect was referring to the walls between yards, the walls of houses, or both. In any case, residents of reed houses would not have seconded his rosy appraisal. Few houses were elevated above the sewage-strewn waters that frequently inundated the suburban landscape, and rot and vermin shortened the life span of reeds to a few years at most, so the material had to be constantly replaced. Reeds are also highly flammable. With almost everyone in the subúrbios cooking on open coals and lighting their rooms at night with kerosene lamps, it was common for fire to set a house alight, sometimes consuming a few dozen homes.[75] The more squeezed the space, the more likely a fire.

Contrary to the architect's theory of reed-based *ubuntu*, the density of settlement kept one's house in often uncomfortable proximity to neighbors and their latrines. People in reed houses complained of a lack of privacy.[76] Clay insulation would have blunted some of the outside sounds and smells and prolonged the useful life of reed walls, but the sandy earth of the subúrbios was too loose to serve this purpose. Therefore, those seeking insulation walked with their empty petroleum cans to the mouth of the Infulene River, a few miles away, to fetch black mud. One resident of Chamanculo, Armando Guilundo, recalled that during his childhood in the 1940s and early 1950s, his mother did the fetching.[77] She would make the trip to the

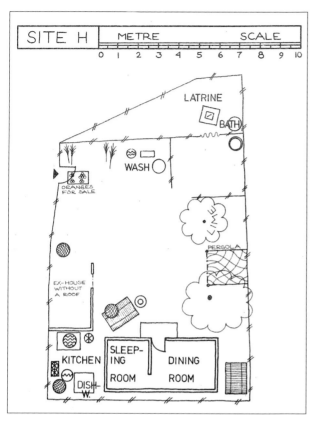

SITE H · METRE SCALE
0 1 2 3 4 5 6 7 8 9 10

LATRINE
BATH
WASH
ORANGES FOR SALE
PERGOLA
EX-HOUSE WITHOUT A ROOF
KITCHEN
DISH-W.
SLEEPING ROOM
DINING ROOM

Figures 1.10 and 1.11 Site plan and reed house floor plan in Maxaquene (formerly Malhangalene), drawn by Swedish architecture student Ruth Näslund in 1976. *The Malhangalene Survey: A Housing Study of an Unplanned Settlement in Maputo, Mozambique, 1976,* vol. 1 (Göteborg, Sweden: Chalmers Tekniska Högskola, Arkitektur, 1977), n.p.

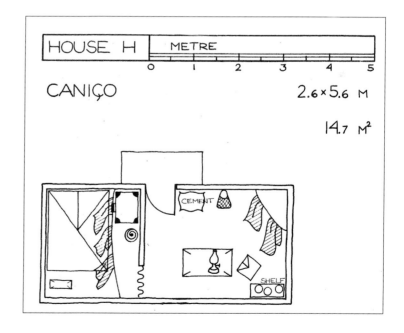

HOUSE H · METRE
0 1 2 3 4 5

CANIÇO · 2.6×5.6 M · 14.7 M²

CEMENT
SHELF

river and back every day for a week, then spread the black mud on the floors of the house and halfway up the inside of the reed walls; when it dried, she would bring the surface to a polish with her palms. "We children would help her carry the mud, but we didn't know how to make the walls," he said. Cracks would appear before long, so she repeated the task two to three times a year. For all the time and resources that people invested in building, maintaining, and occasionally decorating their reed homes, all hoped to one day upgrade to something better.

Reed houses were well suited to the subúrbios in at least one respect, though. They could be dismantled and most of their materials recovered for reassembly elsewhere, a feature that took on a particular importance with the growing threat of displacement beginning in the 1950s. A 1959 chronicle in O Brado Africano entitled "Huts in the Air!" described the pitiful sight of the reeds and wood stakes of dismantled houses being carried on the shoulders of men and the heads of women.[78] Their landlord has sold the lot they rented to make way for new development, and now they must go in search of another plot. They beg another landowner to allow them to settle on his property, but a few months later he sells the land out from under them. The tenants once again strike their huts, as if they were the tents of nomads, and begin their wanderings anew.

HOUSES OF WOOD AND ZINC

Pereira de Lima dated the beginning of the city's "Tumultuous Age of Wood and Zinc" to the 1870s.[79] Transvaal gold may have given Lourenço Marques a new reason for being, but the burgeoning port town was clad in baser metal. Zinc was what the metal panels were called, but to be more precise, they were iron or steel sheets coated with zinc to inhibit corrosion. With that said, deferring to universal practice I will simply refer to them as zinc panels or *chapas*, the Portuguese word for "metal sheet." According to Pereira de Lima, chapas were first introduced to Lourenço Marques in the 1850s, just as Portugal relaxed import controls in the colony. Though the panels were used here and there as roofing, it was not until the 1870s that most Europeans and Asians in the town were living and working in wood-framed buildings with walls and roofs of corrugated zinc. The buildings mimicked the houses and commercial establishments that predominated in Johannesburg.[80]

Along with quinine and railroads, though less remarked upon, the zinc panel was one of the "tools of empire" that facilitated the penetration of African societies by various European interests in the late nineteenth and early twentieth centuries.[81] Lightweight and flat, the panels could be transported easily by ship from foundries in Europe to colonial ports around the globe and then carried into hinterlands by rail, by pack animal, and on the crowns of people's heads. Wood-framed, zinc-paneled structures required no specialized knowledge to build, allowing for the rapid construction of administrative offices, mission stations, and mining camps, and the single-family wood-and-zinc bungalow, a housing type originally developed for British settlers posted in India, was eventually packaged in kits for deployment in Melbourne, Lagos, and Kimberley. Moreover, wood-and-zinc buildings could be easily disassembled as need dictated and conveyed to another site to be rebuilt—an advantage for settler populations uncertain of where the healthiest place to build might prove to be and for prospectors unsure where they might next strike gold. Apart from the more tangible benefits of the wood-and-zinc construction method, the machine-cut wood beams and the factory-made galvanized panels also helped mark a clear distinction between "modern" colonizer and "primitive" colonized at a time when maintaining such a distinction was a matter of great concern and not a little anxiety.[82] At one point, the Baldwin ironworks in England enjoyed a near monopoly on the panels distributed in Mozambique and the rest of southern Africa, and it is somehow appropriate that family scion Stanley Baldwin went on to become Britain's prime minister during the interwar years—the zenith of its African empire.[83]

From the time that the chapa came into common use in Lourenço Marques in the 1870s until independence a century later, Africans of greater means almost always lived in wood-framed, zinc-paneled houses.[84] As we have seen, the changes in the Lourenço Marques building code in the 1910s and 1930s that targeted wood-and-zinc construction in the ringed area were an indirect means of pushing out the African population. In the subúrbios, people continued to build in wood and zinc, just as they had from the city's beginnings. Zinc panels were an upgrade from reeds in that they blocked the wind and dust and did not need to be replaced every few years. Like reed houses, wood-and-zinc houses were useful in suburban conditions for the same reason they were useful in mining camps: they could be quickly disassembled. Actually, it was only because such houses

51

Figure 1.12 The Guambe house, built in Chamanculo in the 1930s, in 2011. (David Morton)

Figure 1.13 Jochua Guambe (*just right of center*) and his family, early 1950s. (Castigo Guambe)

Figure 1.14 The Tembe house, built in Chamanculo in the early 1960s, in 2012. (David Morton)

Figure 1.15 Firewood for sale, Minkadjuíne, 1987. (CDFF)

were considered of "precarious" construction that the municipality allowed them to stand at all, since in the subúrbios, permanent construction was, with very few exceptions, prohibited.[85]

While zinc was relatively durable, it was terrible at regulating the ambient temperature. It magnified outdoor heat, turning rooms into ovens, and it did nothing to insulate against the cold other than fending off the wind. A zinc roof, whether it topped a wood-and-zinc house or a reed house, leaked where nails secured the panels to joists. At night, there was a drizzle indoors even when it was not raining outdoors because moisture would rise from sleeping bodies, condense on the roof panels, and then fall as cold droplets. Zinc-paneled walls did not have to be frequently replaced as reed walls did, but termites fed on wood pillars and rafters, limiting their useful life. For those who could afford it, a common solution was to elevate the house on a concrete plinth, which also elevated it above the frequent water inundations. The low-end wood-and-zinc house was like a simple shed, with a roof inclined in a single direction. The first time the house was expanded in size, a roof incline was added in the direction opposite to the first, just as with the reed house. From the standpoint of status, this second incline was what began to distinguish the house from its neighbors; in fact, such a double incline defined the house. One sought to live in a house of *duas águas*—"two gradients"—to drain off rainwater in opposite directions.[86]

Going from a house of two gradients to the embellishments that truly distinguished a wood-and-zinc house was a leap that few could make. The finest houses of wood and zinc, called *chalés*, featured semienclosed verandas, many gables, and large pigeon coops on the outside (baby pigeons were a Portuguese delicacy) and floors of Oregon pine, false ceilings, and many rooms on the inside.[87] A false ceiling regulated the indoor climate. It caught leaks from above, stopped moisture rising from below, and most importantly formed an attic buffer space that kept hot air from reaching living areas. The higher the roof, the more it drew off heat from below. More zinc panels and more wood were required, so these high-peaked roofs (high, that is, against the low-slung norm of the subúrbios) advertised from some distance away the relative wealth of the people they sheltered. The finest wood-and-zinc houses, perched on concrete plinths and reaching almost to treetops, gave neighborhoods the barest hint of a skyline. The scale was deceiving. Even in the largest houses of the subúrbios, all living quarters were located on a single floor.

Despite the exigencies of the building code, there were still some four hundred houses of wood and zinc within the City of Cement in 1950. One displeased engineer called them "genuine crimes, genuine match-boxes, authentic abortions."[88] At a forum in 1949 on problems facing the municipality, an official called them "obsolete vestiges of the heroic epoch of occupation, almost all of them nests of illness, giving to certain streets the lamentable aspect of shantytowns."[89] He hoped they could be demolished in short order. When they were torn down, the panels often got sold to people in the subúrbios, who used them to build houses that were a mark of relative status. Because the wood-and-zinc houses required greater resources to build, popular memory tends to recall them as out of reach for all but assimilados and mestiços.[90] But this was not the case. Even some of the larger houses were built by people whom no one would consider, by any definition, assimilado. Jochua Guambe, born in rural Inhambane, went to Lourenço Marques in the early 1900s to avoid paying the newly imposed hut tax.[91] He did not work in the city, and he never had need to learn Portuguese. Earning his living as a hunter, he would bag game in Inhambane and then travel to South Africa, mostly on foot, to sell animal skins and claws at a market in Durban. Lourenço Marques was merely a convenient base of operations between his sources of supply and places of demand, and later, the city's subúrbios became the site of Guambe's small real estate empire. In the 1930s, he built a house of wood and zinc for his family, on one of about two dozen lots of property he eventually purchased in Chamanculo. It had the features common to the houses of the suburban elite: a semienclosed veranda, a concrete plinth, a false ceiling, and a pigeon coop perched beside the roof. The house was L-shaped, rather than a conventional rectangle, so instead of two roof inclines, there were four, giving the roof a more complicated profile and a more South African appearance than the more common duas águas. There were two bedrooms, one for himself and one for his sons.

"If you had a house like this, it was a symbol of the fact that you owned land," said Castigo Guambe, Jochua's youngest son. "It wasn't just anybody who owned land." With his native status, Jochua Guambe could not actually be a landowner in the eyes of Portuguese law.[92] But his eldest son, Júlio, who worked in a shoe store downtown, had legally assimilated, and he vouched for his father on titling documents. When Jochua Guambe died in the 1960s, he left his properties and the family house to Júlio, and

55

when Júlio died in the 1980s, the house passed to Castigo, who still lives there today. Guambe replaces the wood-slat interior walls when they rot, and he repaints the exterior zinc panels green when they fade. Recently, he had to cut down the sick mango tree that grew beside the house, the last survivor of the many that his father had once planted in the yard. It was the tree where his father invited the curandeiras of the neighborhood to perform ancestral ceremonies, a practice Castigo continued for years. Studding the trunk were the heads of rusted nails that had secured the drying skins of slaughtered goats for the better part of a century.

House construction stretched the resources even of so-called assimilados. Alsene Cumbana, who had assimilated status, held many jobs over the years—as a deliveryman for a bakery, as a veterinary worker—and when he went to Lourenço Marques in 1947, he was able to buy a simple, two-room house of wood and zinc.[93] A few years later, he married. But as the family grew, eventually including nine children, and as they took in Cumbana's older brother, a miner who had lost the use of his legs, they could not afford to expand the house solely on one salary. Eurica Cumbana, Alsene's wife, worked the family's garden plot in the nearby countryside, did all the food preparation and cleaning, and was responsible for raising the children, but now she asked her husband to buy firewood and charcoal for her to resell in front of the house. "She would split the wood herself," said Elizabeth Cumbana, her daughter, who still lived in the house in 2011. "She wouldn't even get someone to help her do it, because she said that it would be like giving money away." The house's two rooms eventually became five. Eurica told her daughter: "This house grew because I always sacrificed myself for it to grow." Many women in the subúrbios financed house construction through the selling of charcoal, produce, and traditional brews.[94] They also supported each other's projects by participating in lending clubs, called *xitique*.[95]

It will be recalled that the word *assimilado* took on meanings beyond its legal definition and applied colloquially to black Mozambicans of some means. It is likely that some people were thought of as assimilado just because they lived in a house of wood and zinc. That is, the house made the assimilado, rather than the other way around. In the 1930s while working at the counter of a building materials store downtown, Salvador Simão Hunguana built a house in Malhangalene, a lightly populated, almost rural neighborhood north of the city.[96] The house he built was particularly distinguished for the area, having eight rooms and being surrounded by a large citrus grove. Working at the materials store no doubt helped Hunguana with supplies. When his assimilado friends pulled strings to get assimilated status for him as well, his house—just as impressive if not more so than some of the Portuguese-owned homes in the vicinity—allowed him to overcome his shortcomings in regard to other legal requirements. Somewhat indirectly, housing was destiny. Hunguana's children were able to enter government schools and eventually acquire higher-paying jobs because of the house their father had built.

By the 1960s, wood-and-zinc construction predominated in the parts of the subúrbios closest to the city.[97] But in the years following independence, when enforcement of the masonry ban was greatly relaxed, new construction in wood and zinc came to an abrupt halt. Regardless of whatever prestige and comfort it afforded over the reed-built house, the wood-and-zinc house could not compete in either prestige or comfort—or in cost—with construction in concrete block.

CANTINAS

José da Costa shipped off for Mozambique as a young Portuguese army conscript in the 1940s, and upon his discharge a few years later, unexcited about a return to village life in Portugal, he decided to stay in Lourenço Marques.[98] On his own and barely literate, da Costa had few prospects. He took a job as the assistant to a stonemason. Then, he met an enterprising African woman named Glória da Conceiçao Nhambirre. She convinced him to borrow a truck so they could go into business transporting firewood from the countryside. They sold their wood bundles at a stand in Chamanculo, and they lived together in the reed house of her family nearby. Nhambirre possessed the acumen, nimbleness, and entrepreneurial drive that da Costa, as he unabashedly told others, completely lacked. But from birth, da Costa had an important qualification that Nhambirre did not. He was Portuguese and thus could sign official documents and own a business. After a few years of selling firewood, the couple built a cantina.

By the mid-1960s, there were hundreds of cantinas in the subúrbios, about one for every five hundred to six hundred people.[99] The cantina was a commercial and social hub of everyday suburban life, a cross between a general store and a bar, and with few exceptions, it was the only authorized

57

Figure 1.16 João da Costa, a.k.a. "Xibinhana," pours a drink at his Chamanculo cantina, 1960s. (Sérgio da Costa)

business in the subúrbios. To say it catered to people's day-to-day needs is to understate just how much people depended on it. At six in the morning, the first customers of the day filed in, sullen men often on their way to the docks, with an escudo and a half in hand for a roll of bread. Throughout the day, women or their children appeared at the counter with small change to buy a few tablespoons of cooking oil or a cup of rice. Over the years, the municipality installed public fountains here and there in the subúrbios, but they fell far short of demand. The long lines and (for many) the long distance to fetch fountain water were enough to persuade people with a few more cents at their disposal to fill their empty oil cans at the nearest cantina spigot and pay for the privilege. Perhaps the most lucrative time of the day for a cantina proprietor (*cantineiro*) was when men returned from work and gathered to drink. Cantinas were where those with native status could legally purchase alcohol, and from the late nineteenth century onward, they were essential to Lisbon's strategies for making the colonies a profitable market for (cheap) Portuguese wine.[100]

The cantina was a masonry structure of impressive size—impressive, that is, only because there was nothing around to compete with it. Older

Figure 1.17 Dinis Marques and the da Costa children, behind the Xibinhana cantina, mid-1960s. (Dinis Marques)

cantinas, like the many built in the 1930s, had high-peaked roofs and wide pediments supported by fluted iron columns so that the entrance was like a cut-rate Roman temple portico.[101] Cantinas tended to be elevated well above the rainy season high-water mark, and their wide verandas gave clear views of the street life passing by. Even after business hours, when tables were put away, cantina verandas were a place for men to congregate away from home. For many women, the cantina was a necessary stop during the workday; for many men, the cantina was a place to relax.

Fines for public drunkenness were once the local administration's most significant source of revenue, according to Penvenne.[102] Many employers,

59

meanwhile, had long identified cantinas as a threat to a healthy, well-disciplined workforce, and in the 1950s, hours were restricted.[103] African men were said to be spending too much of their earnings getting drunk rather than sustaining their families. Cantineiros locked up in the evening, but customers knew they could enter through the yard at the "horse door," a rear entrance so called because during their nightly patrols, mounted police would also sometimes show up there.[104] Usually, though, an officer could be easily bought off with a beer. Perhaps as a result of the new rules, cantinas built in the 1960s minimized outdoor space. The newer cantinas lacked verandas to command the streetscape. They were turned inward.

A serialized short story that appeared in 1960 in *O Brado Africano,* a newspaper for African readers, was written as a defense of rule-breaking cantineiros and their clientele. The economics of poverty, argues the fictional Chinese cantineiro of the story, require people to make their purchases whenever they get hold of a little cash, a happenstance that follows its own clock. The African customer, he adds,

> likes to converse a little, together with friends someplace, let's
> say a public place, just as whites do, and this place, similar
> to the clubs of white people, can only be a cantina… there
> he feels the pleasure in passing a few convivial hours outside
> work, wooing women, listening to the radio, hearing the latest
> news in a different way than he was used to in the bush. And
> what would be the ideal place for this mutual companionship?
> Obviously the cantina![105]

The cantina was perhaps the only place where non-Africans were compelled to cater to the pleasure of Africans, in part because of competition among cantineiros.[106] At the same time, the cantineiro was often seen as a parasitic figure who schemed for ways to cheat his clientele. He was often so out of his element and reliant on an African employee or companion to communicate with customers that he became a target of ridicule. It was an unequal struggle, but the clientele made ample use of the power to name. Penvenne writes of the generic cantineiro moniker: *mumaji,* which was indirectly derived from the Portuguese phrase meaning "want more?"—the badgering question of a cantineiro seeking to run up a customer's tab.[107] Residents of the subúrbios also categorized individual cantineiros according to an elaborate and uncharitable taxonomy. José da Costa was a fixed, ornery presence behind his cantina counter, and his dog Lisboa (Lisbon) was always seen dozing at the foot of his stool. The similarities between da Costa's snarling features and those of his dog earned him the nickname Xibinhana, which in Ronga means "bulldog," a name that stuck precisely because he hated it. Da Costa and Nhambirre never gave their cantina a name, but everyone called it Xibinhana. Another cantina in Chamanculo, the only one with two levels, was unofficially called Ximajana—meaning "short one"—because of the small-statured Portuguese who owned it. Another cantina was Zestapor, a corruption of *José está porco*—"José is piggish"—because of its owner's generally unhygienic appearance, his practice of storing pig feed in his truck, and his habit of brushing his teeth in the same sink where customers washed their hands. The cantineiro just a hundred feet or so away was nicknamed Agarragajo—"Getthatguy." That is what he would yell from the cantina's steps when a customer slipped away without paying, which apparently occurred with some frequency.[108] In a place without addresses and with few official street names, the local cantina became the most obvious landmark when giving directions to one's house, and it lent its name to the immediate area of the neighborhood.[109]

COMPOUNDS

In a more distant part of Chamanculo, about halfway between the City of Cement and the campus of the São José de Lhanguene Mission, is what must be the largest pigeon coop in Maputo. Most of the larger houses of wood and zinc feature a coop somewhere on the roof or in the yard. This particular one is more like a pigeon apartment block. It features some four hundred separate holes for pigeons to roost, and it rivals in size the elegant wood-and-zinc house beside which it stands. The house was built in the 1920s by a Goan man named José Araújo, but the pigeon coop—expanded several times over the years—was the work of his son António.[110]

António Araújo, whose mother was Ronga, worked for years as a truck driver for the municipality, and as a younger man he sidelined as a journalist for O Brado Africano. In the 1960s, he became an entrepreneur. Calling on his connections in the city government, he was able to open a bar and dance club directly adjacent to his house, and because it was 1962, he

61

called the place Twist Bar. His wife, his brother, and his sons took turns behind the counter and in the kitchen while he was occupied with his other business affairs. One of those businesses, a housing compound built at the other end of his property, was meant to target the clientele coming through the bar doors. With dozens of one-room units, it may have been the largest compound in Chamanculo.[111]

The English word *compound*, when referring to housing, possesses a surprising history. It has nothing to do with a being a mixture of elements, as in a chemical compound or a composition, but probably derives from the Malay word *kampong*, which means "village."[112] The word's almost bucolic origins speak to the radical transformations to which the age of empire subjected it: compounds were what the British called the earliest colonial housing clusters in Southeast Asia—enclosures for European residences and factories. Later, the miserable, fenced-in dormitories where miners were housed on South Africa's Rand were called compounds, and when larger employers in Lourenço Marques built worker housing, often big sheds to shelter hundreds of people under one roof, *compound* became *componde*.[113] In the first decades of the twentieth century, conditions at these various dormitories in Lourenço Marques were considered scandalously abysmal, even by the low standards inherent to a system of forced labor.[114] Neither authorities nor employers showed any sustained interest in financing a housing solution, either through paying higher wages or building livable homes. They were not eager, furthermore, to make permanent a workforce that it usually suited them to treat as transient.

In the 1950s, workers migrating to the city who did not have family to stay with and could not afford to build or rent a reed house of their own had no choice but to live in a compound. The typical compound featured a series of discrete units arranged in long rows on either side of a narrow yard.[115] It was usually of wood-and-zinc construction (and therefore extremely hot), and rooms were often windowless and airless, with the door to the yard being the only opening. Packing people in so close together, it was more pigeon coop than barracks. The average room was less than 100 square feet, smaller than a room in the typical reed house.[116] And people often tried to squeeze many to a room. At Araújo's complex, four pit latrines served several hundred tenants, and the tenants were expected to maintain the facilities themselves. The landlord did give them free use of a water spigot in the yard, however.

Figure 1.18 A compound in Xipamanine, 1978. (*Notícias* archive)

Araújo made no secret of his business plan. It was the same as that of many cantina owners in the subúrbios: build a compound in the back-yard to house sex workers who would cater to the bar's clientele.[117] But even though compounds were often stuck with the reputation of brothels, they were not brothels in the strict sense of being dedicated solely to pros-titution.[118] Not only sex workers lived there, and moreover, sex work was only one of a number of strategies that many of the compound's young women and girls (and some boys), usually new to the city, were com-pelled to pursue. To live in a compound was to live in the slums of the subúrbios, and some homeowners and residents of longer standing in the bairros looked down their noses at their compound-dwelling neighbors. The especially rank conditions of most compounds contributed to the snobbery, as did ethnic chauvinism. To some native Maronga, the speak-ers of Chopi, Tonga, Tswa, and Changana arriving from farther north were unsophisticated country folk at best, unattached and potentially dangerous criminals at worst. That many of the so-called foreigners who lived in the compounds did so as a temporary strategy to accrue savings

63

before returning to the countryside did little to alter the general perception of their rootlessness.

Until the late 1960s, rent in a compound could be very low if one shared a single unit with many others—some 100 to 150 escudos per unit. But when rents skyrocketed in Lourenço Marques and its subúrbios, compound living ceased to be the relative bargain it had once been.[119] In 1971, rent for a single unit could be as high as 500 escudos per month if the compound had a water spigot and illumination. This was more than the rent for an average two-room reed house.

"The compounds exist," argued *Tempo* magazine in 1972, "not for the benefit of the residents, who don't even realize that it would be less harmful to live in houses of reeds—but rather because of attitudes dedicated to exploitation."[120]

THE BAIRRO INDÍGENA

For years, the municipal government made repeated half gestures at the housing problem, always with meager results. In 1913, legislation compelling natives to register with authorities for the purposes of eventual labor impressment also mandated that the municipality dedicate a certain proportion of registration fees to the construction of formal housing for Africans.[121] But over the next two decades, all that the municipality could show for its efforts was a cluster of thirty-three concrete-block houses near the market in Xipamanine, intended for "natives" who worked low-paying jobs for the municipality and the railroad. The houses lacked both piped water and electricity, though at least they were built in solid materials. The city charged a rent so high that few people with native status could afford to live there.[122]

In the mid-1930s, an additional source of funding for native housing was identified: indemnification funds resulting from Mozambicans who had died in the mines of South Africa.[123] These funds had accrued for years, unspent, and the South African Chamber of Mines suggested to the Portuguese that they be used on something to benefit Mozambique's African population. The governor-general of Mozambique revived the long-neglected order to build native housing, and he made the municipality of Lourenço Marques responsible for building it. The city was charged with building "a neighborhood that will come to serve as a model for others and

Figure 1.19 The Bairro Indígena, 1940s. (AHM, icon 42)

to which can be transferred a part of the native population that currently lives, in the subúrbios of the city, in buildings of unpleasant aspect and devoid of the most basic hygienic conditions."[124]

The project, which broke ground in the early 1940s, was called the Bairro Indígena da Munhuana ("the native neighborhood of Munhuana"). It was the colony's first government-led housing development of any size intended for African residents. Other large, government-subsidized projects were under way by the 1960s, in the outlying areas of Matola and Machava and in other parts of Mozambique. But the Bairro Indígena was far more prominently located, and because it stood as the lone public housing intervention of any significance in Lourenço Marques for decades, it took on a symbolic value beyond the numbers it housed—for residents of the subúrbios, for colonial officials, and even for Frelimo both during and after independence. In the 1960s when the legal reforms of the time purged the term *indígena* from official communications, the name of the neighborhood was changed first to Bairro do Ultramar—*ultramar* (overseas) was how Portugal referred collectively to its territories in Africa and Asia—and then to the Bairro Popular da Munhuana. Yet even today, a half century after the name change, few call it anything other than the Bairro Indígena.

65

The 22-hectare site selected for the complex was located along a route that connected the City of Cement with the city's airstrip, and if the project was indeed a superficial gesture—a Potemkin village only "for the English to see," as the expression went—then it made sense to put it there, where many visiting VIPs entered the colonial capital.[125] At the same time, the location was near some of the densest suburban neighborhoods.[126] But there was a good reason the site was not so populous itself. It was a low-lying area that frequently was as inundated as the pestilential ponds that bordered it to the east and west. Reviewing the plan for the complex in 1939, the colony's health director issued dire warnings to Lourenço Marques officials. Prevailing winds passing over the ponds already rendered the site "one of the regions of greatest maleficent influence on the city," he wrote.[127] Locating a housing project in that part of the subúrbios would dangerously aggravate the malaria problem for Europeans downwind, in the City of Cement:

> Without a doubt, it ought not pass through the head of a
> legislator to establish a model neighborhood for natives at the
> very edge of an area that is systematically doomed in terms of
> the city's public hygiene and sanitary precaution in general;
> for the precise reason that it must be a model neighborhood it
> must not be built on the site indicated in the plan.[128]

For the sake of African and European alike, he counseled moving the prospective bairro to a location farther away. A second emphatic opinion followed a month later, in which the director attested to firsthand knowledge of native housing projects in the English and French colonies of West Africa; he said he had never seen a project as "unfortunate" as what was planned for Lourenço Marques.[129] The housing commission, however, disagreed with the health official's negative assessment.[130] The commission's president pointed to several factors in favor of the chosen site, including the low cost of acquiring the land.

Meanwhile, the chief engineer of the regional public works department raged that the houses of the complex were designed without thought to the climate.[131] They lacked verandas, and instead of peaked roofs that would help alleviate indoor heat, architects had, apparently for stylistic reasons, opted for flat roofs of reinforced concrete as if Mozambique were "Scandinavia, Greenland, Canada, etc." Putting people accustomed to living in straw huts in such ovenlike houses was "an extremely grave error,"

the engineer contended, as it would compel them to seek refuge at cantinas and other places where they would "create disturbances, etc., etc." He
blamed the influence of South Africa for the flat roofs, an invasive species
of construction that, to his chagrin, had already become popular in the
European quarters of Lourenço Marques.

During the bairro's first phase of construction, between 1940 and
1943, almost four hundred units were built, the majority of them with
only one room. Each unit had its own narrow yard, and the yards were arranged along streets in half circles around a central plaza, where a police
post and the bairro management office were located. Each property was
supplied with piped water and electricity, but use was restricted to certain
hours of the morning (for water) or evening (for electricity).[132] In terms
of space, the houses were no upgrade from the suburban norm. Rooms
were about 120 square feet, smaller than many reed houses in the vicinity. Nonetheless, the neighborhood initially proved attractive enough
that people who were not designated natives—that is, people of mixed
race and people with assimilado status—occupied many of the units.[133]
Presumably, they did so either through the exchange of favors, as was so
common within the municipal apparatus, or by illegally subletting from
original tenants.

In his report for 1946, the administrator of the concelho harshly criticized the results of the completed development. At enormous expense, the
Bairro Indígena da Munhuana only housed some three thousand people,
and of these, perhaps not even half were the indígenas it was intended for.
"It is possible," he remarked, "that whoever authorized and outlined this
type of housing was possessed of the best of intentions, thinking to give
maximum comfort to the native population of the city. Unfortunately this
goal was not reached and the problem of housing the great mass of the native population of Lourenço Marques remains unresolved."[134] The Bairro
Indígena was "far, very far indeed from meeting needs," wrote the head of
Mozambique's office of native affairs in 1951.[135] Munhuana "seems to us a
drop of water in the ocean." He added that he regretted the municipality
had carried out its plans without regard to social welfare and the "customs
and traditions" of the natives. "This is not just a matter of building houses,"
he argued.[136]

In historian L. Lloys Frates's view, the radial plan of the neighborhood
demonstrated the panoptic ideal of centralized spatial control, the kind one

finds in many prison plans, where everyone and everything can theoretically be monitored at all times.[137] The police station in the Bairro Indígena featured a turret, for instance; a police officer, if he could maintain the attention needed for it, could surveil activity across the spacious central plaza. Because the turret was located at the edge of the plaza, however, rather than at its center, one could not see what was happening at ground level in most of the neighborhood. Perhaps more significant than the turret were the low perimeter walls of every yard, which rose no higher than a person's waist. Clearly, someone intended to keep track of the tenants in this bairro; each unit was given a number and was located on a street with a name, and each tenant established a record with the municipality (that is, the landlord) regarding his or her payment or nonpayment of a monthly rent.

Just about all government initiatives of the time, including forced labor, carried with them the pretension of "civilizing" the natives, and the Bairro Indígena was no exception. Rosa Candla was one of the first residents of the bairro.[138] Born in a rural district, she was orphaned at a young age, and in the early 1940s while she was in her teens, a Portuguese couple drove her to Lourenço Marques so she could try her luck in the city. She was taken in by a railroad worker who had just acquired a house in the Bairro Indígena. They lived together for more than sixty years in a two-room unit near the police post. In a 2009 interview, Candla could not recall much about her life in the neighborhood during the colonial era, but she did relate one story that for her encapsulated the nuisance of living in such close proximity to authorities. Like most of the women in the neighborhood, Candla did her shopping at the nearby Xipamanine market. If she passed the police post with her groceries balanced on her head, the officer on duty would order her to remove her bundles and carry them in her hands at her sides, which presumably was the proper comportment of a civilized Portuguese.[139]

THE PORTUGUESE YARD

For untold numbers of young men and women from southern Mozambique, the daylong bus trip to Lourenço Marques marked their initiation into city life, well before buildings of the City of Cement or its subúrbios came into view. In the rural areas farther north of the city, many young men migrated to the Rand to work on the mines. But during the last decades of

Portuguese rule, the Mozambican capital was the destination of younger brothers and sisters, the more desperate, and tradespeople such as carpenters and stonemasons seeking to establish themselves where there was consistent construction work. For most of the younger passengers, the bus ride was the first time they traveled faster than they could run. They often boarded the bus without a single escudo, without shoes, and without food, and unlike those headed for the mines of "John,"—Johannesburg—most had only a vague sense of where they would stay when they arrived in the city. Many were quite young, preteens and adolescents. Much of what they knew of Lourenço Marques was what they heard on the bus.

A tangle of reasons justified the exodus of these young migrants. Added to forced labor and forced cultivation there were now the perpetual dislocations to make way for Portuguese plantations and other agricultural schemes. One earned only a trickle of cash in the city, but in the countryside, one earned it in dribs and drabs if at all. Still, few Mozambicans cultivated an image of Lourenço Marques as a final destination, a place to build a life and family and to thrive. At best, the city was considered a short- or medium-term measure and a temporary refuge. As soon as they had earned some cash and once the crisis at home had passed, they would return. This, at least, was their thinking when they first came to the city.[140]

A fictional account serialized in *O Brado Africano* in 1959 and 1960 tells the story of Moleque Salomone, a boy from the countryside who tires of laboring in the fields of his Catholic mission school and seeks escape.[141] At the local cantina, he is recruited to work in the home of a Portuguese family in Lourenço Marques. The boy thinks he is twelve years old. The recruiter decides he looks more like fourteen. Salomone discusses his fate with the old miner sharing his seat on the bus to the city. As the landscape rushes past him for the first time, the boy confesses his torn feelings. "No one obligated me to go to the city, but I also didn't abandon home because I wanted to."[142] The miner listens and shares his own misgivings of a life lived mostly away from home. But he offers the boy no consolation. When they arrive at the bus station in Lourenço Marques, the miner has only ominous counsel for him.

> Here, life in the city is different than life in the bush. Here no
> one knows you and you don't know anyone. You'll get to know
> one person or another, but it won't do you any good. Here

The Spaces of Lourenço Marques

you live like a leaf carried from the ground by the wind and that twists in the air without knowing where it's going to fall. The life of a servant is the life of a leaf dragged by the wind. Understand?[143]

He advises Salomone to forget about home; the memory will only distract him from doing a good job. And when he is older, he will realize his mistake in having chosen the urban life, but he will be unable to return home.

Because of the late hour, Salomone must spend the night on the concrete patio of a cantina near the bus stop with other young servant recruits. In the morning, Portuguese men come to claim the boys they signed up to employ. The first building in the City of Cement that Salomone will come to know is the office of the concelho administration, where he will sign the contract that binds him to a Portuguese family for the year. Then, he will be introduced to the family's *quintal* (yard), his new home.

The demand for young male servants grew fierce with the growth of the city's white population.[144] They came cheap, and they were pliable, divorced from family and most other social connections and possible complications. As Penvenne points out, they were preferred to female servants because Portuguese women feared African women would be sexual prey for their husbands, and many African women tried to avoid this type of work in part because they feared the same thing.[145] A young male servant cooked the family breakfast, washed the dishes, made up the beds, fed the dog, and swept the floors. He occupied the very bottom rank, below the cook and the launderer. The cook and launderer usually lived in the subúrbios and walked to work, but the *moleque*, or "kid," as the servant was called, lived on site, occupying a single-room, windowless unit in the yard, usually part of a larger concrete-block structure that was also used for storage. He typically slept on a reed mat. During the day, all servants shared the yard, where most cooking and the washing of clothes took place. Homeowners themselves barely saw the yard, except perhaps when spying it from a window above.

Servants called the head of household *patrão*—a word that combines the senses of the English words *boss* and *patron*. The young servant's daily life was circumscribed by the concrete walls of the yard and the house it served, and so, life stirring beyond the property's boundaries was usually glimpsed only a few hours per week. He could grow quite close to the people he served, and depending on how young he was and the sentiments

of his employers, he might essentially be raised by them. But his utter dependence on his patrões and his near confinement to their home also left
him vulnerable to violent whim. Swift and frequent punishment was levied on servants for lax work, alleged theft, or perceived cheekiness. If the
man of the house did not beat the servant himself, he dragged him to the
police station to have the police administer the beating.[146] The instrument
of choice was a wooden paddle. The *palmatória*, so called because it was
whipped against upturned palms, became a kind of emblem of the arbi-
trariness and brutality of Portuguese rule, long after its use was curtailed in
the late 1950s. The servant's only real protection from an abusive patrão was
the one-year contract—if he could bear the situation that long—coupled
with a fluid market for servants that left few adolescent boys unengaged for
more than a few days.

Adriano Matate arrived in Lourenço Marques in 1950 from rural Gaza;
since he could go no further in school, he needed to secure a job to avoid
chibalo.[147] He found quick employment in the yard of a Portuguese family.
He was sixteen and made 80 escudos per month, a pittance. "They called
us moleque," he recalled years later. "Not 'servant,' not 'workman.' They
called us 'moleque.' You see how it was?" His schedule was simple. When
he was not working or sleeping, he was at church. He left the property to
pray twice a week, on Thursday nights and on Sunday afternoons. Once,
his patrão was away for a week or so. During his absence, police appeared at
the home to question Matate. The wife of his employer had reported him
because surely only a thief, she told them, would be slipping out of the yard
every night. The police searched Matate's small room and then took him to
the station, all the while indicating to him that they did not truly consider
him a suspect in any crime. Unfortunately for Matate, he was detained at a
time when local administrators were being pressured by Lisbon to fill labor
quotas for the cocoa plantations of São Tomé.[148] Within days, he and his
cellmates were on a ship for the remote island colony. Matate was told his
sentence was nine years. His exile lasted twelve.

For many young men working and living in backyards in the City of
Cement, Sunday afternoon was spent in the subúrbios. Out of sight of
patrões and mostly out of sight of police, the bairros were a place to let
off steam. Residents of Chamanculo recall that during the colonial era,
Sunday was actually the most dangerous day of the week. The adolescent
servants dressed themselves up in their most stylish clothes and formed

71

temporary gangs of convenience, roaming suburban lanes in search of other gangs to fight or innocents to rough up. One postindependence novelist, writing in 1985 about the subúrbios in the 1960s, recalled the tranquility that prevailed midweek compared to the weekend, when "fearsome bandits with white trousers" appeared in the neighborhood, "a harmonica on their greedy lips and sugarcane in hand, disemboweling anyone who crossed their path, venting their frustrations and suppressed desires for revenge against the patrões who humiliated them from Monday morning to late Sunday afternoon."[149]

When scholars began in earnest to explore African urban history, they appreciated that what made a city fundamentally different from the countryside—what made it worthy of study in its own right—was its greater diversity within closer confines.[150] People lived side by side with others of different backgrounds and beliefs. They socialized in ways that were entirely new to them.[151] Some tinkered with nationalist ideas. Labor struggles took on a certain edge.[152] New forms of autonomy—cultural, economic, political—emerged among women and men as they found common ground under trying circumstances.[153] In the subúrbios of Lourenço Marques during the last decades of Portuguese rule, women factory workers banded together for mutual support; men shut out of the whites-only football league formed their own; and musicians from around southern Mozambique created a unique style of guitar-driven dance music, *marrabenta*.[154]

Though the social and economic distances between them were usually enormous, Africans of various backgrounds in Lourenço Marques also lived in close proximity to Europeans and people of South Asian descent—mostly as employees. But in many cases, they also met as companions and fellow worshippers and neighbors. Segregationist schemes in cities throughout colonial Africa were halfhearted and incomplete.[155] Even apartheid South Africa, taken as the archetype of racial planning, had its gray zones and people living illegally in outbuildings in white areas; moreover, South African segregation makes no sense without the history of racial proximity and intimacy that it attempted to put an end to.[156] It may seem remarkable that people in Lourenço Marques's City of Cement could be so blind to conditions in subúrbios that were such a short walk away. Then again, ignorance took a great deal of effort.

Figure 1.20 Lídia Manhiça Muhale, Chamanculo, 2011. Muhale and her husband, Filipe Muhale, built their wood-and-zinc house in the 1960s, eventually adding rooms in concrete block to accommodate a growing household. (David Morton)

Figure 2.1 View of the City of Cement from the caniço, 1960s. (Ricardo Rangel/CDFF)

Chapter 2

THE POLITICS OF VISIBILITY

The "City of Reeds" Debate, 1962–65

FEW COLONIZING powers, in any historical context, have been able to resist the appeal of the checkerboard urban grid.[1] The grid demonstrated confidence. It projected, on paper, a controlling authority where otherwise there was little evidence of any. It also worked as a sales pitch: though not yet much to look at, virgin territory, once neatly crisscrossed by streets and avenues, was sure to yield growth. The grid would then harness the growth that followed. The grid "represented a wish, an imagined view of an un-built city," a vision both of European modernity and of universal principles, observes Mark Hinchman, writing about an eighteenth-century town plan for the French outpost at Saint-Louis, Senegal.[2] "Its repetitive form implied the existence of similar forms elsewhere." Europeans were less convinced they needed the grid for cities in Europe; some of the most conspicuous checkerboard plans in the nineteenth century were actually in the industrializing cities of the United States. After Lourenço Marques had grown into much of its own grid, some commentators regretted that planners had opted for the pragmatic "American" approach decades earlier.[3] The grid of Lourenço Marques was monotonous, wrote a Portuguese official in 1945. It "bores us."[4]

Boring, in principle at least, meant predictable. To many, the rational geometries of the City of Cement's streetscape were proof of rational behavior. By contrast, the labyrinthine lanes of the subúrbios meant chaos, "an anarchy without name."[5] Even many residents of the subúrbios thought so. But the curving boundary separating city and subúrbios need not be understood, as it often was, as the line dividing order from disorder.[6] In his work on the outskirts of Zanzibar's Stone Town, Garth Myers describes a "disorderly order," the result of people building where they could and how they could, though still disciplined by custom and patronage.[7] In the subúrbios, the struggle for land and shelter may not have been as institutionalized as it was in Zanzibar, but it still followed established routines. And in Lourenço Marques's City of Cement, the appearance of visual order often hid messier realities. One obvious, if superficial, example was the street grid itself. It may have felt monotonous, but a glance at the map reveals that it was actually full of irregularities. As happened with most grid plans, straight lines were diverted by terrain and existing roads. Surveyors had to work around parcels of land that had previously been surveyed and registered. What was probably a simple miscalculation set one of the city's longest avenues wandering at an angle between parallel thoroughfares.[8] Many city blocks were parallelograms and trapezoids, even if sometimes only subtly so, rather than rectangles. Other odd shapes were produced where the grid met the curve of the old municipal boundary (see Figures I.3 and 1.2).

These imperfections had few consequences. But beginning in the 1950s, a number of architects in Lourenço Marques, for what seem to have been aesthetic reasons, designed buildings that were parallelogram-shaped in plan, rather than rectilinear, to go with parallelogram-shaped or trapezoidal lots. The lack of precise right angles vaguely distorted building facades, but the effect on interiors was almost imperceptible. One imagines the extra work that these slightly off-kilter plans demanded of the tradespeople who cut and fitted tiles and parquet floors—the countless calculations and countless mistakes they made, multiplied across the city, at modest pay and with little discernible result.

As Lourenço Marques doubled in size in the 1950s and doubled again in the 1960s, the City of Cement grew in height. Avenues bristled with new apartment towers, often built on speculation and cheap loans.[9] The government had encouraged banks to loosen credit, allowing many European settlers to build small apartment blocks as investment properties and to give them "confidence in the future," writes José Luís Cabaço.[10] Construction was political stagecraft. For the regime and also for many Portuguese, the skyline became a powerful visible symbol, perhaps *the* symbol, of Portugal's commitment to staying in Mozambique.[11] Long before, many sidewalks downtown were paved in the black-and-white style common to most all Portuguese cities.[12] A worker on his knees laid out mosaics of black basalt and white limestone. He felt for the contours of a small block in his palm, quickly chose a spot for it, and then hammered it into place, thousands of times over, to make a gridded carpet of rock. The walkways of Lourenço Marques established a visual link with the streets of Lisbon, with other far-flung territories of the ultramar, and with the Portuguese past. In the 1960s, as if people had not yet gotten the message, the paving on one of the city's most prominent plazas was relaid so that black stones against a white background spelled out the phrase *Aqui é Portugal*—Here is Portugal.

Ultimately, construction of the City of Cement depended on cheap African labor. Until the 1960s, a certain portion of the workforce was chibalo and therefore coerced. Reforms in the early sixties officially abolished forced labor and systematic workplace abuse, and incomes for many people in the subúrbios rose, but neighborhoods grew more dense and living conditions in some ways more difficult. In large measure, the towers of Lourenço Marques and its well-manicured avenues were possible because African workers were supposed to make do with so little—in wages, in housing, and in basic municipal services. The City of Cement, with its appearance of order, existed thanks to the "anarchy" of the subúrbios.[13]

City and subúrbio shared a single history. They had emerged from the same late nineteenth-century landgrab, when nearly all of the terrain in both the nascent city and its subúrbios, whether already inhabited or not, was parceled out and either titled to people with connections to the municipal bureaucracy or sold for a pittance to foreign speculators. It was a corrupt process no one would call organized, but to this day, the parcels for both city and subúrbios appear on the books at the municipality, on the same chart, much as they did about a century ago.[14] A map of Chamanculo can be pieced together from among parcels numbered 201 through 459. In 1947, an official remarking on the pitiable conditions prevailing in the subúrbios reported, "These unfortunates, besides living miserably in huts constructed of various materials, are still obliged to pay rents for plots on land that might in the past have belonged to their grandparents and are

77

now legally owned and titled by Europeans."[15] A number of titleholders in the subúrbios were also mestiços and Asians, many of them linked to what had been the leading African lineages of the area. Most of the land was in the hands of a very few. By the late 1960s, in fact, an estimated 85 percent of land in the subúrbios not held by the municipality or the state was titled to a mere eleven private landowners, with the rest of it split among several hundred small property owners.[16] According to an overlapping set of norms, much of suburban Lourenço Marques also belonged to a handful of régulos, the traditional leaders appointed by the Portuguese, whom many considered to be "owners of the land" by virtue of inherited right.[17]

Though off the grid, residents of the subúrbios were not illegal squatters. A prospective renter of land found a clear area on which to build a house and agreed to pay the landowner an annual ground rent. The renter and the landlord then informed the local régulo, who received a commission for the transaction. Often, a renter sought permission from the régulo before approaching the landowner—much as a régulo would apportion land in the countryside. Landlords sometimes complained that régulos reached agreements with renters without their knowledge,[18] and sometimes, the régulo *was* the landlord, an especially fraught arrangement for the tenant.[19] Many renters of land built houses that they subsequently rented out. To advertise a vacancy, they affixed sheets of blank white paper to a front window or outside wall, just as one did in the City of Cement.

House construction, too, followed long-established practices. As described in the previous chapter, most houses (except the most elaborate ones of wood and zinc) were built according to almost uniform specifications and with almost uniform methods, with little to distinguish one from the other. Three building types have dominated the subúrbios for most of the last century. The reed house has been built in essentially the same way since at least the 1940s. A wood-and-zinc home built in the 1960s was very similar on the outside to one built two or three generations before (though it was more likely to have a hidden concrete-block interior). The suburban masonry house emerged in the 1960s, and it has been built in roughly the same way and with many of the same stylistic flourishes ever since.[20] Moreover, house construction in the subúrbios was integrated into the regional economy. Nearly all materials used in suburban house construction were purchased at market stalls in and around the subúrbios or at large retailers downtown; it was not uncommon for a downtown store to make a delivery of zinc panels directly to the subúrbios. Some enterprising individuals in the subúrbios became materials suppliers simply by having access to a truck. According to rough estimates from the early 1960s, total investments in reed and wood-and-zinc house construction in the subúrbios amounted to 100 to 200 million escudos, a sum comparable in value to all oil imports to the province in 1962.[21]

Despite the symbolic importance of the curving street between city and subúrbios, colonial-era administrators never quite resolved where they thought the city ended and the bush began. Suburban housing existed in a legal netherworld.[22] Though situated on land that was largely held in private title, many parts of the subúrbios were set aside as "native reserves."[23] Until the 1960s, the reserves theoretically functioned as any rural jurisdiction would, under the customary authority of a régulo. Housing was permitted — that is, it was not illegal — only so long as it was of "precarious" construction, such as in reeds or in wood and zinc. That way, it could be easily demolished to make way for future expansions of the City of Cement. Yet city services were not totally absent from the subúrbios. Municipal police patrolled neighborhoods on horseback. And even though most people used pit latrines, people of greater means in older neighborhoods benefited (if that is the proper word) from a bucket system of sewage removal administered by the municipality.[24] The several thousand households that paid the fee for this service had their pails of waste emptied every evening by men who carted disposal tanks through suburban lanes. One former resident recalled that her parents scheduled dinners early, before the evening passage of the sewage cart, so that the stench would not ruin mealtimes.[25]

In 1967, the man in charge of the bucket disposal teams was a young municipal employee named Carlos Carvalho.[26] Years later, after independence, he became a high-ranking cultural affairs official, but in the 1960s, he was simply the bookish son of a Portuguese family with deep roots in Mozambique — "old colonos," in the local parlance. His uncle was the city manager for Lourenço Marques and part of the "fascist elite" Carvalho said he wanted nothing to do with, but his uncle gave him a job when he needed one. Carvalho gave himself additional work, in addition to his waste-bucket responsibilities. On his own initiative, he instituted suburban street cleanup crews. His superiors initially ignored his requests for personnel, but eventually they gave Carvalho two brigades for the job (well short of the seven brigades dedicated to the much smaller City of Cement).

79

His crews walked suburban roadways picking up litter and filling pools of standing water. People buried household trash in their yards, but Carvalho's crews used a tractor to haul out some of the larger piles that collected in common areas. Still, there was only so much that sixteen men could do; hundreds of thousands of people lived in these neighborhoods. Carvalho marveled at how obsessive many people were in keeping their yards and the spaces in front of their houses swept clean, and how they planted trees and lined their properties with flowers. Sweeping the yard, even if it might not appear to need it, has long been an almost ritualistic practice: it clears the space of malevolent forces, helping people evade misfortunes that others may be wishing upon them.[27] "Some areas of the subúrbios were *impeccable*," Carvalho said, "incredibly beautiful."[28]

Despite the best efforts of suburban residents to maintain comfort and dignity in such conditions, the city's juxtaposition of luxury and neglect made plain the absurdity of Portugal's supposedly color-blind rule. In the subúrbios, the image the regime tried to cultivate as a modernizing, beneficent force ran aground.[29] One of the duties of the official press censor in Lourenço Marques was to keep photographs of African neighborhoods entirely out of the news. The subúrbios also posed a more direct, existential threat: officials feared, justifiably, that they incubated revolt.[30] In 1962, three Mozambican anticolonial groups in exile came together to form FRELIMO (Frente de Libertação de Moçambique, or Mozambique Liberation Front).[31] By 1964, Frelimo guerrillas were waging a war for independence in Mozambique's rural north. Not incidentally, many in the highest ranks of the group had at one time or another called the subúrbios of Lourenço Marques home.

But the war was fought a thousand miles away. Despite the wave of decolonization across the continent, Africans in Lourenço Marques could not organize themselves into any sort of political opposition. There was no sustained nationalist agitation. There were no street demonstrations. And there were hardly any labor actions to speak of. One notable exception was a work stoppage by stevedores at the city docks in 1963, which lasted a few days before it was quashed and led to better pay for dockworkers.[32] Historians have recorded no other strikes in Lourenço Marques until the fall of the Lisbon dictatorship in 1974.[33] For Portuguese propagandists, the lack of evident discontent was proof of African contentment. But the state enforced the silence. Through torture and an expansive network of informers, the secret police—PIDE (Polícia Internacional e de Defesa do Estado)—ruthlessly suppressed meaningful dissent. Officials shut down the major African social organizations, which had functioned, in part, as debating societies, and treated open discussions of racism as acts of subversion.[34] Rarely were Africans in the city able to air their grievances in anything like a public forum. For most of the 1960s, local newspapers fed their readers a low-calorie version of current events: ministerial pronouncements, insubstantial updates on the Cold War, sports recaps, and articles about *American* racism. A would-be dissenter's first step forward was the one that took him or her to safe haven outside Mozambique.

One major issue affecting African life, however, managed to generate a public stir. In the early 1960s, Lisbon was under new pressures to justify its presence in Africa, not just to the many in the international community pushing for decolonization but also to Africans in its territories. The regime's reformist wing partially relaxed censorship, and in 1962, journalists at an upstart daily newspaper called A *Tribuna* took advantage of the opportunity. They launched a campaign to make conditions in the subúrbios visible to the paper's mostly white readership and, by extension, to authorities—or rather, the newspaper forcibly removed the blinders. The campaign lasted less than a year before censorship tightened again, but articles about the need for improved housing in the subúrbios continued to appear on occasion in local media, and the issue continued to be debated in other arenas. This was the shape that politics took in Lourenço Marques in the 1960s. You could not talk frankly about racial discrimination; instead, you talked about it by urging the municipality to improve conditions in the City of Reeds—which is what A *Tribuna* called its series of exposés.

This chapter examines the evolving engagement between those who would govern and those who would be governed: how authorities were compelled to provide for suburban residents in ways they never had before, how people in the subúrbios developed new expectations of what authorities ought to provide for them, and how the problem of housing became the point of friction. The first section addresses the vacuum of governance in the subúrbios, necessary for understanding the full scope of suburban grievance. Because there was no trusted authority in the subúrbios to resolve the disputes that arose between landlords and tenants, residents had to resort to ad hoc solutions of their own. The examples used here are concentrated in the late 1950s and early 1960s, but the circumstances described

81

apply to later years as well. The second section of the chapter discusses the City of Reeds campaign. The third section reveals other ways, usually less publicized, that residents were challenging authorities to improve housing conditions. All these claims rested on a novel premise: that the subúrbios and the city ought to be considered as one.

THE PROBLEM OF FENCES

Older residents remember the Chamanculo of their childhoods as mato — that is, bush. Unlike in the countryside, however, properties in the area were often demarcated by fences. Home dwellers were marking the boundaries of their plots of land as early as the 1940s, most likely much earlier. Giving order to urban space means, in part, being able to divide it, and one often felt the need to define property limits precisely because the conviviality that characterizes so many nostalgic accounts of the past also had its limits.

The simplest boundary marker was a wire suspended on short posts, perhaps no more than knee high. Spiny bushes, which came up to the waist, were more effective as barriers—to corral chickens, for instance. Those who could do so built reed fences or fences of zinc panels or flattened oil drums. Fencing did more than demarcate property: it hid it. Reeds or metal panels shielded latrines and bathing spaces, and they aided anyone who wanted privacy for activities such as brewing alcohol, which, in addition to being a vital source of income to many women, was also illegal and heavily policed. In Chamanculo today, fences are either walls of concrete block built up well above eye level (often with glass shards embedded in the top of the wall like a jagged crown) or old stretches of zinc panels. Behind these walls are trees. The mato that exists in memory did not entirely disappear; rather, high fences put much of it out of the sight of pedestrians. A recent satellite view of Chamanculo shows that the neighborhood is abundantly green, though it seems cement gray and dust brown at street level.

During the colonial era and even until recent times, the reed fence was a source of perpetual friction between neighbors, as explained in 2012 by Bartolomeu Tembe, who soon afterward was appointed Chamanculo's régulo.[35] First, as with any fence, was the matter of who was responsible for it. The fence was built by whoever tackled the job first. Rarely did neighbors share the duty, and the fence builder often justified the expense incurred by pushing out the boundary of his or her property by a foot or two. Revising the boundary this way seriously provoked one's neighbor, the more so as the subúrbios grew more dense. No document recorded the interior lines of a landowner's property, that is, the division between two rented plots. Nor did landowners precisely demarcate which plots belonged to whom. The fence itself was the proof of where the fence ought to be. And since reeds rotted every few years, nerves were not given much time to settle. The boundary between two plots was subject to constant revision.

Landowners did not step in to resolve these kinds of disputes. Presumably, they had the authority to determine where one rental plot within their property ended and another began. And if the adjoining plots were owned in title by different people, the titleholders might have considered the protection of their respective tenants' interests the equivalent to protecting their own. But landowners generally kept out of it. In 1962, a member of the newly installed city council publicly chastised landowners in the subúrbios for neglecting their properties and for not parceling them in orderly fashion.[36] He accused the landowners of being greedy land speculators. Some of them replied that their properties were usually occupied without their knowledge and that they rarely actually charged the tenants rent.

Tenants did not expect landlords to intervene in conflicts among neighbors and rarely asked them to get involved, but those really moved to could take a dispute to the régulo. The job of the régulo and his force of *cipaios* (native police officers) included collecting taxes, suppressing the production and sale of traditional brews, and executing any other of the administration's orders within his jurisdiction.[37] Before forced labor was abolished in 1961, the tasks also included rounding up people for chibalo. In addition, the régulo was the arbiter of customary law, unless overruled by the Portuguese post administrator. From 1945 until he was deposed in 1974, the appointed traditional leader of Chamanculo was Frederico de Almeida Cumba.[38] He was someone to be avoided whenever possible.

Frederico, as he is universally recalled, was living in South Africa when Portuguese administrators called him back to Lourenço Marques and to Chamanculo to be régulo. The previously appointed régulo, Frederico's brother, had been accused of protecting illegal brewers and profiting from it, exactly the kind of activity the régulo and his enforcers were supposed to suppress.[39] (Some years after independence, Frederico recalled his appointment differently; he told a reporter that his brother had been removed for resisting Portuguese authority.)[40] Administrators consulted the Cumba

83

J.A.J. Gumba

family tree in search of a suitable substitute. Frederico was not next in the line of succession, but those ahead of him were not deemed proper régulo material, and so Frederico, an assimilado then in his early thirties, was summoned from the Rand.[41]

According to his youngest daughter, Ana Laura Cumba, administrators had given Frederico little choice but to accept his appointment. The job may not have seemed desirable at first. It was an unsalaried position, and at a 1972 meeting of administrators and traditional leaders, Frederico complained that the expenses of city life made it difficult to get by without a government stipend.[42] In earlier years, before the boom in the suburban population, the complaint might have had some merit. In 1950, a Portuguese official had recommended that, because even traditional leaders had

Figure 2.2 (*opposite*) Frederico de Almeida Cumba, the longtime Portuguese-appointed traditional leader of Chamanculo, 1950s. (Ana Laura Cumba)

Figure 2.3 Traditional leaders, their police officers, and Portuguese administrators of Lourenço Marques, 1950s. Frederico is second from the left. (Ana Laura Cumba)

to rent the land they lived on in the subúrbios, the government ought to secure land and build houses for them "to put them in a position of prominence before their subordinated populations," as if that prominence were not otherwise assured.[43] (It is unclear whether anything came of the idea, but the official evidently put a lot of stock in the persuasive power of architecture, arguing that his suggestion "could bring many advantages to the native policy of the Concelho.") Over the years, however, suburban life proved lucrative for traditional leaders. Living in the heart of the colonial cash economy, they had ample opportunity to fill their pockets through extortion, the acceptance of bribes, and fees—such as the fee charged in rental transactions. Frederico's jurisdiction was more populous than the effective jurisdiction of any traditional leader in Lourenço Marques, and the income he generated was commensurate with the size of his domain.[44] During his almost thirty-year reign, he accumulated a large wood-and-zinc house in Chamanculo with concrete-block interior walls, seven rental homes in Chamanculo and other areas of the subúrbios, a concrete-block house in Matola (a new satellite city of Lourenço Marques), and a car. Until the fall of the colonial regime, he probably had little reason to regret returning home from the South African mines.

Frederico did not have an office in Chamanculo, but he had a courtroom. Every Sunday, his leather-seated armchair—his "throne," as his daughter recalled it—was set under two mango trees beside his house for the weekly court session, called the *bandla* (Figure 2.4). Frederico's counselors arrived before he did and sat in chairs beside the throne, and at about 7:00 a.m., they began to hear cases that had been lodged during the week. Frederico would arrive a few hours later, and he would sit silently for the remaining cases as his counselors asked questions of the various parties. By evening, after consulting the counselors, Frederico would issue his judgments. Most cases involved domestic disputes, such as questions of paternity and spousal abuse. There were also cases of theft—for instance, the theft of chickens or building materials. A thief or assailant who was found guilty would have a sack wrapped around his or her waist, and a cipaio would lash the accused with a hippo-hide whip. The purpose of the sack was to catch what the bowels released. More complex cases were referred upward to the Portuguese officer who manned the Munhuana administrative post—and from there, potentially, to the administrator of the concelho.

Figure 2.4 Frederico and his counselors hold court, 1950s. (Ana Laura Cumba)

People generally recognized the legitimacy of the régulo's authority—in retrospect, at least. Decades later, it is difficult to encounter older people in Maputo, however, who will share a bandla experience. Perhaps the reticence results from sensitivities about the facts that were in dispute (domestic abuse, for example). Perhaps it is because to appear before the bandla was to participate in the second tier of a system of justice that recognized a hierarchy of laws: the Portuguese law, reserved for the so-called civilized, and the law of "customs and traditions" that governed the so-called primitive. Or perhaps people do not have these stories to tell because the bandla was simply a tribunal to be avoided if at all possible. It cost 40 escudos to file a complaint, the equivalent of twenty-five loaves of bread, and the form of justice dispensed by Frederico and his counselors was not widely trusted. The winner of a dispute over a fence—or any dispute, for that matter—was often determined by who offered the higher bribe.

None of the older residents of Chamanculo spoke in interviews of seeking redress with Portuguese authorities, though some clearly did, just as people reluctantly consulted the régulo's authority.[45] In general, colonial officials were approached with great circumspection. The administrative post and the police station were considered places of fear where one went only when absolutely necessary. At least until the early 1960s, they were sites of arbitrary violence, where people were beaten because of perceived defiance or merely disrespect. In the 1930s, an area of the subúrbios where the main suburban police post was located acquired the name Mukumula (meaning, in Ronga, "the one who says 'strip'") because of a notoriously brutal police officer who worked there—before people were whipped, he ordered them to disrobe.[46] Officials eventually decided that rural justice was incompatible with suburban life, and beginning in 1954, natives of the subúrbios, "detribalized" if not legally assimilated, were supposed to be granted their own court system.[47] But such tribunals were never implemented. In the 1960s, all Mozambicans were given the theoretical right of access, as Portuguese citizens, to civil courts, though in reality and due to numerous obstacles—such as the expense and difficulty of filing the necessary paperwork—few could or would exercise that right.[48] Those appealing to higher authority to resolve a complaint were now more likely to seek out post administrators or the municipal police and bypass the régulo altogether.[49] Nonetheless, authorities continued to rely on régulos because they knew the cultural

Figure 2.5 Another important suburban institution: traditional healers, Chamanculo, 1950s. (Castigo Guambe)

terrain, such as customs of inheritance, far better than the authorities did themselves.[50] They also simply knew the terrain. In a place without physical addresses, régulos helped officials locate complainants, defendants, witnesses, and suspects.

Though the emphasis shifted from customary justice to administrative arbitration, this is not to say that post administrators gave complaints an attentive hearing. The daily work logs of Portuguese post administrators at Munhuana from the 1960s are full of dismissive references to mornings and afternoons spent attending to everyday matters called *milandos,* meaning "petty or domestic disputes."[51] It appears that post administrators rarely opened case files or officially registered the existence of individual cases. (At least, such records cannot be located.) Rather, they indicated to superiors that on a given day, "milandos"—not "complaints," not "cases"—had been dealt with. In the subúrbios, the Portuguese passion for bureaucratic procedure was not much in evidence.

Residents of the subúrbios, by contrast, often guarded what few paper records they had in their possession. Most homes in these neighborhoods lacked closets, and people generally could not afford cabinets

89

or armoires. Zinc-panel roofs leaked in the rain, and no walls, not even concrete walls, were a barrier against moisture. For something of the past to have survived to the present—especially something as fragile as paper—required effort. People stored their most valued possessions in suitcases until they could purchase a wood trunk, itself among a family's most valued objects.[52]

In trunks, enclosed in brown envelopes, people have safeguarded wedding photographs and colonial-era forms of identification for years. Many have held on to their *caderneta de indígena*, the pass document that they had to carry at all times more than half a century ago. The small booklet informed any official who asked for it of the holder's name, birthplace, and parentage as well as whether they had permission to live in Lourenço Marques, where they worked, and if an employer or the police at some time or another had found cause to discipline them. The document, replaced by other forms of identification in the 1960s, was necessary in any interaction with officialdom, and the consequences of not having it were steep. In some cases, it might also have contained the only photo that a person had of him- or herself.[53]

In the same envelope with photographs and old IDs, people often keep years of old rental receipts. Although some landowners claimed at the time that they did not charge ground rent, not a single person interviewed for this book said they lived rent-free—unless they owned the plot. Whether one lived in a wood-framed, zinc-paneled home with four rooms, a two-room reed house, or a tiny unit in a compound, one usually received a signed receipt as proof of paying rent, annually if for land or monthly if for shelter. The Guilundo family lived in a house of reeds in Chamanculo that they built themselves. The receipts they received upon paying the annual ground rent were preprinted with the landowner's name, giving them a supposedly official appearance and revealing something of the routinized functioning of the housing market as a whole[54] (Figure 2.6). In the absence of renter's agreements or legal contracts of any sort, receipts were the contracts. They added the veneer of legitimacy to the tenant's presence up to the point the rent was paid, which was not inconsequential given that most people's very presence in Lourenço Marques was highly contingent. A thick pile of receipts officialized, in its own small way, a home dweller's tenure—at least, tenants *hoped* that it would—and so it is little wonder that piles of these receipts

Figure 2.6 An annual ground-rent receipt for a small plot in Chamanculo, 1958. (Armando Guilundo)

from the colonial era survive to the present, existing now as then as a kind of claim before imagined authorities. Jochua Guambe, an African landlord who owned a few dozen properties in Chamanculo, kept copies of receipts for rents received. The receipts are still in the possession of his son Castigo, even though the properties themselves were nationalized decades ago.

A handful of cases from the late 1950s and early 1960s provide a glimpse of the confused relationship between law and authority as it pertained to housing matters. There are only six housing disputes from the 1940s and 1950s in the archives of Mozambique's Native Affairs agency. Until the early 1960s, this agency was charged with protecting the interests and well-being of those with "native" classification and resolving conflicts between them and people who had the status of citizens.[55] From these sparse cases, it is evident why so few housing disputes were resolved through official channels. Administrators, police, and magistrates were befuddled by the cases brought before them and unsure who had jurisdiction in such matters. Nowhere in the documentation of these few cases did an official invoke

91

a law that might be germane to the given situation, perhaps due to unfamiliarity with the law or to a reflexive reluctance to use it to settle what were considered mere milandos.

In 1961, a young carpenter named Joel Chioco Palene sought the help of authorities.[56] Though only nineteen, Palene was already building his own house on a plot he rented in Chamanculo. In two months, he had built everything but the roof. One day, he arrived at the site to work on the roof only to find that his house was gone. In its place, a man named Raimundo had built a house of his own. Palene's first course of action was to complain to Chamanculo's régulo, Frederico, and his counselors. Then, Palene, Raimundo, and the régulo and his counselors went to the Munhuana administrative post, where an agreement was reached: Raimundo would rebuild Palene's house on another part of the same rented plot.

Typical of housing disputes at the time, the owner of the plot in question was absent from the proceedings. But he was not absent from the case file. The owner was identified as Frenque Estevão Nhamana, and he was referred to in the file as a "misto," a person of mixed race, which would have distinguished him from Palene, a mere "native." Yet that was all the file said about Nhamana. He apparently did not involve himself in the dispute's resolution, nor does it appear that anyone sought his involvement—not Palene, Raimundo, the régulo Frederico, or the Portuguese post administrator. As with many conflicts involving housing, the owner's hands-off attitude toward his own property was what had contributed to the problem in the first place. Nhamana had rented land to two people on the same plot without evident concern as to where they built their houses, and for that act of carelessness, no one—not even the affected tenants—held him responsible.

Administrative intervention came to little effect. The agreement between the two tenants did not hold. Six months later, Raimundo still had not followed through on his promise to rebuild Palene's house, arguing that there was no room on the small plot to rebuild it. So Palene returned to the Munhuana administrative post. The administrator might have ordered the landowner to provide Palene a new plot, seemingly the obvious solution, but instead, he wiped his hands of the case. He instructed Palene to bring the matter to the attention of the concelho administration. From there, Palene was sent to the District Court and then to the municipal police.

The police sent him back to where he had started: the Munhuana administrative post. Desperate to find someone in a position of authority to come to his aid, Palene filed his complaint with the Native Affairs agency, and the director of the agency forwarded it, without comment, to the governor of the District of Lourenço Marques. Unfortunately, the case file does not record how the matter was finally resolved, if it ever was.

That Palene continued to press his case until it reached the governor's desk may have owed something to his personal ambition. In 1961, to be nineteen and building one's own house on a plot of land that cost 400 escudos in rent per year was not easy. The person who could accomplish that was perhaps more likely to insist on what he perceived to be his rights, whatever the obstacles might be. The obstacle in this instance was not outright official hostility, and his case was never thrown out as far as we know. Actually, the injustice of his situation made an impression on his various audiences, and his case was repeatedly referred to higher authority, eventually as high as the district governor. Yet the sympathy of some officials for Palene and the sense that something ought to be done for him did not translate into a concerted bureaucratic effort on his behalf. The mechanism to resolve his case existed. What was lacking was an interest in putting the mechanism in motion.

Two years before, in 1959, another carpenter, Chipanela Jentimanhana Macuacua, wrote to the inspector of the Native Affairs agency in hopes that the official could get his rent lowered. Macuacua had lived for eighteen years near Chamanculo, on a plot behind the municipal slaughterhouse. Between 1953 and 1959, the Portuguese who owned the plot had quadrupled Macuacua's annual ground rent to 400 escudos. When he fell behind in payments, the landlord moved another twenty-five people onto the property, knocking down his latrine and bathing stall in the process. In his letter, Macuacua stated: "Because I don't have money to move my shack from the plot in question, knowing that the Illustrious Sir"—the official to whom the letter was addressed—"is the father and mother of all the black people of this Province of Mozambique, I come humbly before your Excellency to request the case be investigated." Macuacua's appeal was forwarded upward, without comment, to the secretary-general of the District of Lourenço Marques. Its final resolution, if any, is unclear. It is significant, however, that in neither of these two cases did the complainants or the officials to whom they presented their situations make mention of the

93

law. In both cases, moreover, legislation may have been applicable: a 1939 measure capped at 40 escudos per hectare the annual rent that could be charged natives who settled on suburban land.[57] Legislation in the 1960s regarding the subúrbios dropped this rent ceiling. Its absence was a "flagrant omission," commented social researcher António Rita-Ferreira in 1968, as it made official the long-standing disinterest of local authorities in resolving suburban landlord-tenant disputes.

Jochua Guambe, a big-game hunter who built a large portfolio of rental properties in Chamanculo (as mentioned earlier), occasionally found himself in a difficult position relative to some of his tenants.[58] Guambe had accomplished what few "natives" at the time managed to do. Without a formal education and without ever having worked for a European employer, he had amassed a small fortune by the 1950s based on suburban property ownership. He was able to do so, in part, because his sons were, according to the law, assimilados; Guambe required the signature of his oldest son to officialize title documents. He himself, though, spoke barely any Portuguese, and despite the fact that his accomplishments earned him a considerable stature in Chamanculo, he did not enjoy the respect of some of his assimilado tenants. According to Guambe's son Castigo, some of these tenants would refuse to pay rent from time to time. The tenants calculated that the landlord, a mere indígena legally, would be unable to collect it.

Once, after unsuccessfully attempting to collect arrears from an assimilado tenant—a nurse—Guambe lodged a complaint with Frederico, the régulo. The nurse did not show up for the bandla, and when Frederico ruled in favor of Guambe, the nurse simply ignored the régulo's order. Guambe then resorted to a tactic said to be common in landlord-tenant disputes of the time. Although the plot of land on which the nurse lived belonged to Guambe, the wood-and-zinc house on the plot had been built by the nurse himself. Guambe waited for an evening when it threatened to storm. With the nurse away, he sent a handyman to the house to tear the zinc panels off the roof. Rain soaked through the nurse's false ceiling and ruined his furniture. Now it was *his* turn to lodge a complaint with the régulo. Guambe was summoned to defend himself. Chamanculo's court of customary law frequently functioned according to régulo Frederico's whim, but in this case at least, documentary evidence—or rather, its absence—held sway. The aggrieved tenant could not produce receipts demonstrating that he had paid his ground rent to Guambe. "You never lived here," Guambe said to the nurse. The ruling went for the landowner.

BEHIND THE "REED CURTAIN"

In early 1961, Eduardo Mondlane took leave from his position at the UN and, preceded by his American wife and children, returned to Mozambique, his homeland, for the first time in a decade.[59] He considered his months-long visit an opportunity to assess Portuguese rule up close. He met with Portuguese officials and asked them pointed questions about the welfare of black Mozambicans.[60] Tailed by the secret police, he held secret discussions with members of the Swiss Mission, the Presbyterians in whose schools he had been educated, and encouraged them to act against the colonial regime. He was taken by surprise by the celebrity treatment he received from the enthusiastic crowds that received him in Lourenço Marques and in the nearby countryside.[61] It appears that Mondlane's visit settled him on the course he would take. The following year, in Dar es Salaam, Mondlane was elected to lead the newly formed Frelimo.

While still in Mozambique, Mondlane already gave some not-so-veiled indications of his thinking. During a sermon at the Presbyterian church in Chamanculo, he invoked a parable of an eagle that was popularized by a Ghanaian-born missionary early in the century. The parable, which was also dear to Kwame Nkrumah, was often taken as a call for African independence, as it was by many in Mondlane's audience.[62] One stonemason recently recalled the day when Mondlane visited his construction site, on the far side of the Infulene River, about 6 miles from downtown Lourenço Marques.[63] The Infulene project was part of a renewed, if halfhearted, effort to build housing for Africans, the first since the Bairro Indígena nearly two decades before. Far from the city and far from where people worked, Infulene was a shoddier version of apartheid planning, but it vividly demonstrated the reality of what Lisbon called its civilizing effort. Mondlane addressed the construction workers with a prophecy. "Brothers, listen well," he said in Changana. "We shall take this land."

Mondlane's time in Mozambique coincided with the most radical reorientation of Portugal's relationship to its African territories since the early 1930s.[64] Portugal had been ruled since 1926 by a right-wing dictatorship,

95

headed from 1932 to 1968 by António de Oliveira Salazar. The Salazar regime instituted what it called the New State (Estado Novo), a corporatist, rigidly Catholic, quasi-fascist restructuring of Portuguese governance. A central pillar of the Salazarist program was the more efficient and comprehensive exploitation of the colonies to serve Portugal's needs, necessitating Lisbon's tighter political and economic control. In the late 1950s and early 1960s, as the other European empires were being rapidly dismantled, Portugal remained steadfast in its refusal to part with its African and Asian possessions. In January 1961, shortly before Mondlane's arrival in Lourenço Marques, a revolt broke out in Angola. In the following months, the Kennedy administration joined the chorus at the United Nations calling for Portuguese decolonization, and Salazar had to outmaneuver a nascent plot against him by regime elements who had lost faith in his Africa policies. Shaken by events, he elevated officials who were pushing liberal reforms.[65]

In Lisbon in 1961, a flurry of legislation sponsored by new minister of the ultramar Adriano Moreira and the regime's more liberal wing wiped from the books the most nakedly abusive laws. The indigenato—the legal apparatus that sustained the system of forced labor that had long been a focus of international criticism—was officially abolished, as was compulsory crop cultivation. The ministry deployed a "psychosocial" campaign to win the loyalty of a wider stratum of Africans, and a small army of social workers from the metropole descended on Portugal's African territories to attend to the "economically infirm." The word indígena was phased out of the official lexicon and was replaced in government reports by autochthone, an awkward locution that carried a vague air of scientific objectivity.[66] Back in 1951, in an effort to deflect external pressures to decolonize, Portugal had refashioned its colonies as noncontiguous provinces of a single, multiracial nation, and the former Ministry of the Colonies was renamed the Ministry of the Ultramar. Now, with pressures intensified, Lisbon attempted to inject new life into an idea of Portuguese exceptionalism that intellectuals had cultivated for decades. Inspired by the Lusotropicalist theories of Brazilian sociologist Gilberto Freyre, regime propagandists and true believers argued that the Portuguese had proven for five hundred years that they were natural colonizers, with an innate respect for other peoples and a talent for assimilating them into European culture[67] (Figure 2.7).

Figure 2.7 1960s-era Lisbon propaganda: "Mozambique only is Mozambique because it is Portugal." (IPAD, no. 14408. See also www.hoteluniverso.wordpress .com/2010/10/29/portugal-is-not-small)

Moreira imbued with a technocratic spirit the various new institutions that Lisbon was establishing in the provinces to replace the now-defunct native affairs agencies. Between 1958 and 1962, responsibility for public housing was incrementally removed from the municipality of Lourenço Marques, whose meager efforts over the decades were widely considered pitiful, and put in the hands of a newly formed entity called the Junta dos Bairros e Casas Populares (Board of People's Neighborhoods and Houses) with its own staff of architects.[68] Providing housing for the poor in Portugal's African cities was an opportunity for the state to showcase social engineering guided by enlightened principles.[69] In the fulfillment of what Moreira called Portugal's "historic task," new multiracial communities in the African provinces, built from scratch, would act as mechanisms of assimilation. In 1962, Mário de Oliveira, a senior architect with the ministry's Department of Urbanism and a Moreira acolyte, elaborated a prototype for multiracial communities on the outskirts of Bissau, the capital of Guiné.[70] Europeans and "evolved" Africans would live side by side with the "less evolved," so that the latter could absorb their "habits, tastes, manners, [and] moral

97

conduct."[71] The plan reflected a new acceptance within Portuguese policy circles that cities were appropriate places for Africans to live, rather than places that would lead inevitably to their ruin. Oliveira, however, cautioned that the process ought to be slow. Houses built for autochthones should be similar to the rustic shelters to which they were accustomed so as to avoid "psychosomatic" disorientation. In these planned integrated communities, he argued, the natives would live "under constant observation, whether at work, in school, or at sport or recreation," and this would mold their personalities accordingly. They would gradually learn to participate in urban society, to support themselves, and to consider themselves "authentic" individuals. Oliveira was emphatic that Portugal's future in Africa was dependent on such social engineering. It was key to developing "humanistic feelings and love for the Motherland" and building a "national community."[72]

On a visit to Mozambique a few years later, Oliveira saw in the subúrbios of Quelimane, a city in central Mozambique, and in Chamanculo, in the capital, favorable conditions for his plans, since in these neighborhoods Europeans were already living among Africans.[73] He reminded his superiors of the importance on the international stage of maintaining appearances. The problem of segregation in Mozambique's cities had to be resolved urgently, so that visitors did not think of a city as exclusively white "but rather [as] an authentic community of whites and blacks—with equal rights for all parties."[74] This, he wrote, was the only way to "free ourselves of certain conflicts" and to defend against "certain criticisms which are assiduously and currently leveled at us by the blacks."

Oliveira's urban vision depended on fuzzy fantasy. Seen up close, the thousands of Europeans living in the subúrbios of Lourenço Marques were hardly evidence of what Oliveira championed as the historical Portuguese "tendency toward living together without ethnic discrimination."[75] Even relatively privileged black Africans were effectively kept out of the City of Cement. The Portuguese who lived in the subúrbios could not afford to live in the City of Cement, and their low status and their cohabitation with African companions stoked fears among other whites of *cafrealização*—a common racist term suggesting Europeans who had been "Africanized" in the tropics.[76] Moreover, though people living in the subúrbios did not agonize over being segregated from whites per se, they did resent being segregated from the basic municipal infrastructure enjoyed by whites in the City of Cement.[77] Most of the African population—and not only Africans—were compelled to live in toxic conditions, yet neither in Oliveira's published work nor in his unpublished remarks to superiors about his visits to various Mozambican subúrbios did the architect mention flooding, sewage, crime, fire, or disease. These were things that he could not see—or chose not to. Nor, apparently, was he impressed by the near absence of schools or health clinics. In a published article, Oliveira, who sidelined as an artist of some note, sketched the traditional huts and handcrafted household objects that he discovered during his explorations of Mozambique's subúrbios, as if in sentimental appreciation.[78] But if he engaged any residents in conversation, his writings offer no evidence of it.

Neglect of the subúrbios bred its own kind of ignorance. With only the barest of services reaching the area, few within the municipal bureaucracy were familiar with the suburban landscape. Moreover, for strategic reasons, the work of social scientists was tightly controlled in Mozambique, and work by foreign researchers in the subúrbios was all but forbidden.[79] The first lengthy surveys of suburban life emerged only later, at the end of the 1960s; both were conducted by Portuguese researchers. One, by Rita-Ferreira, yielded vital insights on the pressures of the suburban housing market and other aspects of everyday life.[80] The other, which provided part of the basis of the 1969 urban plan for Lourenço Marques, was authored in Lisbon by a former official of the ministry of the ultramar who did not set foot in Mozambique until 1970.[81]

The subúrbios were long a wellspring of material for songs and poetry, and everyday life there was chronicled in *O Brado Africano*. But in publications with a largely European readership there was hardly any mention of African neighborhoods, let alone meaningful coverage, until the advent in October 1962 of a daily newspaper called *A Tribuna*.[82] With a staff that included some of the era's leading African cultural figures, such as poet and journalist José Craveirinha, photographer Ricardo Rangel, and writer Luís Bernardo Honwana, as well as journalistic exiles from *Notícias*, the city's proregime flagship paper, *A Tribuna* sought to be an oppositional voice in a place where the censor tolerated no meaningful opposition. The newspaper took advantage of a small opening for provocative reporting. In part to satisfy settler calls for more say in local affairs, the Ministry of the Ultramar had devolved more power to municipalities in Africa, and the deliberations of municipal chambers were made partially public.[83] *A Tribuna* settled almost instantly on the cause that came to define it:

The Politics of Visibility

exposing the conditions behind the "reed curtain." During the paper's second week of existence, editor António Gouvêa Lemos set the tone.[84] He penned an open letter to the newly installed members of the municipal council, saying it was time to recognize that they were responsible for more than just the quarter of the city they inhabited—they also were responsible for the welfare of the three-quarters of the city that rarely received the municipality's attention. "Whoever has flown over the capital of Mozambique knows of what I speak," he wrote. "I'm not preaching, I'm not attacking, I'm not rebelling. I'm reminding. I ask that you understand me. We have to speak clearly to one another—or is it still not the time?" He compared the City of Cement, with the luxuries bestowed upon it, to a frilly "coquette" that would rather embellish itself with "ringlets in girls' hair" than focus on the provision of water, roads, and electricity to the subúrbios. He acknowledged that the municipality was not solely responsible for caniço conditions, but he argued that someone needed to take responsibility. "When are we going to begin? How are we going to begin? Who is going to begin?" In closing, he challenged readers to acknowledge the problem of the subúrbios as their own. "When will we call it, all of us, with equal justification, 'our city'"?

The phrase *our city* embodied an argument new to the public arena: that the conditions of the subúrbios were the result of societal negligence, rather than the result of the low civilizational attainments of suburban residents. In January 1963, the paper launched a running exposé it entitled "The City of Reeds" (*A cidade de caniço*), rhetorically elevating the subúrbios to an independent city to enable readers to see these neighborhoods more vividly as the wretched mirror image of the City of Cement.[85] (The moniker had resonance. In following years, even officials began using it in correspondence.) On the editorial pages that month and frequently thereafter, different residents of the subúrbios gave short summaries of the houses they lived in, the houses they hoped to live in, and how much they could afford in rent if the government were to build new housing. Residents spoke of salaries too meager to construct houses of their own, the great distances to fetch water (or the expense of buying water at the closest cantina), the dangers of walking at night in the absence of street lamps, and the difficulty in maintaining one's dignity—expressed as "tidiness"—under such conditions.

"The mosquitos that appear by the million don't let people sleep," recounted Benedito Fumo.[86] "They are attracted by the unburied trash.

This happens every day because there is no place to bury the trash, because there is no space to dig trash pits. Whenever we dig a pit we see that trash has already been buried there." "And how tragic when there's a fire!" wrote Albino Sive in a published letter.[87] "When one house burns, five or ten more catch fire because as much as the firetrucks may try to get there quickly, there are no roads to get them to the site of the calamity. Only after 20 to 30 minutes are they able to connect hoses across people's yards to get there." Death by fire was one of the most dreaded horrors of suburban life because reeds were such effective kindling.[88]

One of A Tribuna's respondents was Mozambique's future president Armando Guebuza, then twenty-four years old and a resident of Chamanculo. "In the city of reeds we live in intolerable promiscuity," he said.[89] Housing was unaffordable, but people had no choice but to live close to the "stone city" in order to follow a professional career, and also "for the barest of benefits that come to us from contact with civilization." That year, he fled Mozambique to join Frelimo in Tanzania.[90]

Guebuza's few paragraphs in A Tribuna, restrained as they were, nonetheless packed more critical punch than the average "City of Reeds" testimonial. Most adopted a matter-of-fact tone. Perhaps this was the work of the official censor, but it is more likely that those interviewed censored themselves or that editors redlined their more caustic remarks. Not a single one of the suburban residents in the series implicated the municipality or the government at large. None mentioned racism or even race. Moreover, those given voice were exclusively men—most of them apparently in salaried work. Through the drumbeat of testimonials, A Tribuna strategically tailored an argument that few among its readership would dispute: that a male "head of household" who worked hard for his wage ought to be able to provide his family with a decent, healthy home—and a just government ought to help him do so. A Tribuna occasionally demonstrated a willingness to depict the poor whites of the subúrbios, but whites and South Asians and the many people of diverse heritage who lived in these neighborhoods were not represented among the testimonials of the cidade do caniço series. Craveirinha, one of the newspaper's more prominent commentators, conceded that the campaign did not represent the true racial diversity of the subúrbios, but he was cagey in explaining why this was so.[91] Perhaps editors wanted their implicit message about the racially segregated city to also be unambiguous.

101

In June 1963, *A Tribuna* ran a two-page spread by architect Pancho Guedes, entitled "The Sick City."[92] Guedes was a singular figure in late colonial Lourenço Marques, responsible for hundreds of projects in the city and throughout Mozambique.[93] His home and studio became a place where African artists and writers gathered, among them Malangatana Ngwenya and Luís Bernardo Honwana; he also maintained close ties to the Swiss Mission.[94] Though he was not overtly political himself, these were connections that made Guedes a dubious character in the eyes of the secret police, especially after Eduardo Mondlane met with him during his 1961 visit. Guedes also circulated in the subúrbios as no other Portuguese architect or planner did.[95] Lourenço Marques was "schizophrenic," he wrote in *A Tribuna*.[96] A minority lived in luxury in one part of the city, and in the other part, "the city of the poor, the servants, and the maids," people lived without basic services and in "mountains of filth." In the subúrbios, "children come to know hunger, illness, and misery while still young, and lose their charm and their innocence before their time." He criticized the impractical, low-density, Garden City planning represented by the wealthy new Cronistas neighborhood, and he included a shot at the racism that officials claimed did not exist. As if in sly rebuttal to plans for multiracial communities in the subúrbios, Guedes called on the municipality to desegregate the City of Cement instead. Public housing, he argued, "will revitalize downtown" and "will initiate and accelerate a genuine racial integration—or is it that the '*pretos*' only belong in kitchens and at receptions?"[97] (*Preto*, Portuguese for the color black, is considered a cruder way to refer to people than words such as *negro* or *africano*.) The piece was among the harshest to appear anywhere in Lourenço Marques at the time. The censor initially suspended the article, but Guedes later explained how *A Tribuna* smuggled it into print. The article was resubmitted—this time in small sections. For some reason, Guedes's "prescriptions" for the Sick City were easier for the censor to swallow when the words were administered a spoonful at a time.

Ricardo Rangel, *A Tribuna*'s director of photography, followed a similar strategy. For the August feature entitled "The Forge of the Adults of Tomorrow," Rangel first submitted to the censor photos of children, most of them black, at play in suburban yards and in muddy pools.[98] A month later, he submitted more photos of children, most of them white, in ballet class and at school. Once the material was approved, Rangel then juxtaposed the images on the page in a clear demonstration of who were the haves and who were the have-nots. Deadpan photo captions accentuated the point. An image of primly dressed children sitting in a school playground, nearly all of them white, was captioned, "Waiting for lunch, a group of kids of all different races in a world where all are equal." Below was another photo, this one of two black children in rags squatting in the dust as one puts a pen to a notebook. "Anyplace is fine when one wants to learn," read the caption. "Even with rocks from the street serving as desk and chair."

In some respects, *A Tribuna* was simply carrying on a tradition of journalistic dissidence that managed to persist even under the Estado Novo.[99] *O Brado Africano*, the newspaper of the city's African elite, was purchased by a proregime figure in the late 1950s, blunting its sharp edge. For decades, its contributors had criticized policies of the indigenato, and it offered small portraits of life in the subúrbios by writers who lived there, for readers who lived there.[100] *A Tribuna* circulated in the City of Cement so its campaign allowed suburban residents to speak directly to Portuguese readers, many of whom were only vaguely aware of what life in the caniço was like. For the first time, the harsh conditions of the subúrbios became an issue for the public, residents of the subúrbios were themselves part of that public, and Portuguese authorities were implicated as responsible parties. In other words, *A Tribuna* was creating a dialogue for politics and inviting the previously uninvited as participants. It was, of course, a very limited dialogue and a very limited politics. What made this dialogue possible was that in its overt criticism, *A Tribuna* had selected a very narrow target: the municipal administration. The newspaper's explicit recommendations were mostly for better service delivery and for more and better-planned housing. Such demands were in line with Lisbon's stated vision for its African possessions. Reporter Teresa de Sá Nogueira, though, hazarded a sharper interpretation when she wrote that the housing problem was not a technical one that the municipality could solve: "Because it isn't really a problem of houses or of transport. It's a social problem."[101] She suggested raising people's wages. Race, however, was a subject that almost always had to be read between the lines.

A Tribuna's activist phase did not last the year. The paper's owner was forced to sell to a regime sympathizer, resulting in a staff exodus. By November 1963, filler and blank space regularly replaced editorial columns. The most frequently used filler column was a public service announcement

103

made on behalf of ophthalmologists; it called for people to donate their eyes to the blind. Earlier that year, a guerrilla war had erupted in Portuguese Guiné, and in September 1964, Frelimo initiated its own guerrilla war, in Mozambique's distant north. The secret police arrested many suspected Frelimo operatives in Lourenço Marques and its subúrbios, including some who had been affiliated with *A Tribuna,* and the censor tightened its grip on the local press still further.[102] In 1964, a Portuguese crew filmed *Catembe,* a tongue-in-cheek quasi documentary about everyday life in Lourenço Marques, intended primarily for audiences in Portugal.[103] By the time it was screened the next year, censors had cut away almost half of the director's version, later earning it some repute as the most censored film in Portuguese history.[104] Among the deleted material: a scene showing people of different races dancing together at a downtown nightclub, a scene that takes place among rickety fishermen's shanties, and aerial footage of the subúrbios.[105]

AN "ABSOLUTELY NEW SITUATION"

Though its campaign lasted only months, *A Tribuna* helped usher in a debate about government housing that would be carried on beyond its pages. As the newspaper had frequently reported, the government-built housing units in Matola and Machava (where Infulene was located) were disasters.[106] They were far from places of employment in Lourenço Marques and bus service was limited, and few were moving in. By mid-1963, only thirty families had moved into the 100 houses built in Matola at least six months before, and in Machava the picture was worse: just 22 of 350 of units were occupied.[107] Photographs in the newspaper of so many concrete-block houses in Machava sitting derelict amid tall weeds must have been a terrible embarrassment to the housing agency. "This in Mozambique," read the caption to an image of a vacant house.[108]

One of the most elaborate solutions to the housing crisis in these years did not emerge from the government, however. Rather, in October 1963, a working group led by African nurses at Lourenço Marques's central hospital put forth a detailed plan for housing projects that would be located just outside the City of Cement—an initiative directly inspired by *A Tribuna*'s City of Reeds coverage.[109] In Mozambique at the time, to be a nurse was one of the most prestigious positions that a black Mozambican could hope to achieve.

Associational life in the country was heavily regulated, and group gatherings of any kind might be monitored; any professional association of formally educated Africans was likely to raise suspicion. In his speech at the hospital to present the plan, Alvaro Chovane, who headed the initiative, spoke the language that Lisbon would approve of. He defended the right and desire of the "autochthone" to evolve just like anybody else. "All of us have the pride and the clear consciousness of our status as Portuguese," he said, "and thus, we believe that 'luso-tropicalism,' in a real and practical sense, means 'multiracialism.'"[110] The projects in Matola and Machava, he argued, were no more than "encampments." Their great distance from the city was contrary to the worthy goal of "integrating less evolved autochthonous populations" into urban life. No one should interpret people's rejection of these ill-conceived projects as a distaste on the part of Africans for modern housing. Rest assured, he said: Africans knew that reeds were incompatible with city living, let alone life in a capital city. Romantic arguments that reed houses were the appropriate housing for Africans denied "the natural evolution of societies."

The nurses' group had conducted a survey of African staffers at the hospital, and it used the survey to develop its housing plan. The final report included drawings for two-story, medium-density housing with yards. It also provided a careful cost estimate of materials and construction, including the cost of temporary quarters where people could live while displaced by construction. A model of one section of the proposed project was put on display at the hospital, and in February 1964, a debate on the merits of the project was held in the hospital amphitheater. The report itself was authored by a Portuguese psychiatrist. One senses the *padrinho* (godfather) politics typical of colonial-era Mozambique at work here—of whites speaking on behalf of African protégés or dependents.[111] Nurse Chovane's avowed loyalty to Portugal was not in itself sufficient to gain a hearing for the group's proposal. An African initiative required the backing of a white patron. When the city council replied, it addressed itself not to Chovane but to the Portuguese psychiatrist.[112]

Housing was no longer within the municipality's purview, the council members wrote. Having deflected the issue, they then admonished the working group for its characterization of Lourenço Marques. It was not the dual city that they had portrayed it to be. Portugal had never "left room for doubt" about the equality of its citizens, even during the indigenato. Moreover, the municipal administration had "never been divided into city of reeds and city of reinforced cement, expressions that may be used with frequency, but have no official recognition."[113] The nurses' proposal was a rare example in late colonial Mozambique of a grass-roots effort to directly influence government policy, but like most ideas intended to improve sub-urban living conditions, it gained no further traction. When a new master plan for Lourenço Marques was released in 1969, no mention was made of the nurses' effort.[114]

Meanwhile, housing officials, stung by the failures of Matola and Machava, were conducting their own research into how to improve hous-ing delivery. In early 1963 amid the City of Reeds debate, a team of social workers was dispatched to the Bairro Indígena to conduct a survey.[115] Offi-cials hoped that the residents could offer useful advice for future projects based on their experience of living in a government-built complex.[116] In-stead, the residents subverted the intentions of the researchers and boldly used the opportunity to voice their frustrations with government services. A user-satisfaction study of this kind was unprecedented, at least according to those who conducted it. In their final report, the social workers pointed out that people in Munhuana were not accustomed to "meetings with whites in order to say what they think."[117] "The influence of this absolutely new situation," they wrote, had stirred the residents' passions.[118] Respondents were too "emotional" to answer questions with "an objective perspective of realities."[119] This was the social workers' way of saying that the people of the neighborhood had not simply answered their questions but also had surprised them by pressing their own demands.

The dire predictions that some officials made for the Bairro Indígena when it was proposed in the late 1930s proved correct. Flooding was an annual trial for its residents, and by the early 1960s, most of the complex had fallen into disrepair. It did, however, have a new name. To reflect the changing complexion of Portuguese policy, the Bairro Indígena was now the Bairro Popular da Munhuana (the People's Neighborhood of Munhuana). In individual interviews and group meetings, residents complained about the regular inundations, how flooding brought sewage streaming through houses, and how units—most were only one room—were far too small to accommodate a family. Recently built units did not even have doors, ei-ther internally or to the outside, which was a focus of particular outrage. A number of men complained that living in such close quarters with other family members undermined their authority, since discussions could not be had in private. Decency was also compromised. Fathers, for example, could not maintain a respectable distance from daughters. Some residents offered policy prescriptions. Given the government's haplessness, it should simply enable people to build houses for themselves. "It would be better to be given land to make a house," said one.[120] "If the Government doesn't have money to build, it's better to give us land, in a good place, survey lots, give us house plans, to build a house in blocks, with the right to live there forever." Another clarified: "*Our* house, that we would pay for in installments, built by us, with the help of the Government."[121] Rather than being the model it was designed to be, the Bairro Indígena had undermined the regime's prestige. One resident said that the poor conditions of the neighborhood represented "how the Government thinks of us."[122] The spare, doorless new houses built in the neighborhood were like "a materialization of the image that the Government has of the residents of the Bairro," as if "they don't deserve more," wrote the report's authors, summing up some older residents' sentiments.[123]

Few women in Munhuana were consulted for the survey because the social workers did not speak local languages and did not engage a translator. Consequently, the report was something of a compendium of male grievances, though the feelings of disgust must have been universal. It was published in 1964 by the Superior Institute of Social Sciences and Overseas Policy in Lisbon, which meant that people in Munhuana had not just directed their anger at a few social workers in Lourenço Marques but had also managed to broadcast it to the entire ultramar hierarchy. Dissent requires a medium; the survey, despite its stated purpose, had inadvertently helped some people articulate dissent and feelings about the regime that they had perhaps not given shape to before. For one unnamed resident, quoted at length by researchers, the episode was also an opportunity for reflection on the disorientations inflicted by modern urban life. The resident rejected being confined to a single-room house:

> We do not live alone. We have different familial ties than
> Europeans do. Our cousins are our brothers. For the
> European, money is his security—but not for us. Today
> evolution runs its course, runs for its goal without catching its
> breath. Civilization is like a car in motion, but we do not know
> how it goes. We are inside the car and we cannot stop. There

> are some, however, who can no longer keep going. My mother
> is no longer capable of moving forward. The elderly are not
> going to change their ways and they can no longer work. They
> count on us. We are tied from behind. We drag so much
> behind us.

"I liked this conversation," he concluded, "it allowed me to unload my thoughts. It was good."[124]

By 1966, the Bairro Popular da Munhuana had a dedicated social worker, and she conducted her own, updated survey of residents. Lilía Momplé, mentioned in the previous chapter, later became a well-known writer of fiction, and her unpublished report to her superiors reflected greater empathy with its subjects than the average bureaucratic account.[125] In the few years since the first Munhuana survey, people in Lourenço Marques had new reasons to be wary of government workers soliciting people's opinions. War had broken out, and PIDE, the secret police, was assumed to be everywhere. Neighbor distrusted neighbor, often with good reason, and in Munhuana, people were certainly suspicious of the social worker who had gathered them together in group meetings and went house to house asking questions.

The fact that she was of mixed race, rather than white, heightened suspicions that she was a PIDE informant, Momplé wrote, since people thought she was there to lure them into a trap. Meetings began in tense silence. "Little by little, however, standoffishness gave way to true explosions of aggressiveness."[126] Residents leveled direct accusations of negligence at the housing board and, "in a more veiled way," the government. Apparently, living conditions at the complex had changed very little since 1963. Repairs were never made, said one resident—"all the Board wants is to receive the rent!"[127] Another complained of the absurdity of residents being ordered to paint the exterior walls of their houses, while the housing agency did nothing to repair them: "The outside of the house does not matter! We do not live outside! But the Board doesn't care! Animals live in these houses, not us!" And the neighborhood still flooded regularly.

Momplé described one resident who would not receive her into his house:

> He sat in the doorway and calmly said to us: Look girl, I'm not
> so much a child that I would trust the Board. The Board never

did anything for the Bairro, nor did it want to do anything!
Why are you annoying us like this?

He spit on the ground ostentatiously, wanting to demonstrate
his complete lack of respect for the Board, and added: It would
be better if you got another job, because the Board only wants
to let you be disgraced.[128]

An intern was kicked out of another house, with the resident yelling,
"I've had enough of the Board's lies."[129] That Momplé was a young woman
(her intern probably was, as well) and not a young *white* woman likely
emboldened the people she talked to. In interactions she describes with
mostly male heads of household, she was addressed as "girl." Given the
potential consequences at the time of even trivial shows of dissent, however, such disrespect indicated more than a belittling of Momplé—it also
suggested a bold dismissal of the regime. This is likely why Momplé included the details. Perhaps she wanted her superiors to know just how
grave the board's position was. People in Munhuana identified the board
with the government as a whole and with whites, she warned in her report.
"This identification means that everything that the Board 'doesn't do' will
have repercussions that dangerously transcend the specific scope of its activity."[130] Frelimo, for its part, grasped the propaganda advantages of the
Bairro Indígena. In a short piece in its newsletter, published in early 1964
in Dar es Salaam, editors had described the neighborhood as something
"[out of the] sixteenth century."[131]

Momplé sounded a positive note in her report, observing that people's
aggressiveness toward her and indirectly toward the government "is, truly,
an appeal," a desire to be more fully "integrated" into the "larger social
context."[132] She wrote that after venting their complaints, residents appreciated "the unexpected opportunity that had been offered to them to speak
with the Board, and [they] hope as well that soon it would be concretized
in deeds."[133]

Scholars of Lusophone Africa have thoroughly discredited Portugal's claims
to being a peaceable rainbow nation of long standing, a picture that in no
way corresponded to the realities of everyday life in the colonies of the
more distant past and in the so-called provinces of late colonial rule.[134]

109

Maybe, in part, because of the outlandishness of much of the propaganda Lisbon produced, its reform agenda of the 1960s has been dismissed as mere window dressing. In its actual implementation, as the thinking goes, reform impacted too few people to register in the full account of enduring colonial exploitation. But one need not be a regime apologist to acknowledge that initiatives originating in Lisbon, whatever the motivations behind them, had a significant impact on how life was lived in Lourenço Marques and its subúrbios in the 1960s. The most significant changes were the labor reforms and the generalized economic expansion of the period, a subject that will be addressed in the following chapter.[135] Frederick Cooper has explored similar territory for postwar French- and British-controlled Africa. He studied how new strategies of colonial rule—development pushes and welfarism—inspired African workers and intellectuals to demand more, such as higher wages and expanded political rights.[136] But Cooper focuses on labor mobilization and party politics. Cities in Portuguese Africa had nothing like the kind of lasting political agitation witnessed in many cities in British and French Africa.[137] Perhaps this is why the urban dimensions of Lisbon's version of reform are often overlooked. They do not fit neatly into timelines of independence.[138]

In Lourenço Marques, another type of politics emerged within the limited confines of possible debate—not around wages or political rights but around the built environment. It happened this way, in part, because the regime's reformist agenda was simultaneously a modernizing agenda. The cities of Portuguese Africa, with their teeming slums, offered highly visible evidence—to the regime and to the world at large—of what had to be modernized. Reformers in Lisbon looked with scorn upon Mozambique's local officials and powerful settler interests, whom they saw as incompetent, backward, and racist, and whom they saddled with much of the blame for jeopardizing Portugal's position in Mozambique.[139] Allowing some criticism of lower-level administrators in order to expose what was initially construed as a technical problem—housing and infrastructure—fell within the bounds of acceptable discourse.

But setting the terms of the debate did not mean that officials could totally control the debate. Activist journalists found ways around the censor, and even after their voices were stifled, others continued to challenge authorities to do something about housing in the subúrbios. The nurses did so politely and according to social protocols, but the residents of Munhuana did so with undisguised rage and condescension. Meanwhile, many residents of the subúrbios faced other, graver problems. Barely half of the people in one 1971 survey of suburban residents, for instance, were meeting daily caloric minimums, and this included children.[140] But it was harder to make a public case around malnutrition or illiteracy or workplace exploitation. The nature of the evidence did not confront officials in the same way. The spaces of the city, by contrast, were on perpetual display for anyone to see. They were a primary marker of governance and also of its absence.

·

Figure 3.1 Rute Malé inaugurates her family's "clandestine" concrete-block house, Chamanculo, 1963. (Daniel Malé)

Chapter 3

THE POLITICS OF PROXIMITY

Clandestine Masonry House Construction

in the Subúrbios, c. 1960–74

I hardly moved a finger clandestinely
But a militant in fact I am.

—José Craveirinha,
"Unclandestineness" (1980)[1]

ON A Saturday afternoon in 1963, Daniel Malé and his wife, Adelina Cossa, hosted a party to celebrate the completion of their new home.[2] The house was built a few feet from the home of his parents, on a fenced plot the Malé family had long rented in Chamanculo. Among the party's few dozen attendees, two were guests of honor. One was Malé's employer, or patrão, the Portuguese owner of a watch store downtown who had helped him purchase the materials for the house. The other was Cossa's brother, the stonemason who built it. Malé called everyone to attention and read a prepared speech:

The ambition of every man is to have his own house. Among us natives, this ambition becomes even greater—it is in fact a major concern—because it is customary for us to marry only after having built a roof under which we can raise a family. There was a time when a shack was enough, and this is why, without being able to afford much, I built a shack of reeds. These days, however, as one struggles to build a roof, one does so in better financial conditions. Thus, at the cost of many sacrifices and with the help of others, such as the help of my patrão, present here, who contributed with windows, doors, and wood beams, and the help of my brother-in-law, who offered his services as a stonemason, and my own effort, I managed, six years after getting married, to replace the old house of reeds with a house of stone, which still seems a dream to me, a gift from God.[3]

Rute, the couple's six-year-old daughter, was dressed all in white for the occasion, and with a gloved hand she turned the handle of the front door, officially inaugurating the home as open for living.

Daniel Malé did not give the impression that he had anything to hide. But according to municipal officials, his "house of stone," by which he meant a house made of concrete block, was a clandestine construction. In the 1960s, the municipality revived long-dormant regulations that prohibited building in permanent materials such as concrete or ceramic blocks (which were sometimes used in addition to concrete) in the subúrbios of Lourenço Marques.[4] Officials were convinced that there would eventually be up-to-code housing for the middle class, a proper street grid, and the full complement of municipal services, all according to a formal urban plan.[5] The main difficulty would be resettling many African residents on land at some greater remove. Home builders like Malé and Cossa jeopardized this vision, for there could be no modern development for the subúrbios if thousands of substandard concrete houses stood in the way. Clandestine masonry construction only hardened the chaotic suburban landscape into place.

Houses of reeds or wood and zinc were considered suitably precarious. Builders could even lay concrete foundations so long as the slab did not project too far above the ground. But one was officially forbidden from building anything that might give a bulldozer pause. If one was caught building in masonry, the potential consequences were severe. A fine could easily exceed several months' salary, a serious blow for a household that had scrimped on everyday expenses in order to stock up on the necessary materials and hire a stonemason. Demolition, if it came to that, would have been catastrophic. From 1961 to 1971, Lourenço Marques municipal police served violation notices to more than two thousand homeowners for building so-called clandestine structures in the subúrbios.[6]

Some builders were discreet and hid walls of either concrete block or clay block behind zinc panels. Others, like Daniel Malé and Adelina Cossa, built more brazenly. That thousands of people in these neighborhoods were even considering permanent construction was due to the surging local economy and the new ambitions it awakened. But rapid development, beginning in the late 1950s, had its contradictions. On the one hand, many people had more money in their pockets. On the other hand, suburban neighborhoods became far denser with the influx of migrants from the countryside. The municipality, which assumed the subúrbios would eventually be cleared away, did little to improve suburban conditions, with dire consequences for public health. In any case, "improvement" usually meant displacement. Here and there, large swaths of the caniço were cleared for infrastructure that primarily served the City of Cement.[7] Factories and warehouses that now employed many African workers were erected on land where other African workers had been living for years. Competition for space tripled and quadrupled suburban rental rates. One's hold on the small fenced plot one occupied had probably never been so tenuous.[8] Yet even with all this uncertainty—or perhaps because of it—many caniço residents risked investing in masonry construction, illicitly if the law insisted it was illicit.

When people in Maputo talk about the masonry houses they built at the time, they tend to talk about them as Daniel Malé did in 1963: as an achievement won through hard work, patience, good sense, and God's grace. A house of stone meant material comfort and a more secure future for one's family. It also signaled one's entrance into "modern" life.[9] Clandestine masonry home builders represented only a fraction of the people living in the subúrbios, but many more shared their aspirations. They did not necessarily harbor nationalist sentiments or envision independence. They did not think about what they were doing in overtly political terms.

They did, however, defy expectations that they should live in perpetual suspense and wait on a properly urbanized future that never seemed to come. Concrete was the substance and universal symbol of modernization. But like the full promise of modernization itself, concrete was being reserved for the benefit of a privileged minority in the City of Cement.

More was at stake than the carefully cultivated image of what a modern city should look like. The rising ambitions of many African workers, including numerous people of relatively modest means, began to overlap for the first time with those of working-class whites, many of whom lived nearby, also in the subúrbios and also in unauthorized masonry homes. Clandestine builders of various backgrounds were blurring distinctions that had long shaped Lourenço Marques: City of Cement and subúrbio, permanent and precarious, European and African. As Laurent Fourchard might put it, people were imagining difference differently.[10]

THE CONCRETE IMPERATIVE

Portugal's decision to liberalize the colonial economy was much like the African development drives of other European powers not long before.[11] Initially, Lisbon allowed Mozambique to establish more homegrown industry, and then it lifted barriers to foreign investment. The first to enjoy the benefits were Portuguese. Encouraged by the government and attracted by the development boom, tens of thousands fled the poverty and stifling parochialism of home and settled in Lourenço Marques.[12] In the 1960s, as Portugal rolled out programs to win African hearts and minds and then mobilized for war against Frelimo guerrillas, the city also absorbed thousands of military personnel, technical specialists, teachers, and social workers. The service sector grew to meet the demands of all these European newcomers. Neighboring South Africa, the regional economic giant, was rapidly expanding, too, and it pulled the city more definitively into its orbit, not least as a flourishing destination for white South African beachgoers. Lourenço Marques added more new units to its formal housing stock between 1959 and 1967 than it had in its entire history to that point.[13] The making of a more impressive skyline became one of the city's chief industries.[14]

As it was intended to do, growth also boosted employment prospects for a larger stratum of Africans—particularly for African men—and the

Figure 3.2 Daniel Malé and Adelina Cossa at their Chamanculo home, 2011. (David Morton)

conditions of employment improved with the abolition of forced labor in 1961 and the relaxation of movement controls.[15] In addition to the traditional jobs at the railyards and port, on municipal cleanup squads, and in the backyards of Portuguese families, there were now more positions at hotels and restaurants and cafés and social clubs, printing presses and auto shops, and the counters and stockrooms of clothing stores and hardware stores and furniture stores. More Africans entered the job market with skills that were better compensated, such as bookkeeping and typing. And thousands were employed in factories in and around the subúrbios and in Matola, Lourenço Marques's new satellite city. By 1968, eleven thousand African men were working on hundreds of construction sites in the City of Cement.[16] Of course, the gains for many were modest. Wages for those in formal employment continued to trail those of whites by a considerable margin.[17] Opportunities for women improved far less than they did for men.[18] Still, during the last fifteen years or so of Portuguese rule, many people living on the city's margins came to possess more potent buying power. Some households began to think beyond reeds and wood and zinc.

117

Because of the innumerable and seemingly insurmountable barriers to residing in the City of Cement, living there did not register high in the aspirations of many residents of the subúrbios. But concrete did. Some real estate developers recognized a potential new market. An advertisement in a 1963 issue of A *Tribuna* depicted a masonry house in the distant bay shore neighborhood of Triunfo and beckoned, "AFRICANS! A house for you!!! . . . GIVE YOUR CHILDREN A TRUE HOME!"[19] Only the wealthiest suburban residents, though, could have afforded the monthly payment plan. Triunfo's developer disappeared amid a cloud of scandal in the early 1970s, without having provided new homeowners with water, sewers, or paved streets.[20] More within the realm of possibility was a government program through which African civil servants could secure title to a plot and build a house in one of the neighborhoods of Matola, among white and South Asian homeowners.[21] There, from the 1960s onward, the sons and daughters of the suburban elite—if they were able to surmount the considerable bureaucratic obstacles involved—lived in respectable masonry houses with yards ample enough to raise some animals and grow vegetables. The jaunty, high-peaked roofs of many Matola houses became a hallmark of modern living, and in the many years since, they have never gone out of style[22] (Figures 3.3 and 3.4). They have served as the model for tens of thousands of masonry homes built in Maputo's subúrbios after independence and especially since the 1990s.[23] Ana Magaia, the noted actress, recalled that as a child in the 1960s living in Chamanculo, she loved visiting her cousins at their house in Matola. "They weren't houses for rich people," she said, "they were normal houses for people to live in and raise their children with dignity."[24] Magaia went to the toilet several times a day during her visits to Matola just to experience a well-appointed interior bathroom.

With cement now being produced at several plants in Mozambique itself, many people in the subúrbios could afford a few sacks of the material, which they used to lay a thin floor for their houses. Those with more resources plastered their reed walls with cement. The plaster helped insulate the reeds against wind and rot, acquiring the material was much easier than fetching mud, and it also gave a house a more dignified look. Municipal authorities tolerated plastered walls. But a well-applied finish could pass as masonry, and even officials were often fooled.[25] Police circulating through neighborhoods were known to occasionally puncture plastered walls with an iron rod, a test to see whether the homeowner had dared build in concrete block. In any case, plaster was hardly a lasting solution. It was fragile.

Figure 3.3 Mozambique's governor-general awards a property title in a government-assisted housing development, Matola, 1960s. (AHM/cx.61/c-3-4951)

Figure 3.4 "Residence of an African family under construction," Matola, 1960s. Most African residents of the subúrbios could not afford to move to Matola, the capital's new satellite city. But the kind of house being built there, especially its roof profile, became a model of modern living that has never gone out of style. (AHM/cx.61/c-3-4959)

With time, a chunk of the thin shell would break off and then another, revealing the reeds within, like the straw jutting from a scarecrow's shirt. One was forced to acknowledge that a plastered reed wall was a poor imitation of the real thing (Figure 1.9).

In the late 1950s, Chamanculo resident Jaime Tembe, an employee at an auto parts store, plastered the walls of his reed house.[26] For years, the insulation served well enough. But in August 1964, Tembe was shocked to read a newspaper report about a boy who lived in a house just like his own. Following a heavy rain, plaster had broken away from the wall and crushed the boy's head, killing him as he slept. Tembe, a father of four, decided that morning that he would build a house of more solid materials, despite the great cost. He proceeded in typical fashion. He built a wood-framed, zinc-paneled structure, and for the interior divisions he erected walls of concrete block (Figure 1.14). Unlike Daniel Malé and Adelina Cossa's house, where the transgression was on display for anyone to see, a legal exterior often masked an illicit interior (Figure 3.5). With many of Tembe's neighbors in Chamanculo working on downtown construction sites, there was no shortage of builders available to do the job. Tembe's cousin was a carpenter, and the two men discussed how many rooms were needed, what the dimensions would be, and what materials Tembe would purchase.[27] No plans were drawn up, but this is not to say the project lacked planning. A half century later, Tembe could recall the quantity and cost of each material, including the price for each of the half dozen different lengths of zinc panels. (Actually, most people interviewed about houses they built in the 1960s and 1970s remembered what they paid for building materials decades ago. Construction in the subúrbios has never been a rash act.) For the next two years, Tembe "tightened the belt a little" in order to procure materials, and he built a shed to store them. At a time when few people had bank accounts, buying building materials was a way of investing in the future. The construction process was often a long one, subject to any number of interruptions due to cash flow problems, family emergency, or flooding, and moreover, houses were expanded room by room over lifetimes and over generations. There may have been a clear beginning to these projects, but there was no clear end.

The case files for those who were caught building in masonry give us an idea of who these builders were. Approximately 80 percent of the accused

Figure 3.5 (*opposite*) The house of Maria Esperança Tavares, built in Chamanculo in the 1960s, in 2011. Exterior zinc panels mask a concrete-block interior—a common strategy for those building in masonry in the colonial era. (David Morton)

were men, and in the sampled files, most of them were identified as married. This is not to say that women did not play an important role in the planning and construction of the family house. In some cases, wives and other members of the household financed much of the project, such as through the sale of produce and traditional brews. But men were presumed by officials (and often by the men themselves) to head the household, and they were the ones made to account for the illegal construction. Something similar happened in my interviews as well, as men were usually put forward as the sole spokespeople. Single women, however, were named in the case files as transgressors almost as often as single men, giving perhaps a greater indication of the energies that women in general devoted to house construction. Despite having much less access than men to waged work, many single women invested in building simple rental units, sometimes in masonry. As Jeanne Penvenne observed, "Autonomy, a measure of control over one's living space, a secure home, however simple, was a central component of women's strategies to control their lives."[28] It was a way to avoid living with men solely out of necessity.

Josefa Alfonso Maduela has two homes, one in Chamanculo very close to Jaime Tembe's house and one in the nearby countryside.[29] When her husband left her in the early 1960s, she and her three children went to live with Maduela's father, a railroad worker. Every day, she sold bananas in front of a café at the edge of Chamanculo, and every week, she would deposit some of her earnings with a local Chinese cantineiro. (Her children played with the cantineiro's children, and she trusted him not to steal from her savings.) In 1965, she bought an existing house of wood and zinc for 7,000 escudos, a stunning purchase for a sidewalk fruit vendor. The many people being displaced in the neighborhood in these years made Maduela anxious. "One day *xicolone* is going to take us out of here, to expand the city," she told her children, referring to the Portuguese.[30] The family needed a backup, her daughter Isabel recalled. Maduela grew vegetables on a plot she rented about 10 miles from the city, and she decided that instead of upgrading her wood-and-zinc house in Chamanculo, she would build a concrete-block house from scratch out there, where it would be the only such house in sight. She purchased the materials and rented a truck to have them delivered. For roofing, she chose corrugated asbestos-cement panels, locally called Lusalite, which she considered more "civilized" than zinc. She knew something about construction, having watched her father build his own house and helping him fill bags with rocks that would be used as aggregate for concrete. Her father was upset that she was locating her house so far from his. "My daughter is a woman, but her thinking is that of a man," he told others. It took her three years to have her house built; it was finished in 1973. The same house constructed in the subúrbios would have been "clandestine." In the countryside, no building code applied.

Though a number of the owners of clandestine concrete homes were among the suburban elite, many were not. Some were probably called assimilado because they built a concrete-block house, irrespective of what their legal status had once been. Even to use the term *middle class* obscures the fact that in the subúrbios all shared some measure of deprivation, if not equally; virtually no one enjoyed a standard of living that a Portuguese would consider middle class. Nor does the term take into account the complexity of household living situations. Hunger and well-being might coexist under one roof. Certain more fortunate builders benefited from greater connections to Portuguese patrons—as Daniel Malé did—or to Portuguese kin or "godparents."[31] Clandestine home builders were railroad workers, domestic workers, factory workers, clothes makers, truck drivers, schoolteachers, and employees at cafés and retail stores. Those with the highest salaries—office clerks and nurses, for example—turn up in the case files less often. This could be because they may have had the means and connections to ward off police and building inspectors. Or their ambitions may have led them to an apartment in Alto Maé, in the City of Cement, or to a house in Matola.

House construction in contemporary Maputo, as Morten Nielsen has written, is about "preparing the future" and "preserving the future" for one's children.[32] When I asked people to explain why, decades ago, they had risked building in concrete, they often spoke this way. Concrete secured their children against the dangers of climate and fire and ensured them greater comfort and a valuable inheritance. Parents were also concerned about their own comfort; they tended to purchase new furniture when they built a new house. Daniel Malé wanted a concrete house to protect his children, but he also simply thought concrete was "beautiful." A beautiful house, then as now, was generally one that was well constructed, showed no cracks, and had many rooms. Houses at the time tended to be uniform on the outside and left unpainted or painted white, unlike those in the vibrant, multicolored neighborhoods of many other cities in southern Africa and elsewhere.[33] Building a masonry house was about taking defined steps to modern living by dutifully assembling a kit of preselected parts. It was not an opportunity for creative distinction—not when the risks called for modesty.

THE CLANDESTINE NEIGHBORHOOD

José Craveirinha, a journalist and Mozambique's foremost poet, lived for much of his childhood within the curve of the city, before it was truly the City of Cement, with his Portuguese father and Portuguese stepmother.[34] Craveirinha had been born in the subúrbios to a Ronga mother. When his father's wife, who had no children of her own, joined her husband in Mozambique, she insisted on raising his children, and he sent for José and his brother. Ronga, the boys' native tongue, was prohibited in the Portuguese household. Craveirinha spoke the language with friends, and later, his poetry would be punctuated with Ronga shouts and expressions. But he claimed he never commanded it, a loss he later compared to being crippled. He described his youth as a series of rebirths. The first was when, as a child, he moved to the city and discovered there that he was a "mulato." Another was when his mother died, while he was still very young, and he chose Mozambique for his new "mother." Yet another was when his stepmother died, and he, his father, his uncles, and his cousins moved to the subúrbios.

Craveirinha paid homage in poetry to his "handsome ex-Portuguese" father, a retired police officer who, through his children, became Mozambican and who died "as poor as when [he] disembarked in Africa."[35] The only sense we have of his father's life in the subúrbios comes from Craveirinha's newspaper commentaries of the 1950s and 1960s, when he occasionally wrote of humble Portuguese who could not afford the City of Cement but who discovered an agreeable life in African neighborhoods. The subúrbios had recently experienced an influx of working people from Portugal, he wrote in O Brado Africano in 1955.[36] He called upon readers to have sympathy for their new neighbors. In their "isolated contingents," these "unpretentious" immigrants had beautifully restored what had been rundown wood-and-zinc houses, embellished their yards with decorative greenery and vegetable gardens, and generally set a fine example of how people could establish themselves in a place "through love of the land and veneration for the HOUSE."[37] Other Portuguese thought that their poor compatriots had degraded themselves by living in the caniço, he explained. Instead, they should applaud these people for giving other caniço residents a model to look up to. He asserted that too many Africans, now earning more money, were moving to the City of Cement and sacrificing the sociability and open spaces of the subúrbios for the constrictive walls of an apartment high-rise. (Undoubtedly, he was referring to people of mixed race moving to Alto Maé.) Craveirinha's praise for his European neighbors was sincere, as far as it went, but the ironies of the situation were irresistible. The real gift of Portugal's civilizing mission was not modernity, he seemed to say, but rather the lessons offered by lowly Portuguese on living the simple life.

Later, in 1962, the first edition of A Tribuna featured an unattributed article about the problem of children in the subúrbios scavenging for junk near the municipal incinerator.[38] The text avoided what the accompanying images made clear: the children were white—a significant provocation, given what the censor usually deemed acceptable. Still, Craveirinha thought that A Tribuna treated the subject too timidly. During the newspaper's City of Reeds campaign in 1963, he argued that the ongoing series of testimonials by residents, all of them black, presented an "incomplete truth."[39] He felt that diversity in the caniço ought to be openly acknowledged so that whites, blacks, mestiços, and Asians could "join together to face a common enemy"—poverty, which did not discriminate by race. The public assistance agency, however, did discriminate. At the time, it mostly aided whites.[40] Confronted with the embarrassment of having Europeans in the subúrbios, the government moved many of them into subsidized housing in Matola.[41]

In their own way, the Europeans of Lourenço Marques represented a social mosaic.[42] They clustered in neighborhoods and gathered at clubs based on what region of Portugal they were from, and class divisions in the colonial capital could be as rigid as they were in the metropole. Generally speaking, those arriving from Portugal often looked down on whites born in Mozambique, who sometimes called themselves naturais—yet another word for "natives"—but whom others called "second-rate" Portuguese. Until the 1960s, for instance, the higher ranks of civil administration were closed to whites with roots in Mozambique. The poor who arrived as part of rural development schemes in the 1950s, many of whom eventually gravitated to Lourenço Marques, faced the same marginalization they had

125

known in Portugal. The hard, physical labor of colonization was supposed to civilize them, much as forced labor was supposed to civilize Africans. Whites did not necessarily subscribe to a single Portuguese identity, argues Cláudia Castelo.[43] But for those who bought into it, being Portuguese in Mozambique was rooted less in loyalty to Portugal and more in a shared feeling of being under siege by a black majority. The destitute Portuguese who "sank" to living among "the blacks" undermined conceits of white prestige. Over the decades, Lisbon attempted to hinder the emigration to the colonies of unskilled people who might find themselves unemployed or doing the same work as Africans.[44] In 1961, one official warned that given Portugal's obligation to "instill in the black the habit of work," it would be "unacceptable if the white himself demonstrated his laziness or, still worse, his inaptitude."[45] Maintaining appearances—when necessary by rescuing poor Portuguese from comparison with Africans—was a collective responsibility.[46] Anthropologist (and former postindependence minister) José Luís Cabaço, who was born into the city's Portuguese working class, recalled how, growing up in the 1950s, he and his friends never worried about landing a job after they left school, even if they were to drop out. "The community rapidly organized itself to absorb 'its' unemployed," he wrote.[47] Whites considered themselves a "superior caste," and no matter how poor, a white person was always deemed "one of us."

The outbreak of war in Angola in early 1961 inaugurated a year of crisis for Portugal.[48] Images of the brutal killings of white coffee-farming families and their African workers by anticolonial guerrillas set off a panic among Portuguese throughout the ultramar.[49] After years of complacency about the supposed contentedness of the natives, Portuguese in Africa now contemplated their own Mau-Mau emergency. "No one trusted anyone," said Eugénio Lisboa of the reaction of whites in Lourenço Marques.[50] Lisboa, an engineer and literary critic, was one of the more visible members of Mozambique's small circle of white liberals. "Every black person was, in principle, suspect," he wrote in his memoirs. "How could it not be?" To racist fears were added resentments when, within months, Lisbon abolished the indigenato and decreed that the millions of people in the overseas territories with native status could claim Portuguese citizenship.[51] On paper at least, working-class whites now competed for jobs on equal terms with Africans. The regime's gestures at racial pluralism struck some whites as betrayal.[52] Reforms were carried out in an atmosphere of heightened suspicion as the secret police, now on war footing, expanded its operations in the subúrbios. According to Cabaço, some black Mozambicans initially feared that if they dared to exercise newly granted rights, they would risk being denounced as "subversives."[53]

The City of Cement, which had been predominantly European as long as it had been predominantly cement, represented for some a kind of bastion of Portuguese solidarity. Landlords often refused to rent to the relatively few black Mozambicans who could now afford to live in one of the many new apartment blocks. In the subúrbios, though, racial borders were harder to police. Many working-class Portuguese, to say nothing of the poor, could no longer afford decent housing in the city. By the early 1960s, hundreds of whites were living in clandestine concrete-block houses in the Bairro do Aeroporto—the Airport Neighborhood—an unauthorized development in the subúrbios (Figure 3.6).

Figure 3.6 The Bairro Clandestino do Aeroporto, 1969. The street grid of the "clandestine neighborhood" (just below center) blended seamlessly into the caniço (lower left). (MITADER)

127

In the late 1950s, a private real estate concern had divided a large parcel of land adjoining the airport into a grid of unpaved streets, expelled the people living there in reed dwellings, and begun selling inexpensive lots on which buyers built masonry homes.[54] Many of the builders were low-ranking civil servants, including some police officers. A good number of the buyers were South Asian and of mixed race, and there were also a handful of black home builders, including artists Malangatana Ngwenya and Alberto Chissano. The Bairro do Aeroporto had its own kinds of informal segregation, according to Lindo Nhlongo, who has lived in the neighborhood since the early 1960s.[55] Black households purchased properties in the corner of the development that abutted the caniço. Given the bairro's location and who was moving there, the neighborhood looked superficially like the multiracial communities that some in Lisbon hoped to establish in Africa.[56] On the ground in Lourenço Marques, however, officials viewed the unauthorized houses, wedged between the airport and one of the most wretched areas of the caniço, as a serious threat to the urban order. In late 1961, the municipality decided to demolish the bairro.

Officially, the issue was that the "Bairro Clandestino," as it was often called, violated Lourenço Marques's recently updated building code.[57] Such codes had been emanating from Lisbon since the 1930s, as the regime sought to modernize the cities within Portugal's many borders.[58] The clear intention of the 1960 Lourenço Marques law was to regulate construction within the City of Cement. The deeper concerns of authorities, though, lay beyond the curve. The Clandestine Neighborhood, with its dirt streets, its substandard masonry houses, its lack of either electricity or water provision, and its proximity to landing airplanes, became the first target of the new code's enforcement apparatus.

In the press, the controversy pitted those who defended the rule of law against those appealing to economic fairness. One advocate for the illicit home builders used language normally reserved for glorifying the pioneering Portuguese colonizers of the late nineteenth century. Clandestine home builders "perhaps unthinkingly launch[ed] themselves on the adventure of having a home and of maintaining themselves in this land," he wrote. But the true blame rested with bureaucrats, who were throwing up obstacles "so that this land doesn't advance."[59] The municipality eventually relented. It retracted its demolition threat and agreed to supply the neighborhood with street illumination and public fountains, if not direct water service or electricity. Streets remained unpaved.

Clandestine neighborhoods have been part of the urban fabric of Portugal itself for a century, according to planning historian Tiago Castela.[60] Both officially and colloquially, the term *bairros clandestinos* used to refer only to the shacks of squatters that have persistently sprouted up in and around Lisbon and Porto since the end of World War I and are frequently targeted for removal. But since World War II, the term has also referred to a much larger category of housing: unauthorized permanent construction on a city's outskirts, built on once-rural land that enterprising private landowners have subdivided and sold for development. In the 1950s and 1960s, the phenomenon resulted from the same process as the one experienced in the colonies. A liberalizing economy spurred a wave of internal rural-to-urban migration, and affordable housing in city centers was in short supply. After years of being overlooked by municipal authorities, informal concrete developments in Portugal were, from 1958 on, considered in violation of zoning rules and treated as illegal (and in the press described as "criminal"). But they were rarely demolished, in part because there were too many of them. More than half of all new housing in the Lisbon area in the 1960s was in a clandestine neighborhood of this kind. The Bairro Clandestino of Lourenço Marques was simply another.[61]

But because this particular clandestine neighborhood was in Mozambique, it touched a different nerve. This is more evident from what was not said—or could not be said—than what was. Press coverage of the controversy avoided the glaring fact that the unpaved streets of the development blended seamlessly into the caniço. The bairro basically *was* the caniço. Meanwhile, during the coverage of the City of Reeds debate, discussed in the previous chapter, the Bairro Clandestino did not come up at all. Craveirinha's call to think of economic hardship as a shared struggle went unheeded. This bairro was essentially deemed a white problem, and it was treated in isolation, as an aberration. The caniço was a black problem, and the reed and wood-and-zinc housing there was not considered clandestine or even illegal but rather an unfortunate reality natural to the stage of development of the Africans who lived there; it would be phased out in due course. This sensitivity—this anxiety that, in public debates, avoided placing the Bairro Clandestino anywhere near African neighborhoods—may have been what prompted the code enforcement blitz in the first place. Portuguese families with heads of household in respectable employment were occupying an unsettling middle ground between the precariousness of African urban life and the ideal of modern living.[62] The facade of white social cohesion was showing its cracks.

Editors of *O Brado Africano*, for their part, seemed to recognize the stakes involved. The newspaper's critical voice had been muted since coming under proregime ownership several years before. But during the Bairro Clandestino controversy, the onetime organ of elite African opinion managed to flash hints of its subversive past. Under the guise of sympathy for the home builders near the airport, news items seemed to revel in describing the lurid conditions of the predominantly white neighborhood: the open sewers, the flowing trash, and the flies that bred in the filth.

Unreported in the press, however, was the fact that hundreds of African residents in Chamanculo and Mafalala and Xipamanine were *also* building in permanent materials. And following the Bairro Clandestino episode, they started getting punished for it. In 1962, there were 122 violations, the majority of them in the Bairro Clandestino. By 1965, the annual number of violations more than doubled to 295, nearly all of them in other neighborhoods in the subúrbios. The figure peaked at 358 in 1969 and then dropped to 154 in 1970, the last full year for which colonial-era registries are available. Bureaucratic diligence alone cannot explain the aggressiveness of the enforcement push, not when local officials could be so lax in so many other matters. In some respects, the coming of war may have reinforced long-standing racial divides, but development and the wartime economy were also helping to obscure them. The subúrbios and all that they represented just felt too close. It was increasingly unclear where the city ended and the caniço began—and where white lives stood relative to black lives.[63]

Despite the silences surrounding the issue, *O Brado Africano* seemed eager to connect the dots. A commentary on the Bairro Clandestino in 1964 reads as a veiled critique of how home builders were being treated in other, predominantly African neighborhoods. Editors argued that even though the bairro was illegal, it was not "opportune to punish those who, with God knows what sacrifices, built their homes, sometimes little by little, with their own hands."[64] The home builders had not broken laws deliberately or because of a rebellious spirit. Rather, they had seized the opportunity to make homes that were "truly theirs." "And those buildings arose, by the dozens, by the hundreds, because many are those who had and continue to have that very human aspiration" (Figures 3.7 to 3.15).

Figure 3.7 Hulene, 1987. (CDFF)

Figure 3.8 Concrete blocks are often stamped with letters identifying who fabricated them, undated. (CDFF)

Figure 3.9 Hulene, 1987. (CDFF)

Figure 3.10 Concrete blocks, though in storage, already serve as walls, Hulene, 1987. (CDFF)

Officials knew little of the suburban terrain. But they knew it was a hotbed of subversive activity, and they feared what they could not see. In 1964, the secret police arrested dozens in the caniço, crushing Frelimo's nascent Lourenço Marques front.[65] In the latter half of the 1960s, the paving of some of the handful of drivable roads in the subúrbios and the installation of street lamps improved conditions for people who lived there, but residents believed that the upgrades were really designed to enhance police surveillance. The roads facilitated raids by the black-helmeted "shock" police. Actions against clandestine home builders fit within a larger strategy of intimidation.

Nonetheless, these neighborhoods remained largely illegible to officials.[66] Addresses were virtually nonexistent. When the municipality registered a housing code violation in the subúrbios, for instance, and served notice to the alleged transgressor, the location of the house was identified in the case file by the nearest cantina, bakery, lamppost, or factory. In one file, an official left a note saying that he could not follow up with a code violator because he had lost his way trying to find the house.[67] Forty and fifty years afterward, the safety of invisibility was the most common explanation offered by those who built in masonry for why they took the risks they did. The real threat, many said, came not from building inspectors or police happening upon one's illegal house or construction site. The greater danger, according to home builders, was being turned in by a jealous neighbor—someone envious of the prosperity represented by an improved house.[68] Files show that it was common for five, six, or seven years to pass from the time one built a concrete-block house to the time one was caught, even for those houses lacking a zinc-panel disguise. As home builders calculated risk, the law was just one factor among many.

The concrete blocks in Jaime Tembe's house were hidden, for example, but not because he actively sought to hide them. Although there were those who deliberately concealed masonry with other materials, Tembe used exterior zinc paneling because his budget allowed only a limited use of concrete. He did not discover that masonry was officially prohibited until after his project had already gotten off the ground, and he learned it when his neighbor, a railway worker, was caught and heavily fined for having built a similar house. During a search in the subúrbios for weapons,

133

police had entered the house of Tembe's neighbor, and not finding guns or blades, they penalized him for his masonry interior walls. Tembe later said he did not know why his own house escaped their attention.

Many people building houses in masonry, especially in the earlier 1960s, were unaware that what they were building was, from the municipality's perspective, clandestine. This was the usual experience of the law for residents of the subúrbios: one tended to discover the rules when police or the régulo arbitrarily decided to do something about them. Even so, it was not the law, precisely, with which people contended but rather the persons of the police and the régulo. Much of life was governed by rules that had no basis in official decree. Broad areas of the written law were widely flouted, subverted in many cases by the people who were charged with enforcing them. Not only in the subúrbios, but in all of Lourenço Marques, the law was often heard as a distant echo, heeded (if heeded at all) for reasons that had little to do with the mere fact that it was the law. *Tempo*, a weekly magazine that began publication in 1970, dedicated much of its early reportage to exposing the city's clandestine economy. In the year preceding the fall of the Lisbon regime, there were articles on pirate taxi cabs; unlicensed cafés; illegal gambling houses; falsified lottery tickets; and contraband sales of wine, matches, produce, fine clothing, automobiles, and foreign currency.[69] Civil construction in the City of Cement relied on the expertise of falsely credentialed engineers and thrived on padded bills.[70] *Tempo* columnist Rui Cartaxana argued in 1973 that the tendency of Portuguese law toward vagueness and the baroque enabled corruption: the "Law of Hat in Hand."[71] The law was a pretense, an ideal that some in Lisbon aspired to but that many people in the various levels of Mozambique's administrative hierarchy acted upon only when the feeling struck.[72]

The clandestine construction case files do not tell neat narratives. A number of cases appear to have been resolved in ways that were not recorded, or perhaps they were never resolved at all, and one might fill in the blanks with stories of pardons, bribery, and varying degrees of bureaucratic incompetence and disinterest.[73] Not everyone in the subúrbios who built in masonry in the 1960s and early 1970s thought of themselves as taking the same risk. When Daniel Malé was caught in 1968, five years after throwing a party to celebrate his new house, he had his employer on hand to help bail him out. The two went together to the building inspection office and paid "something," and the matter was quickly resolved. Lúcia Joaquim da

Figure 3.11 Zinc, blocks, and reeds used together, 1987. (CDFF)

Figure 3.12 Ceramic block construction, 1987. (CDFF)

Silveira and her husband also built a concrete-block house in Chamanculo in the 1960s, one much larger than Malé and Cossa's. Police did not bother her, she assumed, since the house, located in a blind alley and surrounded by a fence, did not draw too much attention to itself.[74] The couple's standing may have been protection enough. Her husband had been a professional footballer in Portugal.

When African home builders were caught building in permanent materials, their responses to municipal authorities were notably more abject than the defiant grievances voiced by home builders in the Bairro Clandestino. Alleged transgressors were given an opportunity to explain themselves: the case files for code violations are full of statements, dictated to municipal clerks, that read as the scripts of people who understood that they were expected to know their place. The accused played the part of the lowly supplicant and played it with feeling. Most statements were brief. All pleaded ignorance of the law, and almost all pleaded poverty. Most petitioners portrayed themselves as the sole earner responsible for many family members. Most explained the decision to build in masonry as a matter of life and death, given the fires that terrorized everyone living in the caniço.

The statement of Ricardo Niquisse, a thirty-three-year-old office worker who built a three-room house in Maxaquene, sounded many of the common themes:

> The correspondent is poor, the spare salary he receives
> not being enough to pay rent. After some years of work he
> managed to put together some money and with the help of
> friends and people accustomed to protecting him constructed
> a little house in order to be able to shelter in it his wife and the
> six children he possesses. As fires in rustic houses, covered in
> straw and made of reeds, have recently been confirmed, the
> correspondent resolved to make it out of block and covered in
> zinc to provide better protection.[75]

Another petitioner, António Almone, was married with five children and resided in Chamanculo. He explained that he had been living with his family in a reed house, but "one day there was a fire that burned my whole house down and I was left with nothing, only my children were saved, and on the same land where there was a fire there were houses made of blocks and these houses escaped the fire."[76] Alice Malendya, a forty-eight-year-old domestic worker living in Chamanculo, testified that she "built a modest house with the little money that her deceased husband left her, seeking thus to secure a roof for her children"; a harsh penalty would "destroy completely her ability to reserve for her little children the little that their father left them."[77] (She described herself as a "native," but following the new Lisbon-approved nomenclature, an official wrote "African.")

Claims of poverty and fears of conflagration required no exaggeration. These were the everyday realities of life in the caniço. But by playing to the sympathies of the municipal officials in this way, the accused portrayed the building of a masonry house as if it were little more than a desperate act of survival. Perhaps the most poignant moment in each appeal to leniency—poignant because of the self-effacement it demanded—was when the transgressor described the house at issue. Addressing an unseen audience of officials, the homeowner felt obliged to diminish what amounted to one of the principal achievements of his or her working life and possibly that of many family members. The house, no matter its size, was referred to in the statements of the accused as "modest" or as a *casita* or *casazinha* (a little house). António Samora Sebanhana, a sixty-two-year-old toolmaker for the railroad, erected a six-room concrete-block house—larger than most other homes in the neighborhood of Mafalala—but he stressed to officials that it was of the "cafreal type,"[78] "little more than a cafreal construction," and "a dwelling for an autochthone of very feeble economic circumstances."[79] The house that Sebanhana characterized as a crudely built hut was valued by the commission at 10,000 escudos, roughly what he earned in a year.

Similarly, Alice Malendya's "modest house," built to "secure a roof" for her three children, had *seven* rooms. A twenty-one-year-old café employee named Inácio Manjate stated, "My only goal was the shelter of the people of my family in my charge." The report in his case file notes that the structure was initially built not as a house but as a cantina—that is, a business enterprise.[80] And when Daniel Malé received his notice of violation, he explained to officials that "owing to his advanced age"—he was thirty-two when he made the statement—he "was improving his *casita* for the end of his days and living in a house of reeds would offer various dangers. As I have three children, I remain overloaded by the care of my mother, who is a widow, so you can see the difficulties I have in supporting such burdens."[81] Just five years before, as a seemingly much younger man, Malé had thrown a party to celebrate a house that was "a source of great

137

happiness," a "dream" realized through his own effort and the efforts of those close to him.[82]

Occasionally, the accused was more self-assured. Bernardo Ernesto Mário, a twenty-seven-year-old bill collector, introduced himself by stating that he had gone far in school.[83] He then went on to explain that because of the threat of fires and disease, he "resolved, at the cost of many sacrifices, and striving highly" to build a casita of wood and zinc, with concrete-block interior walls. Thus, he "could live in a civilized manner, in harmony with the guidelines of the Government that wishes to elevate the level of the African population." Essau Ezequia Maninguane, a twenty-seven-year-old secretarial assistant at the Agriculture Ministry, adopted a notably officious tone.[84] He reminded authorities that the government faced a housing crisis and that, furthermore, "these days the level of development represents a very important factor"—meaning the higher development of Africans. Words equating one's decision to build in concrete to climbing the evolutionary ladder of civilization—ideals expressed by Portuguese policy makers—may have been spoken in pride and to impress officials.[85] They also may have been a sarcastic jab at official hypocrisy.

Some said they were led to believe that concrete construction was permissible by the fact that so many others seemed to be doing it. One resident of Chamanculo "saw many constructions of the same type being erected with a great naturalness and greater calm, which seemed to the petitioner not to have whatever impediment."[86] It was this very normalization of concrete construction that gave officials reason to worry. As it was, there were just too many cases to process. More than once in the late 1960s, a municipal official noted in a case file that he could not yet schedule an evaluation of the house in question "given that there are many hundreds of cases in identical situations."[87] Social researcher António Rita-Ferreira commented on the futility of enforcement: "The fines and demolition orders, preceded by complicated regulatory formalities, aren't sufficient to repress the activity of builders of all races that inhabit the periphery of the city."[88] How many people actually built clandestinely in masonry is difficult to estimate. An aerial survey conducted in late 1966 counted 1,753 permanent structures in the densest part of the subúrbios.[89] This figure represented only about 5 percent of the total of 33,351 structures in the surveyed area, and it likely included some masonry structures other than residences. But the number and proportion of houses built with blocks likely increased substantially

Figure 3.13 Hulene, 1987. (Daniel Pereta / CDFF)

over the following decade. And the survey figure did not capture (because airborne cameras could not do so) the number of houses whose blocks were masked by zinc panels or even reeds.

NEITHER SOLID NOR PRECARIOUS

In 1965, a few years after the enforcement push had begun, the municipality refashioned the rules.[90] Clandestine home builders were now given an opportunity to keep their houses intact—at least for the time being. A reprieve was good politics. The demolition of hundreds of masonry houses in the name of proper planning that never seemed to come would have needlessly aggravated the discontent that displacements in the subúrbios were already stirring up.[91] But the rules change was not an amnesty. It did not halt code enforcement. Clandestine home builders unable to quickly escape their predicament with a bribe or some other means were now subjected to an arduous process that was seemingly devised for little purpose other than to squeeze them for fines and to enshrine their second-class status.

The municipality sent a team of technical experts to the house in question. They evaluated the quality of its construction, estimated its cost, and

139

then produced a lengthy and detailed report that included necessary improvements. Home builders had to secure permissions from various entities and submit plans and elevations for houses that had already been built without any construction documents. The case files are full of blueprints for many houses that were no more elaborate than a square divided into four rooms. Perhaps the most onerous burden for the homeowner was paying the fine and accumulated back taxes. Fines could total many months' salary or more, and transgressors entered into years-long installment plans to pay them off. The process could sometimes last a decade (if the case ever closed) with demolition being the official penalty if the requisite steps were not followed. In the apparently rare instance that the municipality *did* demolish a clandestine masonry house, it was usually because the transgressor declared outright that he or she would rather lose the house than pay the fine. Most house builders could not afford to factor a potential fine into the costs of construction.

Houses in the Bairro Clandestino, which often had steel-reinforced concrete roofs, were sturdier than concrete houses elsewhere in the subúrbios. Houses in other parts of the subúrbios were usually characterized in technical reports as being both of sound construction and "of clearly provisional character." That is, the houses were built solidly enough not to collapse but not so solidly as to hinder eventual removal. The logical contradiction did not seem to concern officials: if these masonry houses were "of clearly provisional character," just as houses of reeds and of wood and zinc were understood to be, then theoretically they did not violate the ban on permanent construction in the subúrbios. Racial condescension pervaded the process. In their appraisals of houses in African neighborhoods, engineers almost always remarked that they were "intended for the habitation of autochthones" or "for native use" or sufficient "for native habits." If a homeowner in violation completed the necessary steps, he or she was awarded what was called "precarious title." This did little more than affirm the status quo: the house was permitted to stand until future development required a teardown. If the need for demolition arose, the home builder surrendered any right to compensation. It was as if the house had been officially entered into the permanent record of impermanence.

Despite a decade of economic gains for many Africans in Lourenço Marques, much did not change.[92] Whites by and large maintained workplace

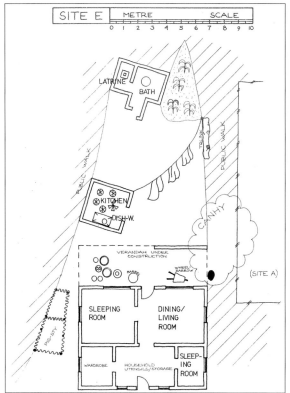

SITE E

LATRINE
BATH

PUBLIC WALK

PUBLIC WALK

TRUNK

KITCHEN
DISH-W.

CANHY

(SITE A)

VERANDAH UNDER CONSTRUCTION

BASKET

WHEEL-BARROW

SLEEPING ROOM

DINING/ LIVING ROOM

PIG-STY

WARDROBE

HOUSEHOLD UTENSILS/STORAGE

SLEEP-ING ROOM

Figures 3.14 and 3.15
Site plan and concrete house floor plan in Maxaquene (formerly Malhangalene), drawn by Swedish architecture student Ruth Näslund in 1976. *The Malhangalene Survey: A Housing Study of an Unplanned Settlement in Maputo, Mozambique, 1976*, vol. 1 (Göteborg, Sweden: Chalmers Tekniska Högskola, Arkitektur, 1977), n.p.

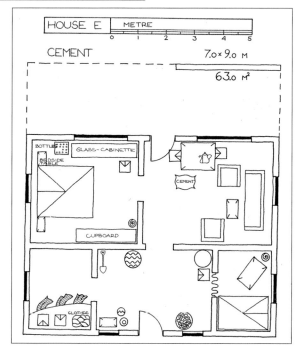

HOUSE E   METRE

CEMENT

7.0 × 9.0 M

63.0 M²

BOTTLES
GLASS-CABINETTE
BEDSIDE TABLE
CEMENT
CUPBOARD
CLOTHES

privileges that they had once feared losing. And PIDE was still widely feared. On a visit to Lourenço Marques in 1970, a former high-ranking official of the Ministry of the Ultramar was shocked to see black workers running home to the caniço just before 9:00 p.m.[93] They were anxious to avoid one of the "posses" that enforced an unofficial curfew for Africans in white neighborhoods. In 1972, the minister of the ultramar was troubled by an internal report about continuing acts of violence and dispossession against Mozambican "autochthones" by local administrators and private citizens.[94] Clearly, deep inequalities still structured life in Lourenço Marques.

According to many recollections, however, police and administrators had dispensed with pettier forms of harassment by the late 1960s. Now, there were some black Mozambicans renting apartments at the fringes of the City of Cement, in Alto Maé. Classrooms in that area had more black students. Men of various backgrounds socialized in certain restaurants and bars, so long as the black men among them could afford to dress as "civilized" persons should.[95] And there continued to be few social barriers to relationships between white men and black women, as long as marriage was not on the horizon. Alto Maé and parts of Matola were more diverse than a good number of neighborhoods in US cities at the time or even today. For many of those living in the City of Cement, the vast gap in living standards between themselves and those living in the subúrbios was understood in much the same way as the average American understands the vast gap between, say, San Diego and Tijuana. The point here is not to exculpate late colonial Mozambique society.

Color blindness was official policy, and the press continued to address the subject of race only obliquely. The only way to discuss racial inequities continued to be via proxy: by discussing conditions in the caniço. In 1972, the city council had a black member representing the subúrbios, and he was asked by a reporter what he thought the solution should be to the conditions there.[96] He replied that the answer ought to be the same for blacks as it had been for whites—though he did not say it so explicitly. Reed houses had to be replaced by cement, he said: the solution for the caniço should be what it had been for the City of Cement. A few weeks later, another city council member drew a connection between the subúrbios and the clandestine construction going on in Portugal, suggesting a link between the trials of people in cities of the metropole and those of Mozambique that few had thought to make.[97]

The regime figure most associated with this period is Baltazar Rebelo de Sousa, who, during his short tenure as Mozambique's governor-general between 1968 and 1970, became known for his charm and his gestures at openness.[98] A dedicated Salazarist, he nonetheless attempted to give the regime what he considered a human face, and after independence, even Frelimo leadership had kind words for him.[99] Probably Rebelo de Sousa's most important initiative was the accelerated construction of schools and health clinics throughout Mozambique. He also relaxed press censorship for a time—though this measure had limited effect because most newspapers were controlled by allies of the regime. In Lourenço Marques, he instituted an office of regional planning, colloquially called the Office of the Caniço, which consolidated government efforts to resolve problems of infrastructure and housing in the subúrbios after years of slack efforts.[100] The sharp drop in enforcement actions against clandestine construction between 1969 and 1970 may have been due to the governor-general's intervention or at least to his influence.

A story told about two of Mozambique's most accomplished artists, involving the governor-general and the issue of clandestine construction, evokes some of the fluid character of the politics of the era. One of the ways Rebelo de Sousa distinguished himself from his predecessors was through his public embrace of Mozambican culture, and he and his wife frequently invited African artists to the governor-general's residence and sponsored exhibitions of their work. It is said that the sculptor Alberto Chissano, however, refused several such invitations. Rebelo de Sousa dispatched an assistant to Chissano's house to find out why. The sculptor answered that African traditions of hospitality dictated that he could not attend: it would be wrong to accept the invitation, he said, if he could not return the kindness. And he could not invite the governor-general to his own house because, being in the Bairro Clandestino, his house was illegal. The story was recalled by Lindo Nhlongo, one of Chissano's former neighbors, and also by anthropologist José Luís Cabaço, the former government minister who was a journalist in Lourenço Marques in the 1960s. Cabaço added that Malangatana handled the situation differently than Chissano did.

Malangatana Ngwenya—Mozambicans knew him by his first name—had been something of a pioneer of clandestine construction. The painter had encouraged several of his friends, including Chissano and Nhlongo, to buy plots in the Bairro Clandestino in the first place, and together they and their families were among the relatively few black residents of the

143

neighborhood. Malangatana's house was made to be seen. It was designed by Pancho Guedes, Mozambique's flashiest architect. After receiving a notice of building violation in 1966, Malangatana paid a hefty fine, and he spent the next five years jumping through bureaucratic hoops attempting to obtain his "precarious title."[101] One wonders if, after accepting the governor-general's many invitations, he ever raised the matter with him. In any case, they became friends, and Malangatana received Rebelo de Sousa's support for a cultural center in the artist's home village, not far from the city.[102] According to Cabaço, when the governor-general and the artist were to make a trip to the village together, Malangatana requested that he be picked up on the way. The request brought an official motorcade through the dirt streets of the Bairro Clandestino. Malangatana had once been imprisoned for more than a year by PIDE. He was no flatterer of power, but he had a shrewd sense of how to leverage it. In a small but symbolic way, the governor-general's visiting motorcade helped legitimate the neighborhood.

Guedes shared a story of his own run-ins with authorities. In the late 1960s, the architect supervised the construction of what he called a clandestine school in Chamanculo, a nursery for the children of women who worked in a nearby cashew-processing factory.[103] It was built in reeds, not concrete. What made it clandestine was that all such establishments had to be built in permanent materials.[104] But the church sponsoring the project could not afford such materials. Guedes recalled that the first time he and workers built it, police told them they had to complete the structure in a single weekend. They could not do so, and the building was torn down. They failed on a second attempt as well. On the third try, though, the police brought over prisoners to help them build the school.

Today, more than a half century later, these stories of bending the will of the establishment have the ring of allegory, not least because of the fabled reputations of the principal players. They reveal something of how law and authority worked in late colonial Lourenço Marques—and how they could be worked. As in Portugal itself, municipal officials in Mozambique used the legalism of "clandestine" to characterize inconvenient realities as deviations from the rule, even when the deviations were common and visible and the idealized norm hard to locate. In Lourenço Marques, only one-quarter of the city lived in conditions that authorities considered both permanent

Figure 3.16 Fabricating concrete blocks, 1982. (António Marmelo/*Notícias* archive)

Figure 3.17 Shoveling stone aggregate, which is mixed with cement to make concrete, 1978. (*Notícias* archive)

Figure 3.18 A street of masonry houses, Hulene, 1987. (CDFF)

and legal. No VIP flying into the capital could miss seeing the Bairro Clandestino from the plane. One imagines that at least one of the police officers who helped Guedes with his clandestine school, after previously helping demolish it, went home to a clandestine house. Scholars of Africa frequently describe the dynamics of life lived under colonial rule as a "negotiation." The concept is intended to transcend the simplifying extremes of resistance and submission, but the picture it conjures up is of a reasonable conversation between parties of equal standing. In the subúrbios of late colonial Lourenço Marques, people's relationship to authorities sometimes looked more like a game of cat and mouse.

In 1972, Alfredo Manjate, a schoolteacher, decided to put to the test his own convictions about equal treatment before the law.[105] In his part of Chamanculo, he saw that white and South Asian merchants built their cantinas and compounds in masonry, apparently without the proper permissions, and so he went ahead and hired a stonemason to build him and his family a concrete-block house.[106] As the walls of Manjate's house got higher and became visible from the street, his neighbors said he was foolish to risk spending so much on something that he would eventually have to tear down. Police threatened him directly. A common police stratagem, though, was to let people build until the walls of their structure reached the roof level. That way, the eventual fine would be steeper, the distress for the homeowner more acute, and the bribe that might be extracted more lucrative. Manjate ignored the warning. He later said he gambled that independence would happen before the house was completed, and either by intent or by coincidence, his timing was almost perfect. The walls were finished a few months after the April 1974 Carnation Revolution in Lisbon that toppled the regime, ending forty-eight years of Portuguese dictatorship and precipitating Mozambique's independence the following year (Figure 3.19).

Despite the illegality ascribed to Manjate's actions, his story asserted the normalcy of his project. The sentiment resonates with the words that began this chapter. José Craveirinha wrote the poem "Unclandestineness" while jailed by PIDE in the 1960s. He characterized his rejection of Portuguese rule not as a conscious revolt but as the natural act of being himself. The lie foisted upon him that he was Portuguese was the truly "clandestine" behavior. "I hardly moved a finger clandestinely," he wrote. "But a militant in fact I am." And yet, even the most assertive clandestine home builders understood their place relative to the municipality and in

147

the scheme of things. Anthropologist Claudia Gastrow writes about un-authorized concrete construction of recent decades in the *musseques* of Luanda, the *subúrbios* of Angola's capital. As the municipality bulldozed whole neighborhoods that were deemed unbefitting of a modern city, concrete home builders registered their defiance. The permanent materials with which they built their homes served as the basis of claims to urban citizenship. "Their houses could no longer simply be dismissed as 'anarchic,'" Gastrow observes, "but had to be taken seriously as objects of good urbanism, through which demands and rights could be articulated."[107] Home builders of late colonial Lourenço Marques could not entertain such expectations. They did not "belong" to the city in the same way that citizens of an independent Angola could claim they did. Their houses were not the basis of further claims; many, in fact, took pains to hide their masonry construction. Concrete was less a confident declaration of the rights of citizenship than a hopeful approximation of what citizenship might feel like.

For all the nonchalance that some attribute to their clandestine building activities a half century or more ago, there were still plenty of people in the 1960s and early 1970s who were more cautious—people who contemplated building in masonry but then decided against it. When the fall of the regime led to a burst of masonry construction in the *subúrbios*, it became clear that thousands had pent up their ambitions.[108] Even though neither the transitional government nor the Frelimo regime that assumed full power in 1975 lifted the ban on permanent materials, the municipality did not demonstrate much interest in enforcing it; other concerns were considered more pressing.[109] The window of opportunity lasted only a few years, however. Shortages dried up the supply of all building materials.[110] Not until the 1990s, following the end of a long civil war, did concrete construction pick up again in earnest, so that today, it is by far the predominant form of construction in the *subúrbios*. Those who are not building in concrete are thinking about building in concrete, and even many with minimal resources are storing up concrete blocks for the day they can start building.

Figure 3.19 (*opposite*) Alfredo Manjate in the courtyard of his Chamanculo home, 2011. He began the house in 1972, defying the police who told him he would eventually be fined for building in concrete. The Lisbon regime collapsed in April 1974, building code enforcement relaxed, and Manjate finished the house. (David Morton)

149

Figure 4.1 The City of Cement, 1994. (*Notícias* archive)

Chapter 4

AN IMMOVABLE LEGACY

The Nationalization of Housing and Its Consequences, 1976–92

SOME MONTHS before independence, Sebastião Chitombe visited a friend's new home in the City of Cement.[1] The friend was doing well for himself. Not long before, he had been a neighbor of Chitombe's in a compound in Chamanculo, but now he was living in a roomy apartment that a Portuguese coworker had left in his care, probably for good. The visit was bewildering. Entering through the apartment's front door rather than the servants' entrance, Chitombe found the bathroom, and he washed his hands. "It was the first time I'd ever been in a bathroom like that for a reason other than to wash the floors," he later said. In the living room, he turned the light switch on and off. He said he took pride in knowing the light was "ours" even though the apartment was not his.

Soon, other Mozambicans were offered a chance to claim apartments of their own. On February 3, 1976, Chitombe was listening on the radio to Samora Machel, Mozambique's president, when he announced the nationalization of rental housing in the country's various cities of cement. Seven months after independence, more than one hundred thousand people had left Mozambique.[2] Much of the European population was gone, as were thousands of others. City centers looked increasingly desolate. By expropriating rental units as well as abandoned properties, the new regime could make vacant units available for new occupants and at the same time undermine landlords. Not only had landlords been deemed an exploiter class, many of them were continuing to collect rents from abroad. The nationalization order also carried enormous symbolism: it ended what the president described as colonial-era apartheid. "The city must have a Mozambican face," he declared. "The people are going to be able to live in their own city and not in the city's backyard."[3] He was referring to the sub-úrbios, using a word for backyard, *quintal,* that to his listeners meant the servants' quarters. To mark the occasion, the capital's Portuguese name was changed to Maputo, after a nearby river.[4]

During the process of decolonization, only a handful of cities in Africa shared circumstances as dramatic as those of Mozambique, among them the cities of Angola, which also gained independence from Portugal in 1975, and those of Algeria, from which the French withdrew in 1962.[5] In all of these cases, urban centers had been developed mostly for the use of white populations—people who left them nearly en masse once new flags were flown. In mid-1974, a year before Mozambique's independence, the majority of the City of Cement, about sixty thousand people, were European.[6] By late 1976, around 90 percent of the Europeans had left, as had much of the Asian population, and tens of thousands of Africans had taken their place.[7]

Independence, according to Frelimo, the armed liberation movement that won it, was to be more than a mere handover of power: it was to be a stage in an ongoing revolution. Uprooting the legacies of colonialism would be an arduous process, and Frelimo dismissed the softer socialism of the earlier wave of independent African states in favor of more radical solutions. Interventionist regimes in Algeria and Tanzania had already appropriated significant chunks of real estate in their cities—vacant and not.[8] Angola did so shortly after Mozambique did.[9] Mozambique, though, went a step further and like Ethiopia's Derg, which had overthrown a feudal aristocracy, abolished private landlords altogether.[10]

Yet even during these revolutionary times, Maputo's City of Cement remained, for the most part, a place for the relatively privileged. It became home to Frelimo elites, war veterans and their families, foreign volunteers and technical workers, and government bureaucrats. For many others who sought shelter in the City of Cement in the late 1970s and 1980s, life proved excruciatingly difficult, even when rents were low. It was not unusual for people to retreat to the subúrbios soon after giving a downtown home a try.[11]

Maputo was like many decolonizing cities in that independence erased long-standing racial divides only for class divides to assert themselves.[12] Scholars of colonial segregation have a simple answer for why: new elites used their leverage to monopolize vacant properties. But this only partially explains what happened in Maputo. Even after the choicest units in the City of Cement were spoken for, thousands of vacant units with rock-bottom rents still remained for anyone to claim. It took more than a year to get them occupied because for many people living in the subúrbios the City of Cement seemed too impractical, too forbidding, or otherwise too unappealing to consider making the move.

As much as he appreciated his friend's apartment, Sebastião Chitombe never gave serious thought to applying for a nationalized unit for himself. He had already found a space in Chamanculo, in the back rooms of a cantina he bought at a cut rate from a departing Portuguese. Others worried that leaving the subúrbios meant abandoning the neighborhood support networks that they relied on. Still others wondered if they could afford the lifestyle that an apartment required. Most could not. For all the clear advantages of the City of Cement—electricity, running water, a central location, and a tendency to stay mostly above seasonal flooding—apartment buildings simply could not accommodate the ways most people eked out a living. Women needed their yards to raise animals, to brew traditional drinks, to pound corn, and to prepare meals on charcoal-burning stoves.[13] None of this activity was allowed in apartment units and few would rush to discard these practices even if they could afford to. To enjoy the privileges of the City of Cement, one had to already have certain privileges. Elites may have been muscling to obtain the best properties, but the built inheritance itself also encouraged social segregation. The City of Cement physically moored the present to the past, with consequences for how we see not just Maputo but all decolonizing cities.

This chapter and the next discuss Maputo in the years shortly after independence and the ways in which the built environment mediated the emerging relationship between Mozambican citizens and Mozambican authorities. Scholarship of the era naturally orbits around Frelimo, either to rationalize its heavy-handed policies or to expose its many failures and

153

abuses.[14] Frelimo was a nationalist guerrilla movement turned authoritarian regime; "revolutionary socialist" since at least independence, it officially branded itself a Marxist-Leninist vanguard party—Mozambique's sole permissible party—in 1977.[15] Leadership was confident that it could remake Mozambican society from scratch, beginning in the countryside, where it attempted to engineer from on high large-scale "transformation." By contrast (and with important exceptions) state action in cities during the first decade of the "People's Republic" was characterized less by centralized planning than by triage and vacillation. The questions of what the state was and what it should do were still open in important ways, and Frelimo's leaders were not the only ones seeking answers. Residents of the suburbios helped give substance to government pronouncements. They sometimes led while seeming to follow.[16]

The nationalization of rental housing, the subject of this chapter, is a case in point. Though the measure may have seemed predictable given Frelimo's revolutionary program, officials cobbled it together in a few days, an improvised response to a flooding emergency in Maputo's suburbios. Others took it from there. The first part of the chapter reconstructs the chaotic context in which the policy was produced, beginning with the fall of the Lisbon regime, in 1974. Then I discuss how, to Frelimo's surprise, Machel's speech nationalizing housing in cities of cement inspired neighborhood activists to spontaneously "nationalize" rental housing in the suburbios. Frelimo officials felt obliged to accept this wider interpretation of the order, and thousands of Mozambican landlords in the bairros of the country were dispossessed as a result. History has essentially silenced this episode. But the nationalizations in the suburbios probably spoke more to what most people expected of the new regime than the nationalizations in cities of cement ever did.

Officials lowered rents across the board. Otherwise, though, expectations were soon frustrated. In the suburbios, the government barely even tried to maintain compounds and other rental units in any kind of shape. In city centers, concrete cityscapes that had been the pride of the colonial state became a burden to the postcolonial state. Nationalized buildings housed a tiny fraction of the country's population, but they absorbed far more than their share of administrative attention and scarce resources. Maintaining them was an absurd cost to bear during years when the economy was in free fall, war ravaged the countryside, and millions were hungry. In the late 1980s and early 1990s, a flood of refugees pushed the limits of Maputo's carrying capacity. The final part of the chapter chronicles how conditions through-out the city rapidly deteriorated, mirroring Mozambique's plummeting for-tunes. For people housed in a run-down building where the government was landlord, state collapse often seemed more than a metaphor.

"STREET OF DESERTERS"

On April 25, 1974, in Lisbon, junior officers in the Portuguese army staged a bloodless coup, toppling a right-wing dictatorship that had ruled Portugal and its overseas possessions since the 1920s. For months, it was unclear if the Carnation Revolution would lead to full independence for Mozambique.[17] Within a few weeks, though, political prisoners held at a facility outside Lourenço Marques were freed. Mass strikes, the first in decades, broke out in the city and around the territory. Frelimo guerrillas faced little resistance as they moved southward. Before long, much of the Portuguese army all but refused to fight. Portuguese who were young at the time remember the euphoric sense of possibility as teachers disappeared from classrooms and censorship of the press and movies faded away.[18] Some students filtered into the subúrbios, where most of them had never been, to teach literacy classes. Local newspapers, staffed by leftist reporters, introduced Frelimo to their readers in the City of Cement.

In the subúrbios, Frelimo was less of an unknown. Much of its leader-ship had lived in the bairros at one time or another, and dozens of Frelimo operatives and sympathizers there had been arrested at the outset of the war.[19] Supporters, old and new, now came out into the open, and they mobilized mass demonstrations to gain leverage for the group in its nego-tiations with Lisbon. The Lusaka Accords, signed on September 7, 1974, set a timetable for Mozambique's independence and established a tran-sitional government for the meantime, to be made up of both Portuguese and Frelimo officials. By the following June, Portugal was to cede control of Mozambique exclusively to Frelimo.

News of the agreement sparked a revolt in Lourenço Marques.[20] Right-wing gunmen seized the strategically important radio station downtown for a few days and called on South Africa and Portuguese military units throughout Mozambique to come to their aid. A throng of supporters formed outside, waving Portuguese flags. Local police remained on the sidelines as militias blocked entrances to the city and briefly took over the airport control tower. For weeks, thugs styling themselves the "Dragons of Death" had been terrorizing perceived Frelimo supporters around town. Now, along with ex-military personnel, they sped through the subúrbios shooting people at random.

Residents of Chamanculo recall the crowds fleeing through suburban lanes to escape from the Dragons firing into the crowds at the Xipamanine market. Barricades manned by people armed with sticks and machetes went up to block the rampaging gunmen. For the first time, the boundary between city and subúrbio became a line of defense, not for the city but for the subúrbios. Groups in the bairros prepared to storm the radio station, but as this growing pro-Frelimo army passed into the City of Cement, Portuguese officials convinced the insurrectionists to surrender, many of whom were able to flee to South Africa. During the days of the crisis, some in the subúrbios exacted vengeance on the nearest targets at hand. White motorists transiting through the area were stopped and their cars flipped over and set on fire. Cantinas were ransacked. Glória Nhambirre, the African co-owner of a cantina in Chamanculo, spirited her Portuguese husband to the safety of one of their houses on the city's outskirts.[21] A crowd appeared at the doorstep of Chamanculo's traditional leader, Frederico Cumba, a man who, during almost three decades of rule, had ordered countless beatings and extorted countless payoffs.[22] But Frederico was not at home. His daughter Ana Laura, twelve at the time, appeared at the door, waving her father's pistol in the air. The crowd moved on. When Frederico returned to Chamanculo sometime later, he was no longer régulo. A friend gave him a job pumping gas at a local service station.[23]

Probably hundreds were killed in the spasm of violence, most of them Africans, before Frelimo guerrillas deployed in the capital alongside Portuguese troops and tensions temporarily abated. There was credible talk of bulldozers digging mass graves for the many African dead, but the human cost of the uprising has never been fully explored.[24] Violence erupted again in the capital the following month. Scores were killed, most of them this time European civilians.[25] Just as the war in Mozambique was supposed to have ended, it seemed to be reigniting in Lourenço Marques, and it was taking on a distinctly racial edge. The flight from Mozambique of the European population as well as thousands of others began in earnest.[26]

Among the first to leave were hard-core Salazarists and those involved in the failed revolt.[27] But even people of more liberal leanings, who were cheered by the prospect of democracy, became increasingly anxious about what was in store for them in Mozambique. António Rita-Ferreira, a social researcher who lived in Mozambique for decades until returning to Portugal a few years after independence, later recalled the shock felt by people of European and Asian backgrounds, as well as a number of African urbanites, as they suddenly faced the new reality.[28] Portugal's wartime propaganda had portrayed the guerrillas as nameless, bloodthirsty terrorists. With censorship lifted, Frelimo had a name and a face, and its leaders now spoke for themselves. But when they did, they did not speak as liberal democrats: Frelimo was a well-organized revolutionary movement with friends in the Eastern bloc that saw the "bourgeoisie" as an obstacle in its mission to destroy colonialism.

In September 1974, Frelimo officials arrived on the ground in what they considered the heart of the colonial complex. Rushed into Lourenço Marques before they felt prepared for it, they were newly convinced that the capital would remain enemy territory even after the enemy had officially withdrawn. Beginning in late October, with the transitional government in place, authorities jailed more than a thousand people in Lourenço Marques considered subversive, often on the barest of pretexts. Arbitrary detention became a running theme of Frelimo's early years in power.[29] Rita-Ferreira ticked off the many reasons people emigrated after 1974, which were his own reasons as well: the threat of arrest, looming dispossession, and the suspicion that followed anyone who employed other people. He emphasized the impact of what has been called Machel's "triumphal journey" from Tanzania to the capital in the month before independence. In speeches delivered in cities throughout Mozambique, the charismatic Frelimo chief assured his audiences that all would be welcome in the new country, whatever their race. But he also vilified the colono.[30] Those who might fit this description came to think they had a lot to lose under Frelimo rule.[31] Not a few of the Lourenço Marques "bourgeoisie" who remained after independence, whatever their complexion, learned that these fears were justified.[32]

In city and subúrbio, the events following Lusaka showed just how fragile the peace would be and how tenuous, when it came, independence would be as well. The wooden shipping crates filled with the possessions of people departing Lourenço Marques began to appear in stacks along city streets and at the port, and yet there was reason to wonder whether those leaving might one day come back (Figure 4.2). Some had deeper roots in Mozambique than others and entertained the possibility of returning whenever the chaos subsided. They left houses and apartments in the City of Cement in the care of friends or older children who opted to stay.[33] Schoolteacher Alfredo Manjate was offered an apartment by a Portuguese colleague who thought he might return, but Manjate later recalled the offer as an insult.[34] He was already building his own house in Chamanculo. "I didn't need to be someone else's caretaker," he said. Another school-teacher, a neighbor of Manjate's, was outright gifted an apartment by a departing Portuguese colleague who had no intention of coming back. But he, too, declined. He worried that accepting the apartment would put him in an unfavorable light with Frelimo.

During late 1974 and throughout 1975, much of the City of Cement assumed the look of a ghost town. A reporter for *Tempo* magazine described

Figure 4.2 Shipping crates of household possessions at the Lourenço Marques docks, destined for Portugal, September 1974. Around two hundred thousand people left Mozambique in the years just before and just after independence in June 1975. (CDFF)

the changing dynamics of local real estate: as apartments in the wealthiest neighborhoods opened up, some people living in predominantly white, working-class districts took them over.[35] But no one took *their* place in the neighborhoods they left behind. Consequently, some streets in these outer areas, conspicuously those that gave direct access to the subúrbios, were left almost entirely vacant, making for an unplanned "buffer zone" much broader than the mere width of street that existed before. Abandonments tended to happen in bunches; a family would leave and inspire a cluster of neighbors to follow. In one area of about a hundred houses in Malhanga-lene, a neighborhood that abutted the subúrbios, all but two houses were vacant by December 1974. One couple who remained noted that some of their former neighbors had stripped their houses of faucets and pipes on their way out. Sidewalk graffiti on abandoned blocks read "Street of Desert-ers" and "Street of Runaways."

According to the *Tempo* reporter, the unwritten code of the City of Cement that effectively barred entry to black tenants appeared to be fixed in place. Landlords preferred units to remain vacant. From a moneymak-ing standpoint, the situation was "illogical." The reporter asked, "Will the owners of buildings in Lourenço Marques continue, as before, with the utterly discriminatory attitude of 'not being exactly interested in renting their houses to the largest segment of our population'? This was what the mentality used to be. It's just that back then this was 'understood.' Now it shouldn't be. It has to be repressed. As severely as necessary."[36] As the City of Cement emptied out, it remained the predominantly European cita-del that it long had been, except now with a widening moat between the shrinking white population and the subúrbios surrounding it on most sides.

Even many months after independence, with the accustomed barriers to entry effectively gone, people in the City of Reeds still did not rush to squat vacant units that, at the very least, offered higher ground and running water. It may seem hard to imagine how they could pass up the opportu-nity, but few considered the abandoned properties to be an opportunity—at least not yet. Squatting, so often romanticized as asserting a "right to the city," was simply not something people were inclined to do.[37] It will be re-called that a host of formalized practices constituted the making of a house and home in the supposedly informal caniço, and paying rent was one of them. Rent seemed to legitimate the occupation of space, as weak as that claim might prove to be when tested. To find a plot and build a house in

159

the subúrbios or even to find a rental unit and make one's home there was a conservative endeavor. Each was marked by deliberation and foresight—a carefully considered bet on one's future in the city. A move to the City of Cement when the future was so unclear was a leap far out of keeping with people's usual strategies.

And people remained anxious about the still unstable political situation. Recent events demonstrated that the subúrbios were defensible in times of danger, a measure of security in turbulent times. A countdown had begun: in less than a year, Frelimo would take full control of Mozambique and, with it, the capital. Any significant move—and changing one's address to the rarefied heights of the City of Cement certainly qualified—ought to have Frelimo's blessing. According to Alfredo Manjate, people awaited orders, out of respect for the government-to-be. None came until early 1976.

"EXPLOITATION OF MAN BY MAN"

On June 25, 1975, Mozambique joined the family of sovereign nations as one of its poorest members. Despite impressive economic growth during the last decade or so of Portuguese rule, as well as some gains in public health and schooling, one in four children did not reach the age of five.[38] Fewer than one in ten Mozambicans spoke Portuguese, yet Frelimo was relying on Portuguese to unite an extensive territory divided into more than a dozen indigenous languages.[39] Through means both deliberate and unintentional, Frelimo had encouraged many people to leave the country, but it appears that officials did not expect such an exodus.[40] Mozambique's store of technical expertise was bare. As one foreign worker at the health ministry later reported, only thirty trained doctors remained at independence to serve a population of about 12 million.[41] Many government administrators were gone or had one foot out the door. Mozambique possessed considerable industry, especially around the capital, but most factory owners and managers were gone or soon to leave, and many took company assets or outright sabotaged their businesses as they left. The rural commercial network neared paralysis and, with it, the ability of people to sell their crops and to purchase food and other necessities. However ambitious Frelimo's plans were upon assuming power, it would be lucky just to avert disaster.

Some of Frelimo's most significant moves in the early going came in the form of nationalizations.[42] The first, a provision of the constitution that went into effect with independence, was the appropriation of all land within the territory of Mozambique so that no one could buy or sell it. This was intended to put a halt to the speculation and alienation of African land that characterized the Portuguese era. It also brought some relief to suburban residents: they no longer had to pay annual ground rents. The month after independence, on July 24, 1975 — called for years afterward the Day of the Nationalizations — the state appropriated all health facilities and schools. Mozambique's remaining private medical services would now be put to more general use, and religious institutions — such as the Catholic Church, which Frelimo reviled as a former partner of the colonial power — would no longer set the educational agenda.[43] Private legal representation was prohibited, so that (theoretically) one could no longer pay for better access to justice. A fourth, seemingly anomalous nationalization that day resulted from the disgust of cabinet members who had just learned there were businesses that profited from death.[44] The state nationalized funeral services and took over the fabrication of coffins and caskets. Frelimo was not eager to nationalize all private enterprise. It sought the dominant role in the economy, and it interfered in many businesses, but it tended to expropriate only those that had "strategic" importance or that had been abandoned.[45]

During these early years, urban policy was something of a hodgepodge. Mozambique was 90 percent rural, and the government had its hands full in the countryside trying to concentrate peasants into "communal villages" and operating the state farms that had been established on abandoned plantations. Cities were not yet places that needed fixing, but rather purging. Frelimo's fears that urban areas were crawling with the "internal enemy" were not totally baseless. The regime had many real enemies. Memories of the September 1974 revolt were still fresh, and neighboring Rhodesia and South Africa operated clandestinely in Maputo and continually threatened attack. But spies and committed counterrevolutionaries were hard to detect, and so Frelimo targeted people that it said subverted the revolution in other ways. Benedito Machava has carefully documented the moralistic campaigns to "cleanse" cities of prostitutes and other "marginals."[46] Beginning in October 1974, urbanites considered corrupted by colonialism were sent to rural reeducation camps, efforts that peaked in 1983–84, when as many as fifty thousand "unproductive" people were rounded up and expelled from Mozambique's cities. The physical conditions of the country's various subúrbios did not top the Frelimo agenda.

An Immovable Legacy

It took a natural disaster to focus attention on the capital's City of Reeds. In late January 1976, a tropical storm hit Lourenço Marques, and for the new regime, the first rainy season in independent Mozambique became its first flood season. Sewage-strewn waters inundated even the bairros that usually escaped serious flooding. Once again, Munhuana suffered the worst of it. Still popularly known as the Bairro Indígena, the "neighborhood for natives," Munhuana had several hundred cube-like units that showcased the carelessness of colonial-era housing efforts. Every year brought some degree of flooding, and this year floodwaters reached depths of 5 feet.[47] The government resolved to shutter the Bairro Indígena for good and to permanently relocate its residents to safer ground, along with residents of other perpetually flooded areas (Figure 4.3). (Munhuana remained abandoned for more than a decade.) Officials evacuated several hundred people to the tourist camping grounds near the beachfront, but there was not room enough there for the thousands more who needed shelter.[48] Only then did officials decide to make use of the many abandoned units in the City of

Figure 4.3 In early 1976, after yet another destructive flood, officials evacuated residents of the Bairro da Munhuana (formerly the Bairro Indígena) to other parts of the city—one of the impetuses for the housing nationalization. Pictured here in 1987, the complex remained empty until the early 1990s. (CDFF)

Cement. The party's Central Committee charged a trio of ministers with drafting legislation that would nationalize all vacant housing.[49] Within a few days, the ministers devised a solution that, in both its intended and unintended effects, more radically impacted people's relationship to urban space in Mozambique's cities than any of the more carefully deliberated master plans drawn up before and since.

Júlio Carrilho was the minister of public works and housing for most of the first decade after independence. Born and raised on an island in Mozambique's far north, he had trained in Lisbon as an architect, later fleeing to Sweden and joining Frelimo. In 1974 when he was appointed to the transition government, he was one of the few university-educated Mozambicans whose skills Frelimo could call upon. Arriving in the capital that September, he had little knowledge of either Lourenço Marques or its subúrbios. At independence, he was twenty-nine. His portfolio, one of the government's vastest, included building and maintaining roads and bridges throughout the country, as well as water provision and urban sanitation infrastructure. Housing was not central to his workload.

Carrilho later explained the initial decision to nationalize much of the City of Cement in practical terms. Landlords had left the country, he said, and just as abandoned businesses were taken over in order to keep them in operation, abandoned housing units were appropriated in order to distribute them to those in need. President Machel was set to announce the new policy on February 3, 1976. But just a day earlier, the regime's Central Committee decided that the draft legislation did not go far enough. The more radical elements insisted that renting out shelter for profit was the "exploitation of man by man," a phrase that echoed through so many Frelimo pronouncements.[50] All rental units in the country's cities of cement, not just abandoned ones, had to be nationalized.[51]

Thousands gathered to hear the president's speech, delivered at a plaza at the far edge of the subúrbios. Machel offered various justifications for the measure. By giving the City of Cement "a Mozambican face," Frelimo was abolishing the racial barriers that had defined the city during the colonial era. By appropriating the buildings, Mozambique was cutting off a source of income to absentee landlords, who, from abroad, were allegedly using the collected rent to fund subversive activities within Mozambique. And finally, Machel declared, the buildings ought to belong to the people who had suffered for their construction, including the building laborers

Figure 4.4 Samora Machel, Mozambique's first president, Maputo, 1980. (Martinho Fernando / CDFF)

working for poor wages, and also the masses of peasants whose exploited labor contributed indirectly to the 1960s building boom. The City of Cement, he said, was "built atop our bones, and the cement, sand, and water in those buildings is none other than the blood of the workers, the sweat of the worker, the blood of the Mozambican people! They are the highest forms of exploitation of our people."[52]

As Machel ended his speech, he added a proviso. The president warned that not everyone who wanted an apartment or a house in the City of Cement would get one. Only those who earned a reasonable income, he said, would be able to afford to live in a nationalized unit. Living there would not be free. Generous loans from the state had financed the buildings; that state was now independent Mozambique, and those loans had to be paid back. This was to say nothing of the costs of just keeping buildings in daily operation. Here was a pragmatic side of Frelimo policy making showing through, and perhaps Frelimo's elitism as well.[53] For all the rhetoric of populating the City of Cement with Mozambicans, the people most likely to benefit from this colonial-era inheritance would be those who, through their rent, could best maintain it.

In fact, much of the best vacant property had already been taken, or soon would be. Many of the units in wealthy districts, such as in Polana Cimento and Sommerschield, were already occupied by Frelimo officials and various state institutions; some were reserved for diplomats and *co-operantes* (aid workers), the many foreigners who arrived in Maputo to lend their skills to the socialist cause. Whole apartment high-rises were requisitioned by ministries for use as offices as well as employee housing.[54] And thousands of former Frelimo guerrillas and their families were offered apartments in the rest of the city; many of those guerrillas were now government bureaucrats. Still, thousands of units, their rents now lowered, remained for those willing to claim them.

Several months after Machel's announcement, much of the City of Cement continued to lie vacant. The president ordered Carrilho to get apartments filled quickly. The result was even lower rents. The government relented on its hope that tenants would fully cover mortgages and maintenance costs. Rent was linked to income, so families who earned less were charged less than higher-income families, no matter the apartment.[55] Three years later, most units in Maputo were occupied.[56] But, according to a government survey, only a small fraction of the city's working-class heads of household lived in the City of Cement.[57] In the majority of units, the head of household was in the service sector, usually a government employee.

As people recalled in recent interviews, rent was not the only cost to living in the City of Cement. One also had to factor in the costs of electricity and water. To cook the meals that most of them were accustomed to and that they could afford, tenants would need their large mortars and pestles to make cornmeal. But they were prohibited from bringing them into apartments because thousands of women pounding corncobs on verandas would compromise the structure of the buildings. Charcoal-burning stoves were also banned. In 1977, on the first anniversary of the nationalizations, a reporter asked how it was, given the space then still available in the City of Cement, that so many people continued to live in suburban flood zones.[58] That rainy season, thousands of people had been washed out of their homes. The answer, the reporter discovered, came down to a matter of furniture. The City of Cement felt foreign: many people interviewed for the article said they did not have the beds and the chairs that they believed were required to live in an apartment—they only had their straw mats. A representative of the municipality, apparently upset that people could not be convinced to leave flood zones, said the displaced people were "poorly informed": subsidies were available to help pay for furniture.[59] Government was often frustrated by its inability to reach people in neighborhoods so near at hand.

165

In 1976, Sebastião Chitombe was twenty-two and living in the back-rooms of his Chamanculo cantina, and he had no interest in making a move (Figure 4.5). As for his friends, most of them were laborers living in the crowded compounds where he used to live, and they were not able to afford the city. Even those in the subúrbios with greater means were reluctant. Helena Macuacua, a young teacher who lived near the airport, thought a move was too risky.[60] "I couldn't put the money together for it," she later said. "I saw the rent was going to be very high, and also my husband wasn't someone I could trust. I preferred to plant myself here where things were accessible rather than go to the city and afterward suffer the consequences." Benjamim Benfica, another schoolteacher, lived in a wood-and-zinc house in Chamanculo that his father, a truck driver, had built. He chose to honor his late father's wish that he never give up the house.[61] "We didn't have electricity, we didn't have a sewage system, but it was *my* house. This was fundamental."

Benfica was young for a homeowner, only twenty-one at independence. Many of his friends, like many of Helena Macuacua's friends, jumped at the chance to live in the City of Cement. Many also returned to the sub-úrbios within a few years when costs proved too much to bear. It was not unusual for people, even those who had a free apartment provided by an employer, to venture to the City of Cement and try to establish a life there only to return after a month or two. Others, like Benfica's father, had spent their adult lives saving up to build a house of their own in the subúrbios. Some families had lived on the same plot for decades. A house was one of the few solid investments that could be passed on to one's children. For an older generation, the City of Cement seemed so distant and the lifestyle it required so unattainable that living there never took shape as an aspiration. New housing rules dictated that a family could only have one house; the situation was still too uncertain to exchange the home one had for a house one had not even hoped for.[62] And a common anxiety had persisted since the period of transition: the fear that the new regime would not survive and the old order would return.

Figure 4.5 (*opposite*) Sebastião Chitombe at his home, 2017. In 1976, Chitombe passed up the opportunity to move to the City of Cement, opting to stay in the backrooms of the Chamanculo cantina he had just purchased at a cut-rate price from a departing Portuguese. (David Morton)

NATIONALIZATIONS FROM BELOW

The nationalizations emerged during a period of improvisation and compromise—years in which Frelimo said it had to make do. The consequences of decisions made on the fly could be as lasting as any of the regime's more deliberate planning—as the housing measure eventually demonstrated. But whether improvising or not, the regime was not alone in making policy. In theory, orders came from Frelimo's Central Committee. In reality, government decrees had to be implemented on the ground, and leadership discovered that people could be creative in how they interpreted them.

In the days after the announcement of the housing nationalizations, a line formed outside the offices of the Public Works and Housing Ministry.[63] As instructed, the current tenants of rental buildings were queued up to register their units with the government, their new landlord. Many thousands waited, and the line snaked through the streets of most of the downtown area. Officials at the ministry were perplexed: there should not be so many renters needing to register their units. Carrilho, the minister, left his desk and questioned people in line. Many of them were not living in the City of Cement, he discovered. Rather, they were people who rented one of the thousands of units built of reeds or wood-and-zinc in the subúrbios.

A new authority had emerged in the subúrbios: the *grupos dinamizadores* (dynamizing groups), usually known as GDs.[64] They were composed of people who had declared their loyalty to Frelimo and their readiness to take orders, and their nomination to the GD was then approved at mass neighborhood meetings. Most GD activists were male, and their credentials to lead usually rested on having a wage-earning job or a higher level of formal education or on having previously run afoul of the Portuguese secret police. During the transition and the early years after independence, Frelimo had only the most tenuous grasp on the city. The hierarchy depended almost entirely on the GDs to communicate and carry out its directives, to keep watch against subversives and counterrevolutionaries, and to settle the disputes of everyday bairro life. Members of the GDs were to "follow the correct ideological line, avoid becoming individualistic, [and] be permanently in contact with the masses, instructing and learning, correcting and being corrected."[65] GDs organized in workplaces as well; their job was to monitor their employers and to take charge if the employers abandoned Mozambique.

The GDs often found themselves translating Frelimo's vague and generalized orders into specific actions in their neighborhoods, usually at mass meetings. According to Carrilho, GDs who heard Machel's speech on Heroes Day and his characterization of exploitative landlords in the City of Cement began "nationalizing" compounds and rental houses in the subúrbios as well.[66] Frelimo had already nationalized all land, including in the subúrbios. But it did not intend to nationalize rental units there. The subject had been broached, but it was recognized that though most building owners in the City of Cement had left the country, many landlords in the subúrbios considered themselves Mozambicans. They were not much wealthier than their tenants, and they had stayed. Setting neighbors against one another made little practical sense. Machel's speech therefore expressly targeted the inequities embodied in the City of Cement, emphasizing how it had been a redoubt of racial exclusion and was built at the cost of unrewarded Mozambican toil. Machel made no mention of compounds, the slums within the subúrbios that more clearly represented how exploitative landlords could be. His speech referred only to the appropriation of rental "buildings" (*prédios*). Policy makers did not imagine that this wording could be open to interpretation. Yet when the Central Committee was informed of the spontaneous nationalizations taking place in Maputo's subúrbios, it decided to go along. If charging rent at a profit was an unacceptable form of exploitation, then indeed it must be unacceptable everywhere. We can only speculate what the effect of reversing suburban nationalizations might have been.

Within days of taking action to relocate flood victims, the government found itself the reluctant landlord to a good share of the City of Reeds. The nationalizations in the subúrbios, as Carrilho later reflected, addressed a long-held and heartfelt desire. They were a demand by caniço dwellers for a meaningful form of citizenship, one in which the government assumed its responsibility for all parts of Maputo. Exactly who was making those demands, however, is difficult to determine: which GDs were responsible, that is, and which suburban tenants (among tens of thousands) may have been pushing them. Frelimo, meanwhile, never publically acknowledged that its housing policy had been diverted from its original intent.

Housing nationalizations in Angola, Algeria, and Tanzania in the 1960s and 1970s left informal areas mostly alone.[67] Algeria and Angola, former settler colonies like Mozambique, appropriated units in formalized sectors

169

that had been abandoned or squatted. As Tanzania's socialist project, *ujamaa*, unfolded in Dar es Salaam, Julius Nyerere avoided provoking the many African landlords of "dog-ribbed" houses whose support he needed.[68] Instead, Tanzania dispossessed wealthier building owners, nearly all of them of South Asian origin, in a 1971 campaign against "landlordism" that seemed racially targeted. Nyerere decried rent as a form of theft before Frelimo did, but Mozambique joined Ethiopia's Derg as the only African regimes to take that notion to its logical extreme.[69] The other countries that had taken a revolutionary path (or something like one) seemed to recognize the limits of their ideology and their power in the vast peripheries of their cities.

How many total units were nationalized in Mozambique is difficult to estimate. The Administração do Parque Imobiliário do Estado (APIE), the state agency created to manage the newly nationalized properties, became responsible for about fifty thousand units of formal residential, commercial, and industrial space in the Maputo-Matola area.[70] (This represented approximately half of the total nationalized buildings in the country.) Though it tried, the agency never managed to complete a nationwide inventory of these units. APIE did not even attempt an inventory for the thousands of properties it officially owned in the subúrbios. In the older neighborhoods, where rental units and especially compounds were densely clustered, most everyone was affected by the nationalization—either they were a landlord or tenant or they knew someone who was. "[H]alf the suburban population lives in a house rented from the other half," reported *Tempo* a few weeks after the nationalizations.[71] The magazine operated in close lockstep with the state, but it empathized with the many caniço dwellers who over time had managed to invest in the construction of small rental units: reed houses, perhaps embellished with a plaster finish and often nicer than the houses the landlords themselves lived in. This was "how many heads of families sustain their own. Many widows live this way. Many abandoned or divorced women, too." These households would be losing their rental income, but *Tempo*'s empathy had its limits: "Thousands of exploited people had no shame in practicing their own exploitation [by] charging high rents for miserable accommodations. It was the blindness of the law of subsistence."

Albertina Amaral's mother, Ana, used the proceeds from making traditional brews to build a wood-and-zinc house in Xipamanine.[72] Eventually,

Ana, Albertina, and Albertina's children moved into the back rooms that Ana had built on the same plot of land, and she rented out the original house. A tenant had been living in the house for only two months when the nationalizations were announced. When interviewed in 2009, Albertina was still full of rancor that the local GD had "snatched" what she called the "mother house."

> Machel said that he was taking the clinics and other houses like that [that is, in the City of Cement], not these shacks. But these people that called themselves régulos, they took the shacks and the rents too. Then they said it was the government that took the shacks . . . I don't think that's what Machel said to do, but humanity is bad, and it was humanity that took these shacks.

The property loss caused heartbreak for many, she said. "Some people had to pay rent in their own house! Do you see? This is something no one can bear."

Benjamim Benfica, the young schoolteacher, had become the note-taker at meetings of his local GD in Chamanculo. He respected the decision to nationalize suburban rental properties, including two rental units his late father had built on nearby plots.[73] But his father built a third unit, a wood-and-zinc house, within a few feet of the family house, and it had become vacant just before the nationalizations. Benfica realized that the unit would now probably go to a tenant he did not know, someone who would not pay Benfica rent and whom he could not evict. He decided to demolish the structure instead.

Jochua Guambe, the hunter who had used the proceeds from decades of selling animal skins and claws to assemble a small real estate empire in Chamanculo of approximately two dozen plots, had died in the mid-1960s.[74] His holdings then passed to his oldest son, Júlio, who lost everything in February 1976—all except for the house that his father had built for his family some four decades before. Júlio died in the mid-1980s, still deeply embittered for having lost his patrimony so soon after inheriting it. Upon his death, his youngest brother, Castigo, moved from an apartment in the City of Cement back to Chamanculo. If he had not moved back, he would have lost the family house to APIE.

During the colonial era, António Araújo ran one of the few African-owned funeral services in Lourenço Marques.[75] His agency fabricated coffins

171

in his yard, in the shadow of his giant, four-hundred-hole pigeon coop. A month after independence, his business, including the hearse, was nationalized (along with all funeral services in Mozambique). And in February 1976, he lost most of the enormous residential compound that he had built a little more than a decade before.[76] The compound was home to many single women who made a living mostly or in part through sex work. For them, the nationalizations meant a reduction in the monthly rent. The more immediate consequence, however, was that Araújo cut off the compound's water supply.

It is unlikely that Araújo's losses would have pricked the conscience of Frelimo officials. Personally subjected to not one but two nationalizations, he fit the profile of the exploiter whom the president was demonizing in countless speeches. But some officials felt immediate remorse for having dispossessed the many people who had built a single rental unit or two in their yards, as the Amarals had done. Within weeks, the government produced a brief clarification of the nationalization law to explicitly include houses of reeds, wood-and-zinc, "or other materials."[77] The elderly and the infirm who had relied on rental income for sustenance were entitled to a monthly subsidy. Those who had yet to recoup their investments in construction at the time of the nationalizations could get partial indemnification. But first, one had to know that these remedies were available. Then, one had to fill out the necessary paperwork downtown. Many, if not most, of the women affected did not speak Portuguese.

Sometime in the 1980s, a man went to Chamanculo and set up a desk under the fig trees at the neighborhood's main crossroads. He claimed that, for a small fee, he could ensure that one's nationalized property was returned. He was soon exposed as a con artist and chased out of the neighborhood, but he no doubt had seen a potentially fertile opportunity in the sense of dispossession that many felt. Today, the resentment still simmers, enough so that some older residents become silent when the subject is raised—not out of fear of speaking ill of the government but for fear of creating problems with neighbors. Former landlords often share their yards with former tenants.

The nationalizations in the subúrbios fundamentally changed the relationships among neighbors. Initially, there was the crude leveling effect of dispossessing many families. As for tenants, those who had once depended on the goodwill of landlords when it came to improving the conditions of rented property now depended on the state, and the state was essentially the GDs, who distributed units and collected rents. As a landlord, the government, such as it was, simply did not have the capacity or the resources to maintain suburban properties. The public works ministry tried to provide tenants with building materials such as zinc panels and bundles of reeds to patch up deteriorating homes, but these efforts fell well short of the need. "Everything ended up destroyed," said Albertina Amaral. She pointed to what had once been the "mother house." It was now in shambles. "When they saw that it was falling apart, they didn't do a thing. And many houses fell into ruins like that. Many houses fell apart."[78]

In the 1980s, APIE offered to reimburse residents of the subúrbios who fixed their own rental units, but officials fretted that so few people knew about the program.[79] The housing agency frequently blamed various difficulties on tenants' "lack of awareness." Information was conveyed by GDs and other neighborhood officials either via the "people's journals" posted on public walls or through large neighborhood meetings. Many people, though, learned of policies secondhand or not at all; clarification, if needed, was not forthcoming. Carrilho, the former minister, recalled a tenant from the subúrbios who was intent on closing the gap between government and governed. The man appeared at the ministry demanding to speak to him. He complained that his front door was crooked and needed fixing. The minister replied that the problem probably was not that the door was crooked but that the whole house was. And unfortunately the ministry could not build the man a new house.

Years later, former government officials characterized the nationalizations in the subúrbios as a catastrophe.[80] Carrilho, who had become a professor of architecture, reflected that Frelimo's fundamental mistake was "turning a technical problem into a political one."[81] Several former GD members who were interviewed for this book said that the nationalization order came to them directly from the Frelimo leadership. They had assumed Frelimo wanted to show that the nationalizations were not racially motivated—that not only white and Asian landlords would lose their properties. Accusing GDs for what happened in the subúrbios was a means, they said, of deflecting responsibility for a policy that still causes some bitterness today.

GDs were often among the first to be blamed when things did not go as planned.[82] Frelimo officials often scolded them for taking orders too far, such as for their role in scaring away business owners or in the mass

173

arbitrary detentions of people deemed enemies of the state. Many activists used their positions in the GD to enrich themselves or settle personal scores. After 1977, Frelimo brought the grupos under tighter control. But what the regime considered to be "indiscipline" in the GD ranks should not be dismissed as a deviation from Frelimo rule, but rather inherent to it. State formation happens in practice, not in theory.[83]

What happened in the subúrbios in February 1976 demonstrated that the Frelimo leadership did not enjoy a monopoly on urban policy. Some, perhaps many, suburban GDs acted on behalf of Mozambican tenants against Mozambican landlords after Frelimo had decided not to. What seemed to be typical GD overreach might instead have represented a parallel vision of what the People's Republic should be, pursued by activists whose ears were differently attuned to the people of that republic.[84]

THE SPIRAL DOWNWARD

In Frelimo political discourse, cities and the people who lived in them posed traps for the revolution, echoing a long tradition in Africa of demonizing urban life as a corruptor of "authentic" African values.[85] Frelimo cadres were urged to steel themselves against the purportedly toxic influence of capitalistic, individualistic, and anti-Mozambican attitudes that anyone who had lived in the former Lourenço Marques inevitably adopted to one degree or another. "Strongholds of evils," President Machel said of cities as he ordered the nationalizations of housing. They were "the factory of reactionaries."[86]

The state bureaucracy relied on the same formally educated urbanites who were so suspect. The government worker who did not follow the political line or meet his goals or who stole public funds was not just lazy or bungling or thieving—he was a saboteur. The stock figure of the internal enemy was a cartoon character named Xiconhoca ("Chico the Worm").[87] Well fed and with a thick cigar hanging from his lips, Xico was the stereotypical self-involved city dweller, in thrall to Western luxury and vice. Xico appeared in newspapers and on posters playing many roles: the government clerk, the merchant hoarding goods for the black market, and the spy on the phone with paymasters in South Africa and Rhodesia. Sometimes, he played all three roles at the same time.

Much about APIE, the agency created to administer nationalized real estate, resembled the caricature. Though less than 2 percent of the population of the largely rural country lived in APIE units, the agency was a large bureaucracy, with offices in all the major urban centers and several in Maputo. Management capacity in Mozambique was thin, and running even the small private enterprises that had been abandoned or in which the state had otherwise "intervened" had proved a struggle. Machel once lamented that the government was operating too many auto shops and hair salons, and not operating them well.[88] But these challenges paled beside the management of much of Mozambique's urban building stock. APIE was overwhelmed by its task from the start, and it soon became notorious for pervasive ineptitude and outrageous levels of corruption.

Throughout the late 1970s and the 1980s, few branches of government received more negative coverage in the state-run media than APIE did. At first, the biggest complaint was that employees were hoarding the best apartments in the City of Cement for themselves.[89] In 1980, amid party concerns about a runaway state bureaucracy, the president launched "offensives" against "indiscipline" and corruption in government, and made APIE one of his principal targets.[90] The director-general of APIE and several of his deputies were not just sacked; they were also arrested for "completely misinterpreting the guidelines set by the President of the Republic."[91] Further investigation led to the arrest of employees who had effectively turned clusters of apartments into personal fiefdoms. APIE employees sold off furniture stripped from apartments, rented out units for personal gain, gave apartments to lovers, and even used some units to operate brothels.[92] As one journalist wrote in 1980, APIE had become a "State within the State."[93]

As bad as it was, corruption was not APIE's central problem. Maintaining the building stock was. Even the best-intentioned office workers would have had difficulties dealing with so many unruly assets, for the government had inherited a built legacy that under ideal circumstances would have stretched the capacities of the state—and circumstances were hardly ideal. Though concrete buildings might seem indestructible, they actually require constant attention, upkeep, and repair, but APIE lacked the trained personnel and the materials to meet those needs. The generalized collapse of the Mozambican economy following Portugal's withdrawal resulted in dire shortages. Nails, paint, wood, zinc panels, cement mix, and tools became scarce, and the careful rationing of fuel restricted the transport of what materials were available.[94] As a result, APIE answered only a fraction of tenant requests for repair.[95] In 1979, fifteen hundred new toilets were

An Immovable Legacy

ordered to replace broken ones, but only twenty were delivered.[96] Elevators, initially a novelty for many people, became something of a curse.[97] Replacement parts, which had to be imported, were hard to come by, as was the expertise to fix the elevators properly. Added to that, APIE stopped paying its elevator maintenance bills. By the mid-1980s, functioning elevators were the exception. Residents were forced to trudge up and down ten, fifteen, or twenty floors several times daily. Older residents found themselves effectively trapped in their apartments.

When the state appropriated Maputo's hundreds of towers and apartment blocks, it also inherited the approximately one thousand men who guarded and cleaned these buildings. Adequately supervising this workforce proved impossible. Guards earned a reputation for acting like free agents—being absent from duty, illegally taking apartments for themselves, and even abetting burglaries.[98] Whether or not this reputation was a fair one, the presence of the guards (and their frequent absences) helped engender a feeling among many tenants that living in the City of Cement meant they were on their own.

From the beginning, APIE had trouble collecting rents. After the first year, almost a third of the tenants in the City of Cement were in arrears.[99] The agency began listing overdue renters in the newspaper to shame them into paying, but the rate of noncompliance hardly budged.[100] People had various reasons for not paying. Some, compelled to make their own repairs to APIE properties, unilaterally deducted their costs from the rent. Others, as APIE acknowledged, interpreted the nationalizations as meaning they did not have to pay rent in the first place. "More awareness is needed," said one official in 1979, echoing what was by then a common refrain.[101] The fact that many government workers were given free accommodation by the ministries they worked for no doubt confused matters among those who did not have free accommodation. And yet, the people whose finances were most precarious—including the thousands of flood victims who had been evacuated to the City of Cement—were the ones who most reliably paid their rent.[102]

Salaried workers expected a well-maintained property. As one apartment dweller put it in 1980, "We fill the holes that APIE's maintenance department do nothing about and this situation cannot continue because we have contracts with APIE, which establish the rights and responsibilities of both parties, and we have paid our rents."[103] But among the very poor, for whom a home in the City of Cement was emergency shelter provided by a benevolent government, paying one's relatively reduced rent was an act of responsibility and a means of solidifying one's link to the state. It was an affirmation of citizenship similar, as Carrilho described them, to the ground-level "nationalizations" of the subúrbios. The nature of the relationship between the Mozambican state and its citizens had yet to assume a predictable pattern, and just what people had a right to and what the government expected of them in return had yet to be determined. For most tenants of the City of Cement, that relationship was mediated to a significant degree through APIE. But not even the people who ran the agency had a firm sense of its proper role relative either to the assets in its charge or the people sheltered under its roofs. "We don't know what we are or what we want to be," said the chief of APIE's Maputo delegation in 1984, eight years after the nationalizations.[104]

Despite APIE's prohibitions and its attempts to tutor tenants in the how-tos of modern living, many tried to preserve their daily routines: cooking on open coals, raising goats and chickens in their apartments, and pounding corn on their verandas. Throughout the late 1970s, journalists played up stories of simple Mozambicans baffled by the use of bathtubs and flushing toilets and of children who relieved themselves in stairwells. Meanwhile, housing officials despaired of the threat to public health and the damage to what they considered the nation's patrimony.[105] To resolve the "cultural problem," the public works ministry embarked on a hygiene awareness campaign: tenants were instructed on the importance of keeping stairs, landings, corridors, and elevator shafts free of trash; they were advised to keep apartments and yards free of animals; and they were educated on what constituted the proper use of a sink.[106] One lesson, increasingly vital for everyone to learn as water shortages and pipe ruptures became more common, was "how to live a normal life alongside excrement."[107]

When the doors to the City of Cement were opened in 1976, the president said he looked forward to seeing how an influx of people from the countryside, with their rural, communitarian values, would influence the city.[108] But even as Frelimo's leadership championed rural values, they considered themselves the clear-eyed agents of modernization and much of the Mozambican populace as mired in backwardness.[109] In one speech, Machel said it was indecent for women to wear headscarves to work—apparently, in João Cravinho's analysis, because the headscarf was considered "a symbol of rural life, unsuited to 'modern' urban living."[110] Many new residents of the City of Cement may have comported themselves as befitted the modern image, but most of their family members did not, including relatives recently arrived from the countryside. Clearly, they did not need the president to tell them that the City of Cement was an uncomfortable fit. For all the condescension directed toward so-called bumpkins who did not know how to use flush toilets and who raised animals in bathtubs and in stairwells, the fundamental issue was not that people's practices were inappropriate to the City of Cement. It was that the City of Cement was fundamentally inappropriate to Mozambique: it was a permanent and immovable reminder of colonialism's colossally bad fit. Yet at independence, the buildings of the City of Cement were not going anywhere, and they would soon fall apart if not properly maintained. Their upkeep required an investment in the buildings themselves, an army of building superintendents to look after them, and a bulky bureaucracy to manage it all. To foot this bill, Frelimo was initially compelled to preserve the kind of economic and social segmentation that it had sworn to dismantle. After lowering rents, there was little the government could do to make apartment living affordable or, for that matter, livable. Many tenants decided they were better off putting their apartments up for sale on the black market—called "selling keys"—and using the proceeds to build a house in the subúrbios.

The sense of dread descending on the City of Cement became a common theme of Mozambican literature.[111] In the macabre 1980s short story entitled "Unexpected Death," by Ungulani Ba Ka Khosa, a man named Simbine checks on the progress of a balky elevator by unwisely peeking his head through a paneless window into the elevator shaft.[112] He becomes stuck there, and the elevator, when it finally comes, crushes his skull. Simbine's mother wonders why the elevator is stuck somewhere above her. She climbs the stairs up to her son's tenth-floor apartment and discovers his corpse still upright, his stiff hands clawing the edges of the elevator portal. Who is to blame for this tragedy? Simbine's mother believes the evil spirits present at her son's birth foretold his premature end. The building's guard expects that *he* will be blamed, since he was drinking at a bar instead of being present on duty when Simbine's children sought help. But the deeper blame, the guard reasons, rests with APIE, for having ignored his advice to replace the missing glass pane in the window of the elevator door.

And ultimately, the guard tells himself, Simbine brought the misfortune on himself by taking three wives, a sure way to stoke jealousies and invite sorcery. The implication is clear: in Maputo, the man of the countryside will meet his doom.

After a brief respite in the early 1980s, when Mozambique showed signs of economic recovery, the revolution entered its terminal phase. By 1983, a long drought was crippling production, rural development schemes were failing, and Mozambique fell deeply into debt. The government had been rationing food for years, but waiting in seemingly endless queues for necessities was now one of the principal occupations of urban life. The rebel group called Renamo (Resistência Nacional Moçambicana, or Mozambican National Resistance) was making alarming headway.[113] These "armed bandits," as Mozambican media invariably called them, had been terrorizing various parts of Mozambique since shortly after independence, when

Figure 4.6 A broken sewage line at an apartment block in the City of Cement, 1989. (Domingos Elias/*Notícias* archive)

Figure 4.7 Several families are evicted from their homes in the City of Cement, 1994. (*Notícias* archive)

Rhodesia's intelligence service cobbled the group together from former elements of the Portuguese secret police and others disaffected by Frelimo. With Zimbabwe's independence, South Africa took over as Renamo's principal patron, and thanks to Pretoria's considerable backing the insurgency wreaked destruction in the countryside and pushed the Frelimo state to near collapse. Many describe the conflict of the 1980s and early 1990s as South Africa's "war of destabilization" against Mozambique. But the violence also fed off the animus of a significant number of Mozambicans toward Frelimo's high-handed rule. And violence fed off itself, helping magnify a conflict sponsored by the apartheid regime into a devastating civil war.

From the mid-1980s onward, the war burned just beyond Maputo's outer edges. By 1989, hundreds of people per day were taking refuge in the capital with relatives or wherever they could find space.[114] Already crowded conditions—ten people to a one- or two-bedroom apartment was common—reached intolerable levels in both the subúrbios and the City of Cement.[115] Gas shortages became more acute. Supplies of food, coal, and wood had been cut off.[116] Tenants of the City of Cement tore up parquet floors to fuel cooking fires. Overcrowding accelerated the deterioration of building structures so that, for many, a house or an apartment in the City of Cement became a dubious privilege at best, a garbage dump and death trap at worst.

Tsendzeleni, a play performed in Maputo in 1989, takes place four years earlier as food and fuel become scarce and trash piles grow higher just outside apartment doors.[117] A woman from the countryside on her way to see her daughter is stranded midway in Maputo when her bus is ambushed by Renamo, and she seeks temporary refuge in Alto Maé, a neighborhood just within the City of Cement. There she witnesses people consumed by their individual problems. In their selfishness, they cannot resolve the problems they have in common—such as the ubiquitous piles of trash. A black marketeer quarrels with sanitation workers. They have requested rice in compensation for carting away the garbage, since they cannot buy any food with their municipal salaries. (There is no food to buy.) A doctor nearly murders his neighbor for moving a trash pile to the front of his door—after the doctor has just moved it to the front of the neighbor's door. The doctor begins building a wall in their shared veranda, though it will block his neighbor's only means of egress. This way, the doctor can protect the space he has declared his own.

The play is ultimately not just about how the City of Cement is the site of corruption but also about how it has somehow corrupted those who live there. In the City of Cement, people are anonymous, black market goods are openly bartered for sexual favors, and no one takes responsibility for their neighbors and community. Anything goes. In the adjoining subúrbios, however, from where most have come—and where conditions, presumably, ought to be worse—the people are disciplined, there is vigilance against crime and corruption, and common spaces are kept clean. It is a romanticized picture of the subúrbios during that time, to be sure, but one that comports with the romantic vision that persists in recollections today. The woman from the countryside, who has suffered more than anyone else, arrives in Maputo and stands as witness to just how distanced from their roots people have become.

In the subúrbios, women swept their dirt yards every morning. In the City of Cement, stairwell landings became trash pits. The spaces of the City of Cement inspired angst, paranoia, neglect, and isolation. The physical qualities of the spaces themselves played a part. In the subúrbios, there were few reliable door locks. When neighbors shared yards, someone always had an eye on what was happening there. Everyday activities, such as getting water, put one in constant contact with others—people, moreover, with whom one generally had years of familiarity. The greater sense of order and community in the subúrbios, under what seemed to be more difficult conditions, was partly due to the very lack of privacy that so many complained about. GDs had an easier time monitoring and directing activities in the bairros than they did in the City of Cement because people in the subúrbios were already accustomed to monitoring their neighbors—and, knowing that neighbors were probably watching, monitoring themselves. In the City of Cement, one spent much of the day behind closed doors. Any common area transformed into a no-man's-land.

In suburban rental properties, tenants simply made repairs themselves when APIE turned out to be like any other disinterested landlord. But in the City of Cement, people could not manage on their own even if they had no other option. When busted plumbing flooded hallways and was left unrepaired and when elevators creaked to a halt and could not be put in motion again, it produced a sense of helplessness and abandonment that living in the subúrbios did not. The quick deterioration of apartment highrises that so recently had looked brand new engendered a sense that the state, such as it was, was itself in free fall—without a single shot being fired in the city. For many people in the City of Cement, living in an apartment was one of the most significant ways that they understood their relationship to the state. Yet in the City of Cement, where people lived next to government ministries and were often neighbors in the same building, the state could still feel impossibly distant.

Figure 4.8 (*opposite*) In the City of Cement, 2002. (Amadeu Marrengula/*Notícias* archive)

Chapter 5

PLANNING IN THE SUBÚRBIOS, 1977–92

IN 1969, the city received its last major urban plan of the Portuguese era, the first plan to pay any real attention to the subúrbios.[1] A lavishly illustrated, never-implemented scheme from 1955 had rendered Lourenço Marques as an elegant Parisian metropolis.[2] The new plan took a more grounded approach. It offered few visuals of what the urban streetscape should look like. Instead, it sketched out regional transport links, vaguely stitching "subintegrated" neighborhoods into the infrastructural fabric. A team of planners and architects, as well as a traffic specialist, a sociologist, and a historian produced dozens of volumes of documentation, a good share of it studies of physical and social conditions in the bairros—quite a change from a time when officials either ignored these neighborhoods or marked them for total erasure.[3]

To coordinate suburban upgrades, Governor-General Baltazar Rebelo de Sousa instituted a new agency: the Office of Urbanization and Housing for the Region of Lourenço Marques.[4] He located it within the caniço itself, in a stripped-down, single-story complex on the road to the airport.

Figure 5.1 (*opposite*) A debate on household plot size during the parceling of Maxaquene, 1978. (Eva Sävfors)

The staff who worked there called it the Office of the Caniço.[5] The people living in the reed houses surrounding the Office of the Caniço came to call their neighborhood Urbanização (meaning "urbanization") in recognition of the government installation in their midst. The agency led efforts to build schools and market facilities and install public water taps. It helped plan housing projects in more distant Matola and Machava.[6] But administrative backing disappeared within a year or two.[7] The local government built so few primary schools in the bairros relative to the children in need that the buildings were little more than novelties.[8] Some came equipped with swimming pools, but the pool at the school built in the Beira-Mar area of Chamanculo, for one, was never filled with water.[9] The 1969 plan gathered dust.

After independence, the Office of the Caniço became home to the National Housing Directorate. Created in 1977, it had fewer resources than the Portuguese agency it replaced, and initially less technical expertise to draw from, but a far greater task. As with all postindependence institutions, its implicit mission was to effect universal, revolutionary change. But every Mozambican city had its subúrbios; it was difficult to know where to even begin.[10] People at the agency had to get to know these neighborhoods, and people in these neighborhoods had to get themselves known. Critics of modern urban planning tend to stress how authorities impose grandiose schemes from above, destroying communities in the process.[11] Lost in these kinds of critiques, however, are the people whom planning never touched. The residents of Maputo's subúrbios had grown tired of decades of neglect. They wanted their new government to think big.

James Scott has been particularly influential in our understanding of how planners—such as urban planners—infiltrate state power into people's lives.[12] "High modernist" states seek to reshape otherwise amorphous populations to make them "legible," he has argued. People and places can then be monitored, controlled, taxed, and potentially "improved"—often through superscaled interventions, frequently with good intentions, but rarely for the better. Places like the subúrbios might function according to a logic understandable to the people who live in them, but to the high modernist planner the visual disorder of the "slums" means chaos. They have to be disciplined into proper shape, like rows of crops, and authorities will demolish unruly neighborhoods if it means they can rebuild on a blank slate. In Scott's portrayal of such thinking, "An efficient, rationally organized city, village, or farm was a city that *looked* regimented and orderly in a geometrical sense."[13]

Between 1977 and 1983, Mozambique adopted high modernist solutions for industry and even more so for the countryside.[14] Taking their cues from Tanzania's ujamaa villagization scheme and from Soviet state farms, Frelimo policy makers tried to "transform" agricultural production by subjecting it to the formulas of scientific socialism. If everything had gone according to plan, nine million peasants—much of the country's population—would have been concentrated in communal villages, each carefully designed as a rectilinear grid. This way the government could better serve the rural population and draw it into collective farming. But despite its efforts (and perhaps because of them), agricultural output not only came up short of high expectations—production declined.[15] Given Frelimo's many failures planning the rural economy, maybe residents of Maputo were fortunate that urban planners made only modest interventions in the subúrbios. The staff of the housing directorate acted when opportunity dictated. They helped suburban victims of floods resettle on safer ground, for instance, and provided several hundred households with building materials. Later, they instituted a latrine-building program.[16]

Yet people in the subúrbios were desperate for a transformative intervention. They wanted ready access to water and roads fit for bus and car traffic. They wanted to feel that they were being looked after—that there was substance to being a Mozambican citizen. The spontaneous nationalization of suburban rental units, the brainchild of ad hoc neighborhood governing groups (the *grupos dinamizadores*) rather than government ministers, was one clear example of where this desperation could lead.[17] During the colonial era and afterward, people in the bairros of Maputo had plenty of reasons to avoid the gaze of authorities. To use Scott's parlance, many tried to make themselves "illegible" to agents of the state. Some hid alcohol stills behind reed fences and others hid concrete blocks behind zinc walls. Sometimes, though, suburban residents inverted the dynamic Scott describes. They took action to make themselves visible, and their neighborhoods legible, to government officials whose attentions were often pulled elsewhere.[18]

This chapter does not address all the planning efforts in Maputo's subúrbios during the first decade or so after independence. Not considered, for instance, is the structural plan of 1985, which, though it could not be implemented at the time, was the first significant urban plan since 1969.[19] Instead, I focus on a few episodes that help reveal how ordinary people attempted to bring government planners and planning into their lives. The chapter centers on the Maxaquene Project of the late 1970s, the first "slum upgrade" scheme in Maputo after independence. I relied for the most part on the perspectives of planners and other people who were attached to the housing agency at the time—individuals who gave the project its official imprimatur. Although I also interviewed several former members of the local grupos dinamizadores, the perspective is primarily from higher up the ranks. It is clear enough, however, that neighborhood residents themselves were the project's driving force. They steered it in unexpected directions, and what was supposed to be a minimal intervention took on much larger dimensions. Residents tried to make their neighborhood look "regimented and orderly," as if according to an official plan—even when no such plan existed.

IMPROVEMENT WITHOUT DISPLACEMENT

In 1977, residents of the neighborhoods of Maxaquene and Polana Caniço were far from downtown, far from sources of drinkable water, and far from feeling that they were part of Maputo[20] (see Figure I.3). Just two years later, a grid of wide, unpaved streets and narrower roads crisscrossed these neighborhoods. Rectangular plots were laid out in neat alignment, and each plot was nearly identical in size to its neighbors. Many homeowners held documentation granting them the right to convert their houses into permanent materials if they wished. Pipes channeled water from the municipal network to taps in the public areas of newly created city blocks. Large sections of each neighborhood had been surveyed and cleared for future schools and health clinics.

The National Housing Directorate was responsible for what was called the Maxaquene Project. A Swedish architect attached to the agency had come up with the idea, and the United Nations Development Program (UNDP) had funded it. And yet, the project was not quite a government initiative, nor was it a foreign import. The project began as a simple concept: to bring more access roads through the subúrbios. Soon residents of the neighborhood transformed that concept into something more ambitious. They themselves demanded the grid plan, the relatively uniform demarcated plots, and the documentation legalizing their masonry houses, and they did most of the organizing, surveying, digging, and building. They turned suburban neighborhoods into what they thought of as proper urban neighborhoods.

None of this was the norm for Africa at the time. In the 1960s and into the 1970s, newly independent countries tended to favor a deluxe version of housing development.[21] Instead of trying to improve existing housing, governments cleared slums and built brand-new houses and apartment blocks. Civil servants, not the poor, tended to occupy the new units, and because these projects were benefiting a privileged few at enormous expense, international lenders and donors looked for other solutions. By the 1970s, many "site-and-service" schemes were in the works; planners surveyed plots on empty land, inevitably at a considerable distance from urban centers, and they linked each plot to a newly constructed infrastructural grid.[22] This left people to build their own houses, but they often had help in the form of funding and technical assistance. Even before Mozambique's independence, a site-and-service scheme was under way in Matola. But the huge up-front cost of building all the infrastructure beforehand, usually far from existing water mains and roads, meant that the site-and-service approach served too few people—only hundreds, in Matola's case—to be practical.

During the 1970s, planners and policy makers began to accept, grudgingly, that unplanned settlements were likely to be permanent fixtures of the urban landscape in Africa and elsewhere in the Global South, and that so-called squatters might be part of a solution. The ideas of an anarchist British architect, John F. C. Turner, filtered into places such as the World Bank, and policies began to shift toward aiding people who were building unauthorized houses, incrementally, on their own.[23] A Swedish architect named Ingemar Sävfors had Turner in mind when, in the mid-1970s, he worked on a small upgrading project in Ouagadougou, the capital of what was then Upper Volta. The objectives for the project were modest.[24] It opened paths of access through tightly packed settlements. Doing so made it instantly possible for ambulances, fire engines, and garbage trucks to circulate—if, that is, the local municipality devoted resources to such services. It also made possible the gradual and more expensive installation of infrastructure over time: water pipes, electricity, sewage lines. The small scale of the project was key. The long period of gestation that a larger-scale project demanded would have forced people currently in need to exercise extreme patience or to be leaped over entirely for the sake of the following generation. A smaller intervention could yield more immediate results.

In 1977, the National Housing Directorate was staffing up with foreign architects and planners, and Sävfors joined them. He had been to Mozambique before. The previous year, he and a number of Swedish architecture students had helped conduct a social and housing study of one of Maputo's bairros.[25] Cooperantes tended to be more radical in outlook than Sävfors. He was being paid by the United Nations, and he thought of himself as a nonideological problem-solver. In this, Sävfors felt he saw mostly eye to eye with the agency's director, José Forjaz, an architect with a decidedly pragmatic bent. But the agency still lacked a clear agenda, and Sävfors cast about for projects to work on. There was an assisted autoconstruction project under way, in which the agency helped people with prefabricated building materials, but it was serving only a few hundred households. Sävfors scorned the ongoing site-and-service project in Matola. He later recalled that some homeowners there, most of them government workers living comfortable lives, complained that their houses lacked garages. He thought back to the bairro that he had recently helped survey. He realized he could do something there along the lines of the project in Ouagadougou. Forjaz gave quick approval for a pilot scheme, and an area of about 150 acres in the neighborhood then called Maxaquene One was chosen for it. A Canadian cooperante, an architect and planner named Barry Pinsky, eventually joined Sävfors as a project lead.

Maxaquene was not an obvious place to intervene. Most of the suburban population was concentrated to the northwest of the City of Cement, in long-established neighborhoods such as Chamanculo, Xipamanine, and Mafalala. But cutting roads through the tightly woven suburban fabric of older neighborhoods would have meant displacing far too many people. Maxaquene was located in a more recently settled area due north of the City of Cement, and its population density was lower. Still, there were enough people in the area, close to ten thousand, for the plan to make a significant impact. Sävfors also knew more about Maxaquene than about most other neighborhoods, thanks to the study, and he had already worked side by side with Maxaquene's grupos dinamizadores (GDs), whose cooperation—and approval—he would need.[26]

The local GD took to Sävfors's proposal with enthusiasm. One section of the neighborhood, with a population of about two thousand people, was chosen as a testing ground. The GD organized a mass meeting to inform residents that opening up access roads in the neighborhood was a necessary first step toward the eventual provision of water, schools, and health clinics. But it would not be painless. Some would have to sacrifice their houses to make way for the new roads. Under the colonial-era administration, people who were displaced by development often received small lump-sum payments to soften the blow, but people whose houses the Maxaquene Project demolished would receive no indemnification. The new government could not afford it.

No one voiced dissent—at least, that is how people recall the meeting. Many were excited by the project's advertised benefits, and any dissenters under such circumstances might have kept their opinions to themselves. The GD gave the planners the go-ahead. But they set one condition: anyone whose house was to be torn down would be given a place to live elsewhere in Maxaquene One; no one, that is, could be displaced completely from the neighborhood. Memories of colonial-era removals were still fresh. The caniço housing just south of the neighborhood had been stamped out by formal development, mostly for working-class Portuguese, in the 1950s and 1960s. An industrial zone to the north had displaced many others. And the area just to the east was populated by a number of people who had been forced from their homes in the 1950s to make way for a new golf course by the bay shore. Given this history, anyone compelled by the new project to give up their home for the betterment of the neighborhood had to benefit from the improvements in some way.

STRAIGHT ROADS (OR STRAIGHT ENOUGH)

The planners conducted an aerial survey, and with overhead photographs in hand they sketched out a rough proposal for roadways. To minimize demolitions, the projected roads meandered around existing houses. In the meantime, the GD appointed an urbanization commission to work with the planners. The members of the commission rejected the road plan: they hated the idea of zigzagging roads. Being "urbanized" meant building straight roadways, just as one saw in the City of Cement—even if they had to knock down more houses. "It's not a real road unless it's straight," Augusto Duvane, the GD member responsible for housing, later said. "If you're going to do something, do it right!"[27] (Figures 5.2 to 5.5).

Figure 5.2 Maxaquene, just as the project began, 1977. (Barry Pinsky)

Figure 5.3 The urbanization commission meets with planners Barry Pinsky and Ingemar Sävfors. (Eva Sävfors)

Figure 5.4 A neighborhood meeting to discuss the progress of the project. (Barry Pinsky)

Figure 5.5 Residents of Maxaquene insisted that the new access roads be straight because this was part of what it meant to be "urbanized." Many homeowners willingly moved their houses by a few feet to accommodate the roads. (Barry Pinsky)

Even so, many of the straight roads that the planners eventually plotted were not exactly straight. The 1969 urban plan, approved in 1972 but never implemented, envisioned new roads and highways running through various suburban neighborhoods, including Maxaquene. Fearing that to tinker with that road plan might invite unforeseen problems in the future, the Maxaquene planners retraced its general outlines. For reasons that are unclear, the main access roads in that plan curved gently away from the principal thoroughfare, like the veins of a leaf. The roads may not have been straight, but the members of the urbanization commission considered them straight enough.[28] The Maxaquene planners then plotted ancillary roads, and made them narrow to minimize disruption to people's existing houses. But again, the neighborhood commissioners objected: they demanded wider roadways. They had a more prosperous urbanized future in mind. In the revised plan, the widest access roads were to be 18 meters, the equivalent of almost five lanes of highway. Fewer than 2 percent of Maxaquene residents at the time owned a car.

To organize the project, the GD divided the neighborhood into a few dozen *quarteirões* (city blocks). It was perhaps the first time in Maputo's history that the word was applied to fluid suburban space. Each block comprised some fifty to eighty households (roughly 250 to 400 people) and elected a committee and a leader. At the center of each block, planners called for a plaza where water spigots would eventually go; the plaza would also serve as a public area for meetings and for children to play. It was more difficult, however, to plan for future schools, clinics, childcare centers, and the like. They required much more land: a quarter of the neighborhood's total area, planners estimated. Some of the land could come out of already existing open space. Most of it, though, would have to come out of people's yards and houses.

This is when the hard work of forming consensus began. Explaining to residents, in the abstract, that houses would have to be demolished was one thing. Convincing individuals to demolish their *own* houses was quite another. But making this case was not the planners' task. It was up to the GD's urbanization commission to resolve the problem. Members of the commission and the project's assigned social worker went house to house, translating the plan into practical realities for each resident who was going to be affected. "There are people who are always resistant," the social worker, Prafulta Jaiantilal, recalled. "But after talking to them many times we overcame their concerns. Neighbors influenced neighbors."[29] As it happened, relatively few people had to be resettled. Many more had to shift their houses by only a few feet, which was not a terrible burden for people living in reed or wood-and-zinc homes. Without too much trouble they could dismantle their houses, recover most of the materials, and rebuild.

But masonry houses situated in planned right-of-ways posed a real problem. Their owners faced a serious loss of investment. And their neighbors had little sympathy. Some concrete home builders had started building in blocks only recently, after independence, and though enforcement of the masonry ban had effectively lapsed, residents had been advised that building in permanent materials would impede future improvements to the neighborhood. Even before the advisory, the construction of a concrete-block house had a way of stoking a neighbor's jealousies. The more one displayed one's good fortune during trying times, the more one raised suspicions that the wealth was ill gained. Shortly before the planning team arrived at Maxaquene, vandals had destroyed two newly built masonry houses in the northern part of the neighborhood. Now, with the roads project in the works, some concrete homes were direct obstacles to the common good. People's image of an appropriately modern plan of urbanization was being threatened by what many perceived as the selfishness of a few.

Suspicions also trailed members of the GD because the planned roadways somehow avoided their houses. This concern may have been partially allayed when the concrete-block house of one prominent GD member was bulldozed to make way for a future school. Meanwhile, the urbanization commission alloted some owners of demolished masonry houses abandoned masonry houses in other parts of the neighborhood. And some were given recently nationalized units outside the neighborhood—thus breaking, at least in some instances, the promise that no one would have to leave Maxaquene One. Overall, though, few enough people were inconvenienced in this way that more than thirty years later, those most involved in the project could recall every troublesome case. One in particular stuck out in many memories: a police officer who steadfastly refused to sacrifice his concrete-block house to the project. The matter went all the way to the desk of Forjaz, the national housing director. No one could remember exactly how it was resolved.

AWAKENED EXPECTATIONS

The second challenge was more strictly technical. Before GPS, working on cleared terrain was the easiest way to survey lines, since there was nothing to

195

obstruct surveying instruments. But in Maxaquene the goal was to do as little damage as possible. Lines for roads had to be surveyed through standing structures that blocked viewing scopes. The solution was to mount strobe lamps on the tops of poles. That way surveyors could see distant points over the roofs of houses. Once the surveying was done, it might only take a few hours to bulldoze the access roads to make a planned block. A number of people from the neighborhood helped technical staff from the housing agency with the surveying and found the leftover land to settle uprooted families, and the work gave them a more personal stake in the project. At the same time, they learned a new skill set. "They were amazed themselves with how they could 'create' space," Sävfors later recalled.[30] As the project spread from the initial test site, a group of men and women now adept at the process circulated from block to block to survey roads and train others.

Participating in the project gave many residents a new perspective on their relationship to the government. Before the planners arrived, expectations were generally very low. People had been given to understand that whatever benefits independence might bring, they would be slow in coming. But as they helped lay out roadways, their expectations quickly changed. If they had found themselves consenting to the planners' proposal at the beginning of the project, they now had quite specific ideas of how the project ought to proceed. On their own, they had already begun squaring up their houses to align with new roadways and paths. Now they wanted their plots to be given precise, equal-sized, rectangular boundaries, which they considered a hallmark of permanence in a modern city.

The desire for some form of secure tenure was long-standing. Participation in the project brought it to the surface. Official recognition of tenure would allow people to invest in their properties, such as through the construction of masonry homes. Some felt the need for security more acutely, including those who had been displaced by the project to a different part of the neighborhood and who were now living on land carved out of another's property. Perhaps because it was less dense than older neighborhoods, Maxaquene had fewer fences, and so it was even less clear where one's land ended and someone else's began. The planners suggested more flexible alternatives to the call for systematic plot parceling because they feared that it would create conflicts among neighbors. The visual disorder of households and yards might have sprung from an organic logic that they should not tamper with. But people were already surveying plots on their own, with the support of block leaders, and they were marking out boundaries with whatever was at hand, such as sticks or rocks. The residents' desires were clear, and the planners and the commission began work on a formal parceling protocol.

By general consensus, residents determined that every plot ought to have the same dimensions. For this to happen, some would have to give land to others and this, in turn, would require a lot of goodwill and neighborly negotiation. The deeper dilemma, though, was what the standard plot size should be. People naturally wanted plots as large as possible. That way they would be able to accommodate animals and a small garden and keep living quarters and cooking areas at a sufficient distance from latrines. Many had in mind the enormous plots that had been hastily laid out for flood victims soon after independence, in an area farther north. But that area had been sparsely settled before the flood victims arrived. The Maxaquene planners demonstrated that the same dimensions that had been used in that neighborhood would, if applied to Maxaquene One, force the expulsion of hundreds of families. Following a great deal of debate, residents reluctantly agreed to plots of 160 square meters, less than half the size most had wanted. The choice forced them to rethink their notions of what urban life entailed—and to recalculate how much of their ideal they were willing to give up so that everyone could benefit.

To demonstrate the viability of the smaller plot, planners developed a dozen hypothetical site plans, each showing a different arrangement of house and latrine and the potential for house expansion. They posted the layouts outside their neighborhood office for everyone to see, and they asked the GD to pick the plans it preferred, part of an ongoing conversation between planners and the people being planned for. Planners, technical staff, and volunteers from the neighborhood then got to work building two model reed homes, based on the selected layouts. People could then see in three dimensions how these arrangements might work. As GD member Augusto Duvane later recalled, the model houses were unrealistic. They were larger and of far better materials and workmanship than people were likely to build on their own—so impressive that they inspired the designs of concrete-block houses that many built later on. But they showed that even the most majestic home could fit comfortably on a smaller plot (Figure 5.6).

With the smaller plot size agreed to, Pinsky produced an illustrated "how-to" manual on the way to properly survey plots and distributed it to each of the block-surveying teams.[31] But after plots were surveyed and lines were

197

drawn, many existing houses straddled the new boundaries. The solution was patience. A house now partially trespassing on someone else's plot did not have to be moved immediately. Residents had already moved and adjusted houses to make room for access roads. A second move could wait for when the reeds of the wayward house rotted and needed replacing. Then the house could be rebuilt so that it was completely within the owner's plot.

Each plot now had a defined place within each block, with a number registered with the neighborhood GD office (Figures 5.7–5.9). To have their newly surveyed plots officialized in this way was the closest that most people had ever come to possessing a title deed or a home address. Those wanting to build in permanent materials consulted with one of the planners or with the main technical worker, and they received building permits. These permits were not officialized by the municipality but were improvised on the spot. Initially, Pinsky and Sävfors typed up "declarations," but soon they were sketching a simple site plan on graph paper. With the pre-printed letterhead of the National Housing Directorate, these "permits" bypassed the convoluted and costly construction approval process that the municipality required.

In April 1978, a favorable update on the Maxaquene Project appeared in *Tempo*, the weekly magazine, noting that the twisting lanes of the neighborhood had disappeared. "In place of these alleys, roads have been opened that allow access from block to block. When 'block' is mentioned, someone might wonder how it is possible to use that word in one of these neighborhoods. Nonetheless, new access roads make it possible to use that word today."[32] As one resident proudly put it to Sävfors following the making of roadways and plots, "Now we are urbanizado."

WHO DECIDES?

What most impressed the planners at the time was how quickly the residents of the neighborhood mobilized. They were astonished at how thousands of people whose previous experience of mass organization was limited to weekly neighborhood cleanups could be inspired to work together for a common purpose; how they could break into smaller, specialized units for

Figure 5.6 (*opposite*) Residents demanded that planners divide land into equal-sized rectilinear plots, but what size should they be? The planning team built model homes to show how smaller plots could work. (Eva Sävfors)

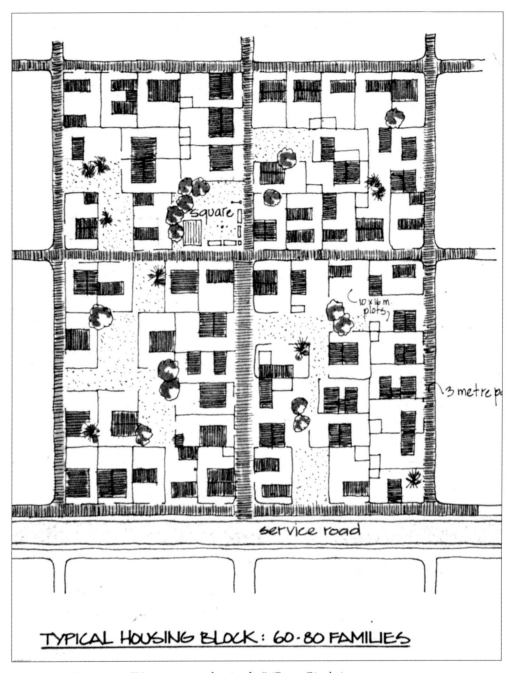

Inside the figure:
square

(10 × 16 m. plots)

3 metre p[

service road

TYPICAL HOUSING BLOCK: 60·80 FAMILIES

Figure 5.7 "Now we are urbanizado." (Barry Pinsky)

Figure 5.8 (*opposite top*) A 2018 satellite image showing the parts of Maxaquene (*center*) and Polana Caniço (*right*) that were parceled in the late 1970s. Areas to the left of the image were not part of the parceling project. (Google Earth)

Figure 5.9 (*opposite bottom*) The making of a new city block in Maxaquene. Mozambique's flag is painted on rubble that was probably from a concrete house demolished to make way for a road. (Eva Sävfors)

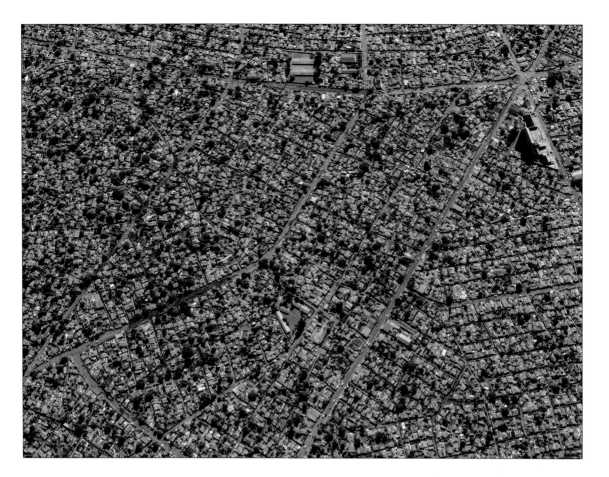

various tasks; how many were willing to make sacrifices for what was perceived as the collective good; and how many others were eager to assist those making the sacrifices. The classic planning dynamic had been inverted. A government agency had not imposed a plan. Rather, two foreign architects had offered some minimal planning suggestions. These suggestions, in turn, inspired neighborhood residents to both demand more elaborate planning and help implement it. Emily Callaci, in her work on postindependence Dar es Salaam, coined the term *popular urbanists* to describe creative people such as writers and musicians who interpreted the urban experience for others—people who were defined "by their ability to shape discourse and to call together an urban public."[33] The residents of Maxaquene were popular urbanists in a more literal sense. They physically shaped urban space.

Yet the question remains: just how participatory was this project of participatory planning? *Mobilization*, the mustering of people toward collective goals, had almost military connotations. The term peppered so many Frelimo policy prescriptions that it seemed to be an end in itself. But one wonders who felt empowered to speak at neighborhood meetings. Those who worked on the project, as well as residents today, recall near-absolute unanimity in the project's execution. The smooth rollout surprised the minister of public works and housing, Júlio Carrilho, when he asked a project technician for a progress report. "Neighbor influenced neighbor," soothing over anxieties, as social worker Jaiantilal put it.[34] Influence, however, can take many forms on a spectrum between persuasion and compulsion. At the time, the planners worried that some people might be harboring doubts but did not feel able to voice them or that people were of a mind to simply accept what the GD told them was best. Meeting after meeting, the women in attendance kept silent. Finally, during one evening meeting, two women spoke up in dissent, and Pinsky recalled that later that night he and Sävfors celebrated with a drink. He could not remember what it was that had moved the women to speak. But there was a chance, at least, that the willingness of the two women to complain meant that women's silence on previous occasions signaled assent.

The molding of consent in the neighborhoods of Maputo after independence was undoubtedly a male-dominated enterprise. Not just men but men with waged work and higher levels of formal education were favored for selection to the grupos dinamizadores. Orders filtered downward from Frelimo officials, and they were posted on neighborhood notice boards.[35] Literacy in Portuguese, though not a requirement, was assumed to be an essential part of the job. To get more female representation in GDs, Frelimo mandated that there always had to be at least one member representing Frelimo's women's organization, the Organização da Mulher Moçambicana (OMM).[36] Without the quota, it is likely that many GDs would have lacked women's representation entirely. Of course, the women's organization itself was not exactly representative of women's interests.[37] According to its statutes, the OMM was to "guarantee the implementation of women's emancipation as defined by the Frelimo Party"—a party whose hierarchy was almost exclusively male.[38]

In Mozambique's cities after independence, the OMM assumed a pedagogical role: teaching women how to properly maintain a male-headed urban household. Lídia Massinge, who was the organization's representative in Polana Caniço in the 1970s and 1980s, said that she instructed women in hygiene, how to dress well, and how to comport oneself with one's husband. Women were taught not to argue with their husbands in public or in front of the children.[39] They were advised on how to plan, with their husbands, the household finances so there was enough money for food and other expenses. "I grew up in a mission and I was always given advice on how to live in a home," Massinge said, recalling her credentials. Many women in the neighborhood were recent arrivals from the countryside, and Massinge instructed them on how to tend to the urban male. In the country, men left in the morning for work without eating, but in Maputo, women had to learn to cook breakfast and lunch for their husbands and to keep them scrubbed and tidy. Yet even as some women were learning how to maintain the New Man of the revolution in presentable and productive shape, their own husbands often discouraged participation in the OMM. Anastásia Titos Mahumane, a resident of Maxaquene, said that her husband would beat her whenever he discovered that she had attended one of the organization's meetings.[40]

There were other, unofficial women's groups, such as lending clubs,[41] and women led the weekly neighborhood cleanups. Their labor was disproportionately relied upon in any collective neighborhood endeavor, since many men were said to be otherwise engaged in proper jobs. The report of the OMM national conference in 1976 lamented that social inequality had been institutionalized in the home, so that girls grew up learning only how to serve the needs of men.[42] But a separate resolution, one that addressed social problems, warned that women fell into prostitution and dissolution because of "liberal" ideas—that is, that women in the city were prone to "the abuse of individual liberty."[43] It went on to cast blame on the urban

203

housewife who demanded that household chores be split equally, "without her having other tasks to justify it."[44]

In the Maxaquene Project, too, women were involved in much of the manual work. In films showing the construction of model reed houses, for instance, men are seen nailing the frames together and managing the job; women haul the materials to the site.[45] Once the neighborhood was divided into blocks, however, women were immediately elevated in stature. Partly, this was because the block committees, which managed how blocks were parceled up, were intentionally divided evenly between men and women. The impact of women's improved status on decision making is hard to discern. According to Pinsky, women began to be more active in open meetings, more likely to speak up, and more involved in the details of the rollout.[46] And about six months after the completion of most of the roadways and plots, women were probably the motivating force behind the project's next stage. They were not shy in voicing their anger over the issue that affected them most of all: water.

Residents had grown impatient. When the Maxaquene Project was initially presented to them, they were told that creating paths of access was a necessary prelude to essential infrastructural improvement. Many remembered the statement as a promise: open the roadways, and infrastructure will follow. People wanted roads and street illumination, but they were desperate for water access. Only a handful of private taps served a neighborhood of some ten thousand people, and as a result most women walked a half mile or so to get to a public fountain. In the late colonial era, in what had become a weekly ritual, women from Maxaquene would go to the apartment towers and townhouses at the edge of the City of Cement and beg Portuguese families to let them use their taps.[47] Before the project began, the frustration over water did not coalesce into any kind of activism to pressure the new government to do something about it. But the Maxaquene Project unintentionally created a channel for complaint and a language of justification. If the City of Cement had water, why was there not water in Maxaquene, which was now also urbanizado?[48]

The anger spread from household to household, and the GD organized a neighborhood mass meeting to address the issue. For the planners, this was a particularly tense moment. They had been acting in the role of the government, but they were largely independent of it, and they received virtually no cooperation from the municipality. Now, though, they were being held accountable for services that it was the responsibility of the municipal water utility to provide. Sävfors had attempted to convince a representative of the housing agency to speak at the meeting, but he received no response. In front of a crowd of more than a thousand people, an older resident confronted him, demanding to know how it was that lawns downtown were being watered, but "there's not a drop to kill the people's thirst?"[49]

The planners eventually struck a deal with the municipal utility. The city would pump water to taps located in the central plaza of each neighborhood block. But residents themselves would have to do the labor of building the infrastructure. Planners and residents alike recalled that people were so animated by the prospect of water that they virtually ran to shovels to begin digging the trenches for pipes (Figure 5.10). People in Polana Caniço, the neighborhood directly to the east, liked what they saw happening for their neighbors, and the project soon expanded there, as well as to a part of Maxaquene just to the north. By the middle of 1979, two years after the start of the Maxaquene Project, more than forty thousand people had benefited from access roadways and were surveying their plots. Yet with much work still to be done, the project simply ended. Residents were left to wonder why.

Municipal officials were openly hostile to the Maxaquene Project, as were some staffers at the National Housing Directorate, and many within Frelimo and the Ministry of Public Works and Housing were similarly unconvinced.

Figure 5.10 The most pressing demand in Maxaquene, after the need for secure tenure, was for ready access to water. (Barry Pinsky)

205

The subúrbios were seen as a colonial creation, the very embodiment of Portuguese-era inequities. Upgrading them meant accepting them as a permanent reality. To its critics, the Maxaquene Project was "Salvation Army-style patchwork," Sävfors said, as if incremental infrastructural improvements were unworthy of the housing agency of a modernizing movement that sought the socialist transformation of Mozambique.[50] A Portuguese couple working at the Housing Directorate—one a sociologist, the other an architect and urban planner—circulated a memo in October 1978 calling the project both "technically incorrect" and "dangerous."[51] The relatively low densities that the project was hardening into place were financially unsustainable in the long run, and the cost of installing similar infrastructure for the entire city would be exorbitant. The ideal for many at the housing agency was the kind of high-density government-built housing that one saw in the Eastern bloc, but this option was well out of reach for Mozambique at the time. Therefore, the memo argued, it was better to wait until resources became available for such a project than to act precipitously. The Maxaquene planners agreed with this call for higher densities, and they set aside areas for eventual multistory housing blocks. The housing blocks have never been built.

But the critique went beyond a cost-benefit analysis. According to the memo, a city brought people into close contact and thereby promoted "collective living."[52] The Maxaquene Project, in its unforeseen turn toward parceling out lots for single households, compromised the socialist ideal in favor of individualistic ambition.

> The fact that families demand having concrete limits to their land, so that they can invest in it their power of savings in terms of housing, seems to us indefensible in a society that is constructing a collective life in the socialist mold. That they do it with the idea in mind of securing possession for their children . . . means that the dynamic of such a [socialist] society wasn't understood.[53]

The memo's argument that Maxaquene had too many rural characteristics ran counter to the opinion of most people in the neighborhood that it was not rural enough. Residents continued to question the wisdom of plots that seemed too small to them.[54] Both sides of the argument were sure that what they had in mind constituted a "modern" city.

Despite the criticisms within the housing agency and ambivalence among higher circles of the government, Forjaz, who headed the agency, kept the project running. "No one fully believed in it," he later recalled.[55] Most in the Frelimo hierarchy, he said, had only a "superficial" knowledge of the subúrbios and could not appreciate that most people there expected infrastructure, not government-built housing.

In mid-1979, Sävfors's contract expired, and he returned to Sweden. Responsibility for the Maxaquene Project (and other planning and infrastructure functions) soon shifted from the housing agency to Maputo's municipal government. This did not bode well for the project. The municipal staff was skeletal, and what few technical workers were left tended to consider themselves defenders of the building code. The municipality rejected the legitimacy of the hundreds of ad hoc building permits that had been issued in Maxaquene. Those who had built in permanent materials, or who planned to, were told to submit the proper documentation, including blueprints and the other costly paperwork normally associated with building in the City of Cement. An official building permit cost almost twice the average monthly salary, but the expense was largely irrelevant: most of the houses built in Maxaquene would not have met code in any case.[56] By late 1980, new construction in Maxaquene came to a halt, at least for a while. Some people who had, over time, accrued concrete blocks to build a house went ahead and erected their homes. But they stacked the blocks loosely and did not mortar them together so that—if need be—they could dismantle the structure and recover the materials.[57]

Resources were the central issue, according to Jaiantilal. A municipal official told her that the Maxaquene Project, as modest as it was, was still too expensive to implement in every neighborhood. If everyone could not benefit, no one should. Donor funding lapsed, and as independent Mozambique entered its darkest years, the costs of keeping the Maxaquene Project going just in the neighborhoods where it began were prohibitive.[58] Before embarking on the project, Sävfors had been advised by an official at the donor agency, the UNDP, to avoid building a West Berlin—that is, an island of privilege in a city of need. In the eyes of some, that was what had happened. As Sävfors later observed, the kinds of expectations kindled by the Maxaquene Project, if not met elsewhere, could easily have jeopardized the legitimacy of the city's already threadbare administration and perhaps Frelimo's legitimacy as well.

THE FATHER OF FOUR CHAMANCULOS

In early 1979, Frelimo organized a conference to lay out for the first time its principles for urban policy.[59] In preparation for the conference, a delegation

207

of officials toured Maxaquene to observe the project then still in the works, and they came away favorably impressed. Government support for the Maxaquene Project was generally tepid, but some saw its symbolic value. This was the era of "people's power." Maxaquene was a model of what Mozambicans could accomplish when they "counted on their own efforts," as Frelimo frequently exhorted them to do. Several resolutions published at the conference's conclusion bore the Maxaquene stamp—most notably in the call for participatory planning.[60] The focus of the conference, though, was not how to improve living conditions in Mozambique's cities, but how Frelimo could gain control of cities.

People were flocking to Maputo. By 1980, the city's population had grown to more than 755,000, just about double what it had been in 1970.[61] Mozambique faced the classic predicament of rapidly urbanizing societies: once farmers left their fields for the city, they no longer provided food either for city dwellers or for themselves. And because of the decline in Mozambique's buying power, imports could not make up the difference. As Oscar Monteiro, the chief of the cities conference, said in his opening speech, Mozambique's cities, built to accommodate a settler minority, did not have the infrastructural capacity for so many people, and the sudden population growth was exacerbating food and water shortages and worsening levels of urban unemployment and crime.[62] The solution to making "unproductive" people productive was to establish "communal neighborhoods." The idea was to bottle the spirit of the wartime "liberated zones," the communal villages getting under way in the countryside, and the citizen activism of the type observed in Maxaquene. The conference did not chart a specific course for government intervention. There were no drawings or plans visualizing what an ideal neighborhood ought to look like, for instance. Unlike a communal village, which physically took people spread out across the countryside and concentrated them in one location, the communal neighborhood was mostly a figurative device. It would be the place that resulted when officials gave an existing urban area precise boundaries and political definition within party and state structures and then "mobilized" residents toward collective goals.

Frelimo policy makers were attempting to make the subúrbios legible. Motivated by a desire to turn what had been centers of colonial power into what Monteiro called socialist "red cities," Frelimo was also driven by a need to police the "internal enemy."[63] The two objectives went hand in hand. In his speech, Monteiro quoted Samora Machel's words of the year before, when, in addressing the Popular Assembly, the president first called for the making of communal neighborhoods: "We don't know ourselves because we don't live in an organized way. We don't know ourselves and that is why the enemy slips through the cracks, that's how he infiltrates. The first measure above all in our cities is to constitute ourselves in communal neighborhoods for better vigilance, for blowing the whistle, for neutralization of all type of agents."[64]

Officials launched the first population census since independence, and the work of dividing cities into smaller and more manageable units began. The drawing of boundaries for suburban neighborhoods marked the first time the constituent bairros of Maputo's City of Reeds had ever been given clear-cut spatial definition, after decades of not even appearing on many maps. Frelimo portrayed the identification of distinct neighborhoods as a promise that after a century of neglect, the subúrbios were now fields of government action. What would seem to be little more than the plotting of lines on a map prompted considerable hand-wringing within the party's highest circles. The General Resolution of the cities conference specified that for a communal neighborhood to function properly, its population should be about twelve thousand people.[65] Sometime in 1980, Adriano Matate learned just how sacrosanct this figure was.[66]

Matate will be recalled from the extraordinary travails he suffered as a new arrival to Lourenço Marques, described in chapter 1. In the 1950s, while working as a servant for a Portuguese family, he was briefly detained by police, and then summarily dispatched to the cocoa plantations of São Tomé. There he became the leader of a plantation work crew. He participated in an islandwide strike. He married. After twelve years in exile, he returned to Lourenço Marques with his family, eventually finding work at the gas utility. He settled in Chamanculo, and during the transition to independence he became a member of the local grupo dinamizador. A few years later, soon after the launch of the communal neighborhoods, the Frelimo Central Committee summoned Matate, now the neighborhood secretary, to its offices. The matter was urgent. A black Mercedes sedan with small Mozambican flags flying from the hood came to fetch him.

Matate was given an audience with the most powerful men in Mozambique: President Machel, Vice President Marcelino dos Santos, and

209

Minister of the Interior Armando Guebuza. They were joined by several others whom Matate understood were "experts." All were on their feet because the president was in an animated mood, as he often was, and as long as he was standing, everyone else had to be standing as well. Machel explained to Matate that Chamanculo was far too populous to be governed as a single neighborhood. He ordered Matate to figure out how to divide it in three. "Comrade President, I can't do that," Matate responded. "It must be four."

The president went silent. He paced up and down the room and then blurted, "It must be three!" Years later, Matate played up the drama of the moment. He recalled that Guebuza, a future president himself, put his face in his hands as if in sympathy with Matate's fate and that he heard him mutter how this meant jail for the poor neighborhood secretary. Matate had contradicted an order from the Maximum Leader, and many people at the time were jailed for far less. Matate, however, had faith in his calculations. He had counted homes in Chamanculo in the course of his various duties, and he knew that if divided into three neighborhoods, each new division would be too large. But divided into four, they would be more manageable and yet still meet the prescribed minimum population.

The vice president now spoke on Matate's behalf. "He's the owner of Chamanculo," dos Santos reminded the president. "If anyone knows how to divide it, it is him." To be "owner" of a neighborhood was once a designation reserved for traditional leaders. Dos Santos, who knew the area, was vouching for Matate's authority and his wisdom.

"Chamanculo!" Machel addressed Matate as if Chamanculo were his title. "Okay, four neighborhoods. But I don't want any neighborhood with 9,000 or 10,000 people. It has to be 12,000!"

Three days later, Matate was again picked up by the black Mercedes for a meeting with the president. He carried four maps, one for each new neighborhood—Chamanculo A through Chamanculo D—and spread them out on a table. The president was eager to review Matate's work in detail, insisting that they go over every significant boundary marker: the bus depot, the two big fig trees, the notary's office, the "Dlembula" grocery. The president was familiar with each of them. "He knew it like he lived here," Matate later said. The importance of the episode to Matate is clear enough. He talked about his role in boundary setting as if, in the process, he had fathered not just one but four neighborhoods through the courage and insight that had won over the president himself. The partition of Chamanculo also reveals a great deal about the nature of Frelimo governance at the time, particularly the president's habit of micromanaging his way through major initiatives, and the leadership's desperate faith that the right formulas would trigger socialist transformation.

During the 1980s, it was Dutch aid that triggered the most signifcant transformation in the subúrbios. Beginning in 1982, the Netherlands funded the construction of large drainage trenches beside some of the city's most flood-prone neighborhoods.[67] When completed in 1987, the trenches dramatically reduced the inundations that annually befell neighborhoods such as Munhuana, Mafalala, and Lagoas, making a far more decisive mark on the timeline of Maputo history than is usually acknowledged.[68] For the most part, though, these were years in which people were expected to get by with little help from above. Older neighborhoods tended to be passed over for improvements in favor of newer neighborhoods that lay at the outer edges of the city.[69] People had been living in these distant areas in some numbers since the 1960s, many of them displaced by an expanding City of Cement.[70] Some had even been displaced twice over when private interests began developing these outer areas for residences destined mostly for Portuguese, accounting for what little infrastructure there was. Due to this previous development, large stretches of outer terrain had already been surveyed for plots. These areas were now the principal destinations for people immigrating from the countryside, and even a minimal intervention, such as the subdivision of existing plots, could make a major difference. The primary schools, health clinics, and roofed marketplaces being built there were usually the first within miles. The wells that were dug had to serve thousands.

By focusing on these still semirural neighborhoods, Frelimo planners hoped to stimulate a more concerted cultivation of a belt of agricultural "Green Zones" around the city, especially along the Infulene River that divided Maputo from Matola.[71] Many women in the outer areas were already cultivating land on abandoned Portuguese *quintas* (small farms), and officials formed cooperatives in the hope that crop production at the city's edges could help feed Maputo. The capital would cease to be the "parasite" on the rest of Mozambique that it had been, and at the same time the Green Zones would give some substance to Frelimo's professed desire to take the city to the countryside and the countryside to the city.[72]

211

The areas of Hulene, Malhazine, and Benfica were all given specific boundaries and reborn as communal neighborhoods, and concrete monoliths topped with red stars were erected in each to mark the transition. In Hulene and Malhazine, neighborhood makeovers became opportunities to flush out religious groups that Frelimo saw as threats. An article in *Tempo* in 1979 noted that in Hulene, "religious sects abound, seeking to exploit the people through their obscurantist intrigues," and the church of one independent congregation, still under construction, was seized to make a neighborhood cultural center, reportedly at the request of neighborhood residents.[73] Benfica, named for the famed Lisbon soccer club, was renamed in honor of Georgi Dimitrov, the Bulgarian communist leader.[74] Residents had trouble pronouncing the new name, but some hoped that the gesture would encourage Bulgaria to come to the neighborhood's aid.[75] The name never stuck.

By 1983, a drought in many parts of Mozambique undermined Frelimo's remaining hopes for stimulating agricultural production.[76] Maputo residents remember it as the Year of Cabbage because it seemed that was all there was to eat. Exasperated by what it frequently portrayed as Maputo's surplus population, Frelimo now took more draconian steps to make the city self-sufficient. Through Operação Produção (Operation Production), it sought to rid the city of all "unproductive elements," "undesirables," and "delinquents" and put them to work on state farms.[77] During the initial, voluntary phase, those without formal, waged work were given trips back to their "homelands." In the subsequent compulsory phase, those without the proper proof of employment were swiftly "evacuated," sometimes by jetliner or military air transport, to farms in remote Niassa or Cabo Delgado, more than 1,400 miles away. Operação Produção relocated tens of thousands of urbanites before Frelimo abandoned the policy the following year. In terms of numbers and the distances to which people were removed, the expulsion was far worse than the piecemeal urban displacements of the colonial era and was more akin to the forced urban-to-rural dislocations of Tanzania's ujamaa, from which Frelimo had taken its inspiration. Operação Produção turned into a massive exercise of arbitrary force. Neighborhood officials in charge of the expulsions used their task as cover for vendettas and extortion.[78] As during the transition period, many women were targeted, accused of prostitution.[79]

Operação Produção was probably the clearest example, in Maputo at least, of what Scott would call high-modernist policy making. But what seemed a strong exertion of the state's control over urban space at the same time betrayed the state's great weakness. It bears mentioning that many people in Maputo welcomed the measure at first: finally, Frelimo was doing something meaningful about the chaos that enveloped them.[80] The state's intervention, however, only added to the chaos.

THE GOLF CLUB

From about 1984 onward, the Renamo insurgency entered a new phase of destruction, expanding farther into southern Mozambique.[81] Violence in the areas surrounding Maputo intensified, and shacks and emergency tents appeared nearly everywhere in the city, filling up the few open spaces in the inner subúrbios.[82] Those who could not find space under a relative's roof or in a backyard erected reed shelters or set up their donated tents along roadsides. Some suburban residents, already wanting for public space, resented losing what little there was to the refugees. One night in Chamanculo, some kids from the neighborhood set alight several shelters erected in what had been a small soccer pitch beside the Beira-Mar clubhouse. Still, despite the near state of siege that Maputo faced in the late 1980s and early 1990s, a kind of order could sometimes prevail. Perhaps more telling than where the refugees built their shelters is where they did not build shelters.

The Polana Golf Club was originally established in 1908, and in the 1950s, it moved to its current location on the flatlands beside the bay shore, below Polana Caniço.[83] The people who lived in reed houses that were in the way of the links were pushed up the slope, and those who resisted were burned out of their homes. During the colonial era, the club was a playground not just for the Lourenço Marques elite but also and more specifically for British and South African businesspeople. Boys who lived on the plateau above the golf course, many of them children of the families who not long before had been displaced by it, earned money by fetching balls. As they got older, they worked as caddies.[84]

In 1970, the club installed a barbed-wire fence around the course perimeter and patrolled it with dogs. Children from the neighborhood up the slope had been wandering onto the course at night to pick fruit from trees, and people were crossing the greens on their way to the beach, where they fished and trapped crabs in the shallows. They were now forced to take the long way around the course. After independence, though, the club's

213

membership vanished. People from the neighborhood took down the wire fence, and they put the wire to other uses. Polana Caniço's population increased significantly in 1976, when the government surveyed large plots to resettle thousands of people who had been flooded out of Maxaquene, and women began to cultivate machambas at the edges of the golf course.

Yet the course continued to operate. A few caddies, then in their late teens, became the establishment's grupo dinamizador, and they took charge, just like many workplace GDs that were running businesses whose management had abandoned the country. Wooden tournament plaques hanging in the main hall of the clubhouse listed the names of champions going back decades; now, with more black golfers playing the course, unambiguously African names appeared for the first time. The grass was not mowed, except by goats and cows from the neighborhood that pastured on the greens. In the 1980s, the course became a favorite in-town escape for some cooperantes who found playing a round of golf there to be an adventure.[85]

In 1988, hundreds of refugees who had been living in temporary shelter elsewhere in the city were resettled on plots surveyed along the course's west margin (Figure 5.11). But the strip of lost land did not dramatically change how the course was played. People were now freely crossing the fairways, but the course managers marked out two paths for foot traffic so they would not disrupt play too much. Most kept to the paths. During a time of emergency, when space was dear and wood for cooking scarce, perhaps the largest single open space in Maputo other than the airport remained mostly open, its venerable fig trees untouched. The golf course had been a site of trauma for the people who had once lived there and a place of exclusion afterward, and few activities more fully embodied elite privilege and imported taste than golf. Yet there was no pressure from the municipality or the Frelimo hierarchy—or from the increasingly crowded neighborhood just beyond the back nine—to significantly alter the status quo.

For the managers of the club, this was no mystery. They had kept the facility in operation and put it to use. Like any functioning institution (in a place where there were so few), people felt it deserved to be left alone. "They respected it," said Alfredo Dique Fumo, the golf club's longtime director, of the course's neighbors. "At least the Maronga did," he added, referring to the area's original inhabitants, such as himself.[86] After the war ended in 1992, a number of families of demobilized Renamo militants settled in the sodden areas to the north and east of the course, where no one

Figure 5.11 Polana Caniço and the Polana Golf Club, 2018. Within the stripe of dense housing at the west edge of the golf course are the homes of people who were settled there as refugees in the late 1980s, during Mozambique's civil war. (Google Earth)

else would live. The golf course became a kind of buffer zone, keeping the stigmatized population at some distance from Polana Caniço. When people on the road did not get out of the way of cars entering the club or when they idled on the fairways and obstructed play, Fumo said they were the newcomers being difficult. Frelimo's interest in maintaining the golf course can probably be chalked up to a desire to please foreign dignitaries. Why war refugees respected the club's managers and the vague wishes of government officials, however, requires further explanation. The refugees were mostly on their own. Perhaps they acted as if authority were in force and holding them back because only by doing so could they feel that authority was present, and while present, protecting them.

Anthropologists have done much to advance our understanding of how people relate to the inchoate entity we think of as "the state"—how we always seem to imagine it as a constellation of fixed institutions, one that exists apart from and above the people it governs.[87] When the institutions understood to comprise the state are barely functioning or very distant, then the abstraction can also be quite spectral. People at the margins of governance, who are particularly needy for the embrace of the state, often mimic state rituals and functions.[88] Some indigenous Peruvians, living outside the gaze of the faraway capital, march annually in strict, military-like discipline and wave the national flag to demonstrate that they, too, are members of both their state and their nation. In parts of Guatemala, the civic leaders of towns officially unrecognized by the central government act as if theirs were towns like any other, and they construct central squares with all the customary public installations. In many parts of the world, people without ready access to local courts fabricate official-looking documents to legitimate transactions. Anthropologist Morten Nielsen studied a community at the distant fringes of Maputo that the government established in 2000.[89] Planning officials intended it to serve as a model neighborhood for the resettlement of thousands of people displaced by catastrophic flooding earlier in the year. The government's presence at the site soon evaporated. The grid layout of the neighborhood might have fragmented into a planning free-for-all. Instead, Nielsen writes, residents took matters into their own hands. Many of them hired professional land surveyors to lay out plots. By surveying house plots according to the way it was thought officials would have wanted them surveyed, people in the neighborhood thus imagined an active state and imagined it governing. Nielsen describes this kind of mimicry as an aspirational performance. It reasserted people's sense of belonging to a state that was either unwilling or unable to serve them.

The episodes in this chapter write these observations further back into Maputo's history. They were instances of state formation when the state was closer to scratch. By obeying authorities otherwise not much in evidence, the people who kept to the margins of the golf course were trying to bring government into their lives. Adriano Matate was doing the same when he personally tried to make Chamanculo more legible to the president. The residents of Maxaquene, in adopting the grid and other common markers of modernist urbanism, were signaling that they, too, belonged to the city and deserved the benefits that belonging should convey. Planning is not just something conceived in cloistered meeting rooms, subjected to careful review, and then implemented on the ground with all intentions fulfilled. Such a placid reality never truly exists—still less so in a country stumbling into being. In Maputo after independence, lines traced roughly on the ground were lines of communication, allowing suburban citizens to call out to the would-be state.

Figure 5.12 (*opposite*) Maxaquene, 1978–79. (Eva Sävfors)

Figure C.1 Graça Ferreira builds her house, Matola, 2011. (David Morton)

MULTIPLE TRAJECTORIES

IN 1987, a new era officially began in Mozambique as Frelimo started to implement market-oriented reforms according to conditions set by the International Monetary Fund.[1] Or perhaps the new era began in 1989, when Frelimo shed Marxism-Leninism as official state doctrine. Then again, perhaps both changes were only truly rendered significant a few years later with the signing, in 1992, of the Rome peace accords between Frelimo and Renamo, ending a long, catastrophic war and enabling the new policies of structural adjustment to take effect throughout the country. Peace also heralded Mozambique's new birth as a "donor darling" of European development agencies, a status solidified in 1994 with the country's first multiparty democratic elections, and it opened wide the door to nongovernmental organizations (NGOs) in the functioning of government services.

But some who lamented Mozambique's abandonment of socialist principles saw an earlier date, 1984, as the disastrous year of capitulation to capitalism.[2] That was when impending state collapse compelled Maputo to reach a nonaggression pact with apartheid South Africa, the patron of Renamo violence—an agreement that included provisions for greater South African investment in Mozambique. In fact, private enterprise had never disappeared entirely from Maputo after independence, and one must also account for the active black market that made life in the city possible during the 1980s.

For many Mozambicans today, the decisive year of change was 1986, when President Samora Machel was killed, along with thirty-three others, in a plane crash on a South African mountain within sight of Mozambique. Crime and corruption are said to date from that tragedy at Mbuzini. Relative to the disorder and uncertainty of today, nostalgia often characterizes the "time of Samora" as a golden age of alleged order achieved by the imposition of harsh discipline and tireless vigilance, inseparable from the memory of Comrade Samora himself.

In the late 1980s, Renamo guerrillas harassed the edges of Maputo but did not enter the city, enabling the economic restructuring to take effect there before most anywhere else in Mozambique. One of the first major initiatives to be implemented was the reform of APIE, the state real estate agency that, since the 1976 nationalization of rental properties, was landlord to some fifty thousand units in the urban cores of Maputo and Matola, in addition to uncounted (though many thousands) of compound units and houses in the subúrbios.[3] Rents were to be allowed to rise to reflect market demand, and a bargain sell-off of properties to their tenants began. By the late 1980s, living in the City of Cement had taken on a hellish quality, as will be recalled from chapter 4. With frequent blackouts, paralyzed elevators, avenues lined with piles of trash, and seemingly endless water stoppages, life there was hardly more livable than it was in the subúrbios, and in many ways, it actually was less so. The costs of living in the City of Cement, moreover, even when rent-free, had long before compelled many people to return to the subúrbios if they had family there and space waiting for them. The market reforms took on real significance after 1992 with the advent of new demand: an influx into Maputo first of UN peacekeepers and then, shortly thereafter, a legion of NGOs, all in need of office space and housing for staff. Those residents of the City of Cement who had managed to stay through the most trying years now possessed valuable assets that only appreciated in value with time and the ever-greater foreign presence. A new rentier class came into being, seeming to at last fulfill the destiny of the many buildings erected during a flurry of speculation in the last years of Portuguese rule. Many government workers who had received units in the City of Cement as a perk of employment now used proceeds from renting those units to fund construction of new houses in the subúrbios or on larger plots at the fringes of the city and in Matola. In the early 2000s, Maputo's first new office tower in decades was completed and named for its primary tenant, a Portuguese cement company. The first four floors were occupied by the nation's first shopping mall. The changing face of Maputo led one critic of Mozambique's development model to refer to the "recolonization" of the City of Cement.[4]

By the 2000s, a Maputo economy stimulated by donor largesse became more fully a node of foreign direct investment. Following democratic elections in South Africa in 1994, South African capital flowed into Mozambique, notably into the "Maputo corridor," a revitalization and expansion of the pitted road joining the Rand and Maputo.[5] The investments reasserted the historical link as an axis of regional economic growth. By 2015, the exploitation by multinational corporations of vast coal reserves in Mozambique's Tete Province (largely to meet Chinese demand) as well as natural gas reserves was helping produce some of the highest annual national growth figures in Africa.[6] Mozambique's links to China were resulting in massive new infrastructural projects, such as a new bridge to join downtown Maputo to Catembe, a community across the bay.[7] Beijing also built a new presidency building, a new national assembly building, new airport terminals, and a new national soccer stadium.

Meanwhile, households in the subúrbios of Maputo and other cities were being hooked up to electrical and water infrastructure at a rapid pace. Many users of electricity pilfered it, but most was paid for using a prepaid credit system. A new building type emerged in the subúrbios in the 1990s consonant with the greater activity at Maputo's port: metal shipping containers, often repurposed to shelter bars or other businesses. The most far-reaching visible change in the subúrbios, however, has been the proliferation of concrete-block construction.[8] Since the 1990s, local production capacity for cement has boomed. Early in that decade, Castigo Guambe, whose family has appeared several times in this book, was already fabricating and selling concrete blocks on his property, as many in Maputo were doing if they had space to spare and a modicum of capital to invest (Figure C.2). In the nationalizations of 1976, the family had lost the Chamanculo real estate portfolio that Guambe's father had assembled during the first half of the twentieth century. Now, however, Guambe was able to build several rental units in his yard, and he also rented space for people to park their cars. He built a small unit near the street that he rented out to a

Figure C.2 Castigo Guambe, with the blocks he fabricates and sells in his yard, Chamanculo, 2011. (David Morton)

shopkeeper, and he opened a bar in his front yard, with one of the few billiard tables around.

The classic upward growth curve promised by neoliberal economic policy making took a nosedive after 2015 with rising public debt and revelations that the government had secretly guaranteed billions in dubious loans.[9] Mozambique was unable to make its payments, and the debt crisis hit people in the subúrbios hard as the currency collapsed, consumer prices rose, and health services were cut. And yet, even before the crisis, the singular focus on a rising gross domestic product obscured countless other trajectories—many of them downward and many that cannot be so easily charted. Years of growth were also years of impoverishment, as government employment and services were slashed.[10] It is often pointed out that the benefits of Mozambique's economic growth have been concentrated disproportionately in the capital, but it is also true that economic growth in Maputo has itself been narrowly concentrated. That much of the population manages to *desenrascar* (scrape by)—through daily improvisations, petty trade, and linkages with the countryside—has been the subject of a great deal of scholarship, and it will not be expanded upon here.[11]

Suffice it to say that upgrading from reed construction to shelter in concrete blocks does not mark the end of hardship. Even in what seems a prosperous household, prosperity may not be equally shared; in fact, it may coexist alongside great want, sometimes in the same room. Furthermore, many people rent the units they live in, and so what might appear on the outside to be evidence of greater permanence may be nothing of the kind. One of the remarkable facts of Maputo's building culture is that even people living on scant and unsteady incomes invest in concrete blocks little by little, perhaps stashing them just outside their small compound unit, in the hope of eventually building a house. Maputo and its fringes are dotted by countless concrete-block dwellings lacking doors and roofs, and many other projects may rise no higher than a few courses of block. For many, concrete is the index of one's aspirations, which may far exceed the measure of one's affluence.[12]

The proliferation of concrete, moreover, has changed the dynamic of neighborly relationships in ways that cannot be said to be better or worse—just different. Between yards, concrete walls would seem to have settled, once and for all, the problem of flexible boundaries that bedeviled relationships between neighbors when reed or zinc fences divided plots. Yet the expense of concrete wall construction and its material permanence can preclude negotiated settlement and raise the stakes of conflict. Block chiefs are frequently called in to settle disputes when, seemingly overnight, one resident builds a concrete-block wall that encloses part of a neighbor's plot.[13] Since the late 1980s, Anastásia Titos Mahumane has lived on a plot she purchased in Maxaquene, in a location that, back in the late 1970s, had been one of the pilot areas of the Maxaquene Project.[14] She moved there following her separation from her husband. She let him keep what had been their shared house for his life with his new wife, saying she did not want "to make a commotion." Mahumane's income largely derives from selling charcoal, which earns her 20 to 40 cents per sale. She was only able to convert her house into concrete block in the late 1990s with help from her church. She uses what little land she has around the house to cultivate cassava roots, which she then replants in a machamba in the countryside.

A few years ago while she was away from Maputo, one of her neighbors built a concrete wall several inches into her yard on one side. This minor land grab, however, was nothing compared to the 6 feet or so of land that

Conclusion

her neighbor to the other side later took from her plot. Indeed, he took almost a quarter of her open space. As he built his wall, Mahumane sat in her yard and scowled at him. "I wasn't going to say anything," she said. When the neighbor started building around her water spigot, which would have denied her access to it, she at last called on the block chief to intervene. He ordered the neighbor to dismantle that part of the wall. But the block chief would not order the man to take down the entire wall: the builder had put too much money into the project. This was a common response—or rather a common nonresponse—to the problem of wealthier residents encroaching on more vulnerable neighbors. Another block chief, in nearby Polana Caniço B, said of such situations, "You have to have patience, you have to have understanding. . . . When someone is away at work, and the other builds a wall, you're not going to knock it down. We are a poor country, so you can't knock down a concrete wall."[15]

In Chamanculo, concrete divided two brothers. Benjamim and Paulo Benfica had inherited their wood-and-zinc house from their father, a truck driver, in the 1960s.[16] Benjamim later enjoyed good fortune as a schoolteacher. He eventually ran his own technical school in northern Mozambique, before returning to Maputo to open a private school and live at the family homestead in Chamanculo. The brothers split the property between them and built adjoining concrete-block houses. But Paulo had not fared as well as his younger brother, and he wanted to sell off pieces of their common property to raise cash. Benjamim refused to break up the property that their father had purchased in the 1940s. "My brother just has the spirit to sell!" he said.[17] The resulting animosity was such that, some years ago, Benjamim returned home one day to find that his brother had started building a concrete-block wall that divided the property between them. With funds lacking to finish it, Paulo's barrier rose no higher than one's knees. In early 2013, Benjamim unilaterally dismantled what he called the "Berlin Wall." "History has been made," he joked.

Maputo's built environment, I have argued in this book, is not merely an inert stage for other historical dramas; rather, it embodies some of the central dramas of urban life. The making of suburban space has historically

Figure C.3 (*opposite*) The City of Cement, 2017. The building is decorated with an armillary sphere, a symbol of Portugal's overseas expansion that also features on the Portuguese flag. (David Morton)

conditioned people's relationship to the state and shaped their image of what it means to belong to the modern world. A kind of politics and a set of claims have been engendered through the medium of urban space that cannot be understood solely in terms of nationalist movements, the mobilization of political parties, or the plans and intentions of ruling regimes—the typical framing elements for histories of African decolonization and postindependence state formation. And this politics certainly cannot be restricted to the "before" and "after" language of colonialism and postcolonialism because, in the spaces of the city, far too much of the past remains embedded in the present and keeps a tight grip on possibilities for the future.

The built environment has long served as a ready metaphor for theories of modernization and human development, from primitive shack to civilized apartment tower.[18] The Age of Concrete, however, cannot be considered a story of progress or for that matter of decline. We must use a different scale.

GLOSSARY

águas   Roof inclines.

APIE   Acronym for Administração do Parque Imobiliário do Estado, the government agency that administered all state-owned real estate following the nationalizations of rental buildings in 1976.

assimilado   During most of the colonial era, one of several thousand black Mozambicans legally considered Portuguese citizens. To "assimilate," an African had to establish that he or she was sufficiently "civilized," a standard that included reading and writing Portuguese, eating and dressing as a European was said to eat and dress, and achieving a certain level of income and formal education.

bairro   Neighborhood.

bandla   Group meeting, discussed in this book as the weekly gathering at which, during the colonial era, a traditional leader and his advisers would adjudicate disputes and petty crimes.

cafre   The Portuguese equivalent of *kaffir*, a racist slur referring to black people, with a meaning that approximates "savage." In the colonial era, *cafrealização* referred to the supposed Africanization of Portuguese who lived in the subúrbios or in rural areas, often with African companions.

caniço   A type of reed that was the most common building material in Maputo's subúrbios until recent decades. The band of suburban settlements around the city was often collectively called the *caniço* or the *Cidade do Caniço* (City of Reeds), a phrase coined in the early 1960s by the newspaper *A Tribuna*.

cantina	A center of social and commercial life in the subúrbios that functioned as a general store and bar.
chibalo	Forced labor, officially abolished in 1961.
Cidade de Cimento	City of Cement, the predominantly European formalized core of Lourenço Marques/Maputo.
cipaio	During the colonial era, a "native" policeman.
colonato	One of several agricultural schemes in Mozambique during the colonial era, largely made up of Portuguese immigrants.
colono	Portuguese settler.
componde	The basest form of housing found in the subúrbios, usually comprising single-room units arranged in rows, with each unit shared by multiple people. Derived from the English word *compound*, as in the compounds where Mozambican men lived when employed in the mines of South Africa.
cooperante	Foreigner who went to Mozambique in the years after independence to offer assistance at a time when technical and managerial expertise was in desperately short supply.
curandeiro	Traditional healer.
escudo	The unit of currency used in Mozambique until 1980.
Frelimo	Portmanteau of Frente de Libertação de Moçambique (Mozambique Liberation Front), the anticolonial movement formed in 1962 that has governed Mozambique since independence in 1975.
grupos dinamizadores (GDs)	During the transition to independence and in the years afterward, the committees that governed neighborhoods. Initially, GDs were largely ad hoc, but they were later brought under greater centralized control.
indígena	Portuguese word meaning "native," this was the legal classification of the vast majority of Mozambicans for most of the colonial era. Those with indígena status were denied the rights of Portuguese citizenship and, until 1961, were subject to terms of forced labor, called chibalo.
mato	Undifferentiated bush.
mestiço	A person of racially diverse origins, specifically of African and European or Asian descent. Somewhat more dismissive terms include *misto* and *mulato*.
metical	The unit of Mozambican currency from 1980 onward.

milando	A domestic dispute or a dispute between neighbors. During the colonial era, milandos were generally considered to be under the purview of customary authorities rather than Portuguese officials, who thought of them as trivial affairs of the so-called natives.
moleque	During the colonial era, a belittling term referring to black teenaged boys (or preteens) who worked as domestic servants in households in the City of Cement or in cantinas, generally living in a unit in the backyard.
palmatória	Wood paddle used to whip someone's palms as a punishment and frequently employed as a symbol of the arbitrary violence of colonial rule.
quarteirão	City block, used as a unit of governance in the subúrbios from the late 1970s onward.
quintal	An enclosed yard in either the City of Cement or its subúrbios where cooking and laundering often take place. When, with the nationalizations of much of the City of Cement in 1976, President Samora Machel announced that Mozambicans would no longer live in the quintal of the city, he meant that they would no longer live in the equivalent of the servants' quarters.
régulo	During the colonial era, a traditional leader who served at the pleasure of Portuguese authorities and whose duties included collecting hut taxes and rounding up "natives" for forced labor. Appointments were based on an interpretation of existing practices of inherited rule. Frelimo abolished the institution following independence, though in recent years the position has been resurrected, with functions and importance varying widely throughout the country.
Renamo	Portmanteau of Resistência Nacional Moçambicana (Mozambican National Resistance, or MNR). Formerly an armed Mozambican insurgency against the Frelimo regime, initially organized by the Rhodesian intelligence service following Mozambique's independence and later backed by apartheid South Africa. The Renamo-Frelimo conflict lasted approximately sixteen years (there is some dispute as to when the war began and when it can be said to have become a civil war), and it cost an estimated 1 million Mozambican lives before ending in 1992. Renamo became a political party, and since 1994, it has been Frelimo's

principal opposition in multiparty elections and in the national assembly.

suburbios Neighborhoods located outside what were once the official boundaries of the city—and thus generally not served with municipal infrastructure. In the late colonial era, about three-quarters of the population of Lourenço Marques lived in the suburbios, including the vast majority of its African population. The suburbios are not to be confused with *suburbs* as that term is understood in Anglophone contexts, though for the sake of convenience, the adjective *suburban* is used when referring to them in this book.

ultramar Portugal's overseas possessions. In 1951, the Portuguese colonial ministry was refashioned as the Ministério do Ultramar as part of Lisbon's effort to establish that its African and Asian territories were not colonies but rather noncontiguous provinces of a single Portuguese nation.

NOTES

(The full terms for the abbreviations used in the notes are provided in Sources.)

Introduction

1. Calane da Silva, "Poema incompleto à minha mãe," in *Dos meninos da Malanga* (Maputo: Cadernos Tempo, 1982), 39. Given the sheer volume of Portuguese-language citations, titles will not be translated.

2. Rui Gonçalves, interview with author via Skype, August 23, 2018. In 2011, Gonçalves let me review the presentations the students made of their research, and we visited a materials stand in the subúrbios where reeds were still being sold.

3. On caniço construction, see Amâncio d'Alpoim Guedes, "The Caniços of Mozambique," in *Shelter in Africa*, ed. Paul Oliver (London: Barrie and Jenkins, 1971), 200–209; Gabinete de Urbanização e Habitação da Região de Lourenço Marques, "Estudo do 'Caniço,'" Plano Director de urbanização de Lourenço Marques, no. 44, 1969, MITADER; Björn Brandberg, "Constructions," in *The Malhangalene Survey: A Housing Study of an Unplanned Settlement in Maputo, Mozambique, 1976, pt. 2* (Göteborg: Chalmers Tekniska Högskola, Arkitektur, 1977), 1–69; Sandro Bruschi, Júlio Carrilho, and Luís Lage, *Era uma vez uma palhota: História da casa moçambicana* (Maputo: Edições FAPF, 2005); Pedro Guedes, ed., *As Áfricas de Pancho Guedes* (Lisbon: Sextante Editora, 2010), 300–301.

4. Rui Gonçalves interview.

5. Luís Bernardo Honwana, "A velha casa de madeira e zinco," in *A velha casa de madeira e zinco*, 2nd ed. (Maputo: Alcance, 2017), 21–42.

6. Extrapolated from 1970 census figures published in Serviços de Centralização e Coordenação de Informações de Moçambique, *Moçambique na actualidade* (Lourenço Marques: Imprensa Nacional de Moçambique, 1974), 39.

7. Alexandre Lobato, *Lourenço Marques, Xilunguíne: Biografia da cidade* (Lisbon: Agência-Geral do Ultramar, 1970). On the city/subúrbio binary as it is employed in contemporary Maputo, see Isabel Raposo and Cristina Salvador, "Há diferença: Ali é cidade, aqui é subúrbio—Urbanidade dos bairros, tipos e estratégias de

habitação em Luanda e Maputo," in *Subúrbios de Luanda e Maputo,* ed. Jochen Oppenheimer and Isabel Raposo (Lisbon: Edições Calibri, 2007), 105–38; Bjørn Enge Bertelsen, Inge Tvedten, and Sandra Roque, "Engaging, Transcending, and Subverting Dichotomies: Discursive Dynamics of Maputo's Urban Space," *Urban Studies* 51, no. 13 (2014): 2752–69.

8. Cement itself (technically, "portland cement") is made of a number of ingredients, the principal one being lime, often from crushed limestone. Edward Allen and Joseph Iano, *Fundamentals of Building Construction: Materials and Methods,* 4th ed. (Hoboken, NJ: John Wiley and Sons, 2004), 467–75.

9. As is common practice in Mozambican historiography, *Africans* here refers to black Mozambicans as well as to people who were of mixed indigenous and European or Asian origins, but this is not to dismiss the fluidity of an African identity, then and now.

10. Karen Tranberg Hansen, *Keeping House in Lusaka* (New York: Columbia University Press, 1997); Garth Andrew Myers, "Sticks and Stones: Colonialism and Zanzibari Housing," *Africa* 67, no. 2 (1997): 252–72; Rebekah Lee, *African Women and Apartheid: Migration and Settlement in Urban South Africa* (London: Tauris Academic Studies, 2009), 81–105; Anne-Maria Makhulu, *Making Freedom: Apartheid, Squatter Politics, and the Struggle for Home* (Durham, NC: Duke University Press, 2015); Claudia Gastrow, "Cement Citizens: Housing, Demolition and Political Belonging in Luanda, Angola," *Citizenship Studies* 21, no. 2 (2017): 224–39; James Holston, *Insurgent Citizenship: Disjunctions of Democracy and Modernity in Brazil* (Princeton, NJ: Princeton University Press, 2008); John F. C. Turner, "Barriers and Channels for Housing Development in Modernizing Countries," *Journal of the American Institute of Planners* 33, no. 3 (1967): 167–81; Caroline Melly, "Inside-Out Houses: Urban Belonging and Imagined Futures in Dakar, Senegal," *Comparative Studies in Society and History* 52, no. 1 (2010): 37–65.

11. Hansen, *Keeping House in Lusaka,* 60; Gastrow, "Cement Citizens," 226.

12. Jeanne Marie Penvenne, "Fotografando Lourenço Marques: A cidade e os seus habitantes de 1960 a 1975," in *Os outros da colonização: Ensaios sobre o colonialismo tardio em Moçambique,* ed. Cláudia Castelo et al. (Lisbon: Imprensa de Ciências Sociais, 2012), 173–92.

13. For a critique of "slum" discourse, see Alan Mayne, *Slums: The History of a Global Injustice* (London: Reaktion Books, 2017).

14. On the city as a place inspiring different and perhaps conflicting ideas of what constitutes "modern" life, see also James Ferguson, *Expectations of Modernity: Myths and Meanings of Urban Life on the Zambian Copperbelt* (Berkeley: University of California Press, 1999); Emily Callaci, *Street Archives and City Life: Popular Intellectuals in Postcolonial Tanzania* (Durham, NC: Duke University Press, 2017).

15. Ato Quayson, writing of Accra, speaks of the "relations of complicity and overlap between top and bottom that have constituted the African city," including

during the colonial era. Quayson, *Oxford Street, Accra: City Life and the Itineraries of Transnationalism* (Durham, NC: Duke University Press, 2014), 8. On avoiding binary explanations of power and urban governance, see also Clifton C. Crais, "Introduction," in *The Culture of Power in Southern Africa: Essays on State Formation and the Political Imagination*, ed. Clifton C. Crais (Portsmouth, NH: Heinemann, 2003), 21; Simon Bekker and Laurent Fourchard, "Introduction," in *Governing Cities in Africa: Politics and Policies*, ed. Simon Bekker and Laurent Fourchard (Cape Town: HSRC Press, 2013), 1–12.

16. Maputo has about 1.1 million people, according to preliminary 2017 figures, and adjacent Matola recently surpassed it, with more than 1.6 million. Instituto Nacional de Estatística, "Divulgação os resultados preliminares: IV Recenseamento Geral da Populaçao e Habitação 2017" (Maputo: INE, 2017), n.p., http://www.ine.gov.mz/operacoes-estatisticas/censos/censo-2007/censo-2017/divulgacao-os-resultados-preliminares-iv-rgph-2017.

17. Catherine Coquery-Vidrovitch, "African Urban Spaces: History and Culture," in *African Urban Spaces in Historical Perspective*, ed. Steven J. Salm and Toyin Falola (Rochester, NY: University of Rochester Press, 2005), xxiv; Anthony D. King, "The Social Production of Building Form: Theory and Research," *Environment and Planning Development: Society and Space* 2 (1984): 429–46.

18. Frantz Fanon, *The Wretched of the Earth*, trans. Richard Philcox (New York: Grove Press, 2004), 4–5.

19. Janet L. Abu-Lughod, *Rabat: Urban Apartheid in Morocco* (Princeton, NJ: Princeton University Press, 1980); Gwendolyn Wright, *The Politics of Design in French Colonial Urbanism* (Chicago: University of Chicago Press, 1991); Zeynep Çelik, *Urban Forms and Colonial Confrontations: Algiers under French Rule* (Berkeley: University of California Press, 1997); Odile Goerg, "From Hill Station (Freetown) to Downtown Conakry (First Ward): Comparing French and British Approaches to Segregation in Colonial Cities at the Beginning of the Twentieth Century," *Canadian Journal of African Studies* 32, no. 1 (1998): 1–31; Hilton Judin and Ivan Vladislavić, eds., *Blank: Architecture, Apartheid, and After* (Rotterdam: NAi Publishers, 1999); Garth Andrew Myers, *Verandahs of Power: Colonialism and Space in Urban Africa* (Syracuse, NY: Syracuse University Press, 2003); Jennifer Robinson, "Johannesburg's 1936 Empire Exhibition: Interaction, Segregation and Modernity in a South African City," *Journal of Southern African Studies* 29, no. 3 (2003): 759–89; Mia Fuller, *Moderns Abroad: Architecture, Cities, and Italian Imperialism* (London: Routledge, 2007); A. J. Njoh, "Colonial Philosophies, Urban Space, and Racial Segregation in British and French Colonial Africa," *Journal of Black Studies* 38, no. 4 (2008): 579–99; Fassil Demissie, ed., *Colonial Architecture and Urbanism in Africa: Intertwined and Contested Histories* (Farnham, UK: Ashgate, 2012); Carl H. Nightingale, *Segregation: A Global History of Divided Cities* (Chicago: University of Chicago Press, 2012); Robert Home, *Of Planting and Planning: The Making of British Colonial Cities*, 2nd ed. (New York: Routledge, 2013);

233

234

Carlos Nunes Silva, ed., *Urban Planning in Sub-Saharan Africa: Colonial and Post-colonial Planning Cultures* (Abingdon, UK: Routledge, 2015).

20. Laurent Fourchard, "Between World History and State Formation: New Perspectives on Africa's Cities," *Journal of African History* 52, no. 2 (2011): 229. Historian and journalist Jacob Dlamini makes a similar case with his memoir of growing up in a township outside Johannesburg. Dlamini, *Native Nostalgia* (Johannesburg: Jacana Media, 2009).

21. Garth Andrew Myers, "Reconstructing Ng'ambo: Town Planning and Development on the Other Side of Zanzibar" (PhD diss., University of California–Los Angeles, 1993); Myers, "Sticks and Stones." See also William Cunningham Bissell, *Urban Design, Chaos, and Colonial Power in Zanzibar* (Bloomington: Indiana University Press, 2011).

22. Myers, "Sticks and Stones," 266.

23. Makhulu, *Making Freedom*, 60.

24. There is a rich literature on apartheid-era spatial regimes and how people challenged or resisted them, sometimes in subtle ways. Rebecca Ginsburg, "'Now I Stay in a House': Renovating the Matchbox in Apartheid-Era Soweto," *African Studies* 55, no. 2 (1996): 127–39; Belinda Bozzoli, *Theatres of Struggle and the End of Apartheid* (Athens: Ohio University Press, 2004); Lee, *African Women and Apartheid*, 81–105; Leslie J. Bank, *Home Spaces, Street Styles: Contesting Power and Identity in a South African City* (New York: Pluto Press, 2011); Ginsburg, *At Home with Apartheid: The Hidden Landscapes of Domestic Service in Johannesburg* (Charlottesville: University of Virginia Press, 2011); Koni Benson, "Crossroads Continues: Histories of Women Mobilizing against Forced Removals and for Housing in Cape Town, South Africa, 1975–2005" (PhD diss., University of Minnesota, 2009).

25. James R. Brennan, *Taifa: Making Race and Nation in Urban Tanzania* (Athens: Ohio University Press, 2012).

26. For critiques of the concept, see Karen Tranberg Hansen and Mariken Vaa, eds., *Reconsidering Informality: Perspectives from Urban Africa* (Uppsala: Nordiska Afrikainstitutet, 2004); Ananya Roy and Nezar AlSayyad, eds., *Urban Informality: Transnational Perspectives from the Middle East, Latin America, and South Asia* (Lanham, MD: Lexington Books, 2004).

27. Allen F. Isaacman and Barbara Isaacman, *The Tradition of Resistance in Mozambique: The Zambesi Valley, 1850–1921* (Berkeley: University of California Press, 1976); Allen F. Isaacman, *Cotton Is the Mother of Poverty: Peasants, Work, and Rural Struggle in Colonial Mozambique, 1938–1961* (Portsmouth, NH: Heinemann, 1996); Isaacman and Isaacman, *Dams, Displacement, and the Delusion of Development: Cahora Bassa and Its Legacies in Mozambique, 1965–2007* (Athens: Ohio University Press, 2013).

28. James Ferguson writes of a man in rural Lesotho who built what the man called a "European-style" house: it "was not a matter of blind copying; it was a

powerful claim to a chance for transformed conditions of life—a place-in-the-world, a standard of living, a 'direction we would like to move in.'" Ferguson, *Global Shadows: Africa in the Neoliberal World Order* (Durham, NC: Duke University Press, 2006), 19.

29. James Holston, ed., *Cities and Citizenship* (Durham, NC: Duke University Press, 1999); Rainer Bauböck, "Reinventing Urban Citizenship," *Citizenship Studies* 7, no. 2 (2003): 139–60; Holston, *Insurgent Citizenship*; Adam M. Pine, "The Performativity of Urban Citizenship," *Environment and Planning* A 42 (2010): 1103–20; Morten Nielsen, "In the Vicinity of the State: House Construction, Personhood, and the State in Maputo, Mozambique" (PhD diss., University of Copenhagen, 2008); Brodwyn Fischer, *A Poverty of Rights: Citizenship and Inequality in Twentieth-Century Rio de Janeiro* (Stanford, CA: Stanford University Press, 2008); Nielsen, "Mimesis of the State: From Natural Disaster to Urban Citizenship on the Outskirts of Maputo, Mozambique," *Social Analysis* 54, no. 3 (2010): 153–73; Brennan, *Taifa*; Patricia Burke Wood, "Citizenship in the 'In-Between City,'" *Canadian Journal of Urban Research* 22, no. 1 (2013): 111–25; Claudia Gastrow, "Negotiated Settlements: Housing and the Aesthetics of Citizenship in Luanda, Angola" (PhD diss., University of Chicago, 2014); Felicitas Becker and Joel Cabrita, "Introduction: Performing Citizenship and Enacting Exclusion on Africa's Indian Ocean Littoral," *Journal of African History* 55, no. 2 (2014): 161–71; Leslie Bank, "City Slums, Rural Homesteads: Migrant Culture, Displaced Urbanism and the Citizenship of the Serviced House," *Journal of Southern African Studies* 41, no. 5 (2015): 1067–81; Nikhil Anand, *Hydraulic City: Water and the Infrastructures of Citizenship in Mumbai* (Durham, NC: Duke University Press, 2017); Gastrow, "Cement Citizens."

30. John L. Comaroff, "Reflections on the Colonial State, in South Africa and Elsewhere: Factions, Fragments, Facts, and Fictions," *Social Identities* 4, no. 3 (1998): 341.

31. Frelimo at independence was still spelled as FRELIMO, a portmanteau of FREnte de LIbertação de MOçambique (Mozambique Liberation Front). A few years later, when the independence movement transformed itself into a political party, it changed the styling of the name to Frelimo. For the purposes of readability, this is how the name will appear in the book.

32. For the ways in which ordinary people adopted the language of new regimes to give legitimacy to their own claims and initiatives, see Donald L. Donham, *Marxist Modern: An Ethnographic History of the Ethiopian Revolution* (Berkeley: University of California Press, 1999); Priya Lal, *African Socialism in Postcolonial Tanzania: Between the Village and the World* (Cambridge: Cambridge University Press, 2015); Jeffrey S. Ahlman, *Living with Nkrumahism: Nation, State, and Pan-Africanism in Ghana* (Athens: Ohio University Press, 2017).

33. Architecture and urbanism "constitute an essential part of the human experience," writes architectural historian Zeynep Çelik, "and their experiential

235

qualities make them accessible to everybody. They express cultural values, but they are also firmly grounded in material and daily life. Their connection to the everyday world is so substantial that they can never transcend or be divorced from worldly associations—a phenomenon often observed in other cultural and artistic formations." Çelik, *Urban Forms and Colonial Confrontations*, 2.

34. Adrian Forty, *Concrete and Culture: A Material History* (London: Reaktion Books, 2012), 14.

35. Filipe Mata, "O mar vai beber do 'xitala-mati,'" *Tempo*, May 16, 1982; Aldino Muianga, *Xitala mati* (Maputo: Associação dos Escritores Moçambicanos, 1987).

36. Cristina Delgado Henriques, *Maputo: Cinco décadas de mudança territorial* (Lisbon: IPAD, 2008), 78–80. Chamanculo is currently split into four neighborhood units; according to the 2007 census, it had about sixty-four thousand inhabitants. Officials have recently begun to spell Chamanculo as Nhlamankulo to more closely approximate its correct Ronga pronunciation.

37. Fernando Bismarque, "Moradores abrangidos pelo projecto reclamam do valor das indemnizações," *O País*, February 8, 2012, http://opais.sapo.mz/index.php /sociedade/45-sociedade/18903-moradores-abrangidos-pelo-projecto-reclamam -do-valor-das-indemnizacoes.html.

38. Nadja Manghezi, *O meu coração, está nas maos de um negro: Uma história da vida de Janet Mondlane* (Maputo: Livraria Universitária, 1999), 184. The original text of the letter was in English, but it was translated into Portuguese for publication. The text as I have quoted it is therefore a reverse translation and may not perfectly match the English original.

39. Ana Laura Cumba, interview with author, April 29, 2011.

40. Ferreira's story is from: Margarida Ferreira, interviews with author, April 11, April 13, 2011, and September 28, 2011, and June 13, 2012; Gilmar Ferreira, interview with author, May 3, 2011; and Graça Ferreira, interviews with author November 2, 2011, and May 7, 2013.

41. See Marcia C. Schenck, "From Luanda and Maputo to Berlin: Uncovering Angolan and Mozambican Migrants' Motives to Move to the German Democratic Republic (1970–1990)," *African Economic History* 44 (2016): 202–34.

42. Castigo Guambe, interviews with author, April 14, April 26, and May 17, 2011.

43. On the meanings of home and/or house construction in contemporary Maputo, see Ana Bénard da Costa, *O preço da sombra: Sobrevivência e reprodução social entre famílias de Maputo* (Lisbon: Livros Horizonte, 2007); Nielsen, "In the Vicinity of the State"; Nielsen, "Futures Within: Reversible Time and House-Building in Maputo, Mozambique," *Anthropological Theory* 11, no. 4 (2011): 397–423; Jørgen Eskemose Andersen, Silje Erøy Sollien, and Khadidja Ouis, "Built Environment Study," in *Home Space Maputo*, 2012, http://www.homespace .dk/tl_files/uploads/publications/Full%20reports/HomeSpace_Built_Environment _Study.pdf; Paul Jenkins, *Urbanization, Urbanism, and Urbanity in an African City: Home Spaces and House Cultures* (New York: Palgrave Macmillan, 2013).

Julie Soleil Archambault has recently addressed concrete house construction and aspiration on the outskirts of Inhambane, a small city in southern Mozambique: Archambault, "'One Beer, One Block': Concrete Aspiration and the Stuff of Transformation in a Mozambican Suburb," *Journal of the Royal Anthropological Institute* 24, no. 4 (2018): 692–708.

44. Luise White, "Hodgepodge Historiography: Documents, Itineraries, and the Absence of Archives," *History in Africa* 42 (2015): 309–18.

45. The place of the suburban "dream house" in American history has been thoroughly explored. See Kenneth T. Jackson, *Crabgrass Frontier: The Suburbanization of the United States* (New York: Oxford University Press, 1985); Dolores Hayden, *Building Suburbia: Green Fields and Urban Growth, 1820–2000* (New York: Vintage, 2004); Andrew Wiese, *Places of Their Own: African American Suburbanization in the Twentieth Century* (Chicago: University of Chicago Press, 2005).

46. Hansen, *Keeping House in Lusaka*, 94–117. Hansen's work is rare. She was able to do research in the same household over more than two decades, resulting in an illuminating work of historical anthropology that did not depend on looking backward. See also Jane I. Guyer, "Household and Community in African Studies," *African Studies Review* 24, no. 2–3 (1981): 87–137.

Chapter 1: The Spaces of Lourenço Marques

1. Samora Machel, "Independência implica benefícios para as massas exploradas," in *A nossa luta é uma revolução: Nacionalizações—Moçambique* (Lisbon: CIDA-C, 1976), 35.

2. Machel, "Independência implica benefícios," 56.

3. Lília Momplé, "Caniço," in *Ninguém matou Suhura*, 4th ed. (Maputo: CIEDIMA, 2008), 23–38. The collection was originally published in 1988; the story won an award linked to the city's centenary celebration in 1987.

4. Momplé, "Caniço," 32.

5. José Catorze, "'Apartheid' na habitação," *Tempo*, October 27, 1974, 19–20. See also Keith Middlemas, "Twentieth Century White Society in Mozambique," *Tarikh* 6, no. 2 (1979): 37; Honwana, "A velha casa," 33.

6. The literature on how the Lisbon regime repackaged the Lusotropicalist theories of Brazilian sociologist Gilberto Freyre (sometimes with Freyre's help) is vast, as is the literature debunking its premises. See Freyre, *Um brasileiro em terras portuguêsas* (Rio de Janeiro: J. Olympio, 1953); Gerald J. Bender, *Angola under the Portuguese: The Myth and the Reality* (Berkeley: University of California Press, 1978); Cláudia Castelo, *O modo português de estar no mundo: O lusotropicalismo e a ideologia colonial portuguesa (1933–1961)* (Porto: Afrontamento, 2001); José Luís Cabaço, *Moçambique: Identidades, colonialismo e libertação* (Maputo: Marimbique, 2010).

7. Janet Abu-Lughod, in her study of colonial urban planning in Morocco, uses "apartheid" with a similar objective in mind—that is, precisely because French

237

planners had vehemently denied accusations of racism. See Abu-Lughod, *Rabat*, xvii.n.

8. [José Craveirinha,] "Maulide Rifāi na Mafalala," *O Brado Africano*, February 26, 1955, 6. Craveirinha frequently used a pseudonym or his initials, and sometimes (as in this case), he left his contribution unsigned. (This piece also appeared in a collection of his essays published decades later.)

9. Jeanne Marie Penvenne, "Two Tales of a City: Lourenço Marques, 1945–1975," *Portuguese Studies Review* 19, no. 1–2 (2011): 257–60.

10. Penvenne, "Two Tales of a City."

11. J. Craveirinha, "Não se fazem quaisquer diferenças . . . ," *O Brado Africano*, August 8, 1956, 1.

12. Honwana, "A velha casa," 33.

13. L. Lloys Frates, "Memory of Place, the Place of Memory: Women's Narrations of Late Colonial Lourenço Marques, Mozambique" (PhD diss., University of California–Los Angeles, 2002), 189.

14. The contrast with South Africa's apartheid cities certainly struck one of the few foreign researchers allowed access to the subúrbios, a South African. Hilary Flegg Mitchell, *Aspects of Urbanisation and Age Structure in Lourenço Marques, 1957* (Lusaka: NECZAM and Institute for African Studies, University of Zambia, 1975), xii.

15. Mitchell describes this as a "laissez-faire" approach. Mitchell, *Aspects of Urbanisation*, xii.

16. There were also (brief) Dutch and Austrian attempts at settlement, in the eighteenth century. The following account of early Lourenço Marques is based primarily on: Alexandre Lobato, *História do presídio de Lourenço Marques, 1782–1786*, vol. 1, Estudos moçambicanos (Lisbon: Gráfica Boa Nova, 1949); Lobato, *História do presídio de Lourenço Marques, 1787–1799*, vol. 2, Estudos moçambicanos (Lisbon: Junta de Investigações do Ultramar, 1960); Lobato, *Quatro estudos e uma evocação para a história de Lourenço Marques*, Estudos moçambicanos (Lisbon: Junta de Investigações do Ultramar, 1961); Lobato, *Lourenço Marques, Xilunguíne*; Alfredo Pereira de Lima, "Casas que fizeram Lourenço Marques," *Studia*, no. 24 (1968): 7–71; Pereira de Lima, "Para um estudo da evolução urbana de Lourenço Marques," *Boletim Municipal*, no. 7 (December 31, 1970): 7–16; Pereira de Lima, *Pedras que já não falam* (Lourenço Marques: Tipografia Notícias, 1972); Jeanne Marie Penvenne, "A History of African Labor in Lourenço Marques, Mozambique, 1877–1950" (PhD diss., Boston University, 1982); Maria Clara Mendes, *Maputo antes da independência: Geografia de uma cidade colonial*, vol. 68, Memórias do Instituto de Investigação Científica Tropical (Lisbon: IICT, 1985), 17–27; Gerhard Liesegang, "Lourenço Marques antes de 1895: Aspectos da história dos estados vizinhos, da interacção entre a povoação e aqueles estados e do comércio na baía e na povoação," *Arquivo: Boletim do Arquivo Histórico de Moçambique*, no. 2 (1987): 19–75; Penvenne, *African Workers and Colonial Racism: Mozambican Strategies*

and Struggles in Lourenço Marques, 1877–1962 (Portsmouth, NH: Heinemann, 1995); Valdemir Donizette Zamparoni, "Entre *narros* e *mulungos*: Colonialismo e paisagem social em Lourenço Marques, c. 1890–c. 1940" (PhD diss., Universidade de São Paulo, 1998); Nuno Domingos, *Football and Colonialism: Body and Popular Culture in Urban Mozambique* (Athens: Ohio University Press, 2017), 61–79.

17. British maps called it Delagoa Bay and called the estuary the English River.

18. Convicts and political dissidents were often exiled to the colonies.

19. Pereira de Lima, "Casas que fizeram Lourenço Marques," 11.

20. Olga Martins, "'Va ka Mpfumu,' Lourenço Marques, e Maputo: Uma inter-relação problemática" (undergraduate thesis, Universidade Eduardo Mondlane, 1995).

21. Liesegang, "Lourenço Marques antes de 1895," 43. In 1862, only 84 of 1,021 residents counted in the census were European. By 1896, the European proportion had risen significantly, to 1,544 of 3,672 residents.

22. Penvenne, *African Workers*, 38–39.

23. Zamparoni, "Entre *narros* e *mulungos*," 252–55.

24. Zamparoni, 254–55.

25. We ought not take Portugal's claim to effective occupation on its face. Colonial control was never complete, nor was it unchallenged. See Isaacman and Isaacman, *The Tradition of Resistance in Mozambique*.

26. Lourenço Marques was designated the new capital in 1898.

27. João José Soares-Zilhão, "Lourenço Marques: Ensaio geográfico," *Boletim da Sociedade de Estudos de Moçambique*, no. 36 (1938): 16–18.

28. João Sousa Morais, *Maputo: Património da estrutura e forma urbana, topologia do lugar* (Lisbon: Livros Horizonte, 2001), 106.

29. Zamparoni, "Entre *narros* e *mulungos*," 256.

30. Magda Pinheiro, "O subúrbio entre o arrabalde antigo e a metrópole: Identidade e temporalidade—Os territórios do urbano," *Ler História* 48 (2005): 11–32.

31. Soares-Zilhão, "Lourenço Marques," 16, and map on p. 6. "Subúrbios" also appear in a 1919 plan for Bissau, later the capital of Portuguese Guiné. Ana Vaz Milheiro, "The City under the First Republic in the Former Portuguese Africa," in *Urban Planning in Lusophone African Countries*, ed. Carlos Nunes Silva (Abingdon, UK: Routledge, 2015), 36.

32. Soares-Zilhão, "Lourenço Marques," 16; Alfredo Rodrigues dos Santos, "O regime municipal em Lourenço Marques," *Moçambique: Documentário Trimestral*, no. 34 (1943): 68; António Rita-Ferreira, "Os africanos de Lourenço Marques," *Memórias do Instituto Científica de Moçambique*, series C, 9 (1967–68): 182. The official designation *subúrbios* may predate 1903.

33. See comments of Mouzinho de Albuquerque, as quoted in Rita-Ferreira, "Os africanos de Lourenço Marques," 182–83.

34. James Duffy, *Portugal in Africa* (Baltimore: Penguin Books, 1962); Eduardo Mondlane, *The Struggle for Mozambique* (Baltimore: Penguin Books, 1969); Leroy

239

240

Vail and Landeg White, *Capitalism and Colonialism in Mozambique: A Study of Quelimane District* (Minneapolis: University of Minnesota Press, 1980); Penvenne, *African Workers*; Kathleen Sheldon, *Pounders of Grain: A History of Women, Work, and Politics in Mozambique* (Portsmouth, NH: Heinemann, 2002), 50–53; Eric Allina, *Slavery by Any Other Name: African Life under Company Rule in Colonial Mozambique* (Charlottesville: University of Virginia Press, 2012); Zachary Kagan Guthrie, *Bound for Work: Labor, Mobility, and Colonial Rule in Central Mozambique, 1940–1965* (Charlottesville: University of Virginia Press, 2018).

35. Due to international pressure, forced labor was made illegal from 1928 to 1942, but this did not put a total halt to the practice during that time.

36. See, for instance, Zachary Kagan Guthrie, "'This Was Being Done Only to Help': Development and Forced Labor in Barue, Mozambique, 1959–1965," *International Labor and Working-Class History* 92 (2017): 134–54.

37. Penvenne, *African Workers*, 36–39 and 136–37; Zamparoni, "Entre *narros* e *mulungos*," 13–42.

38. Lilly Havstad, "Multiracial Women and the African Press in Post–World War II Lourenço Marques, Mozambique," *South African Historical Journal* 68, no. 3 (2016): 390–414.

39. Raúl Bernardo Manuel Honwana, *The Life History of Raúl Honwana: An Inside View of Mozambique from Colonialism to Independence, 1905–1975*, ed. Allen F. Isaacman, trans. Tamara L. Bender (Boulder, CO: Lynne Rienner, 1988), 105–6.

40. Penvenne, *African Workers*, 65–69.

41. Alexander Keese, *Living with Ambiguity: Integrating an African Elite in French and Portuguese Africa, 1930–1961* (Stuttgart: Franz Steiner Verlag, 2007).

42. There were 4,554 registered assimilados as of 1955. Cláudia Castelo, *Passagens para África: O povoamento de Angola e Moçambique com naturais da Metrópole (1920–1974)* (Porto: Edições Afrontamento, 2007), 295.

43. Cabaço, *Moçambique*, 220–21.

44. For typical (and stereotypical) postindependence sendups of the supposedly selfish and ultimately self-destructive assimilado, see Albino Magaia, *Malungate* (Maputo: Associação dos Escritores Moçambicanos, 1987); Sant'Ana Afonso, "Eu não sou eu," in *"Eu não sou eu" e outras peças de teatro* (Maputo: Imprensa Nacional de Moçambique, 1981), 97–126.

45. See, for instance, Jeanne Marie Penvenne, "João dos Santos Albasini (1876–1922): The Contradictions of Politics and Identity in Colonial Mozambique," *Journal of African History* 37, no. 3 (1996): 419–64.

46. Honwana, "A velha casa," 33.

47. Penvenne, *African Workers*, 97–102.

48. Jeanne Marie Penvenne, "'Here We All Walked with Fear': The Mozambican Labor System and the Workers of Lourenço Marques, 1945–1962," in *Struggle for the City: Migrant Labor, Capital, and the State in Urban Africa*, ed. Frederick Cooper (Beverly Hills, CA: Sage, 1983), 153.

49. Emblematic of their second-class citizenship, the document assimilados carried was different than the identity card carried by other "Portuguese."

50. Zamparoni, "Entre *narros* e *mulungos*," 308–29; Frates, "Memory of Place," 89–127.

51. Zamparoni, "Entre *narros* e *mulungos*," 309.

52. Zamparoni, 321–29; Catherine Coquery-Vidrovitch, "Residential Segregation in African Cities," in *Urbanization and African Cultures*, ed. Steven J. Salm and Toyin Falola (Durham, NC: Carolina Academic Press, 2005), 343–56.

53. Pereira de Lima, "Casas que fizeram Lourenço Marques," 64. It is unclear why a wood-and-zinc house in itself would be considered unsanitary.

54. Zamparoni, "Entre *narros* e *mulungos*," 309.

55. Governo-Geral da Província de Moçambique, Diploma Legislativo No. 616, November 16, 1938. I consulted a copy of the legislation found in the "Aldeamentos indígenas 1948" file in AHM/DSNI/cx.528.

56. Jeanne Penvenne, "A Luta Continua! Recent Literature on Mozambique," *International Journal of African Historical Studies* 18, no. 1 (1985): 116.

57. Penvenne, "History of African Labor," 255–67; José Capela, *O movimento operário em Lourenço Marques, 1898–1927* (Porto: Afrontamento, 1981), 12–13.

58. The census distinguished between the "city" and Munhuana, the administrative jurisdiction that closely approximated the subúrbios. Província de Moçambique, *III Recenseamento geral da população na Província de Lourenço Marques* (Lourenço Marques: Direcção Provincial dos Serviços de Estatística Geral, 1960), 23.

59. Colónia de Moçambique, *Censo de população em 1940, I: População não-indígena* (Lourenço Marques: Repartição Técnica de Estatística, 1942); Colónia de Moçambique, *Censo de população em 1940, II: População indígena* (Lourenço Marques: Repartição Técnica de Estatística, 1943); Província de Moçambique, *III Recenseamento geral*.

60. Penvenne, "Fotografando Lourenço Marques."

61. Frates, "Memory of Place."

62. Mitchell, *Aspects of Urbanisation*, 5. See also the play created by the troupe Grupo Mutumbela Gogo, *Nove hora* (Maputo, 1989), based on the poetry of Rui Nogar and inspired by the nine o'clock curfew.

63. André-Daniel Clerc [with Eduardo Mondlane], *Chitlangou, Son of a Chief*, trans. Margaret A. Bryan (repr., Westport, CT: Negro Universities Press, 1971), 16; Henri Alexandre Junod, *The Life of a South African Tribe*, vol. 2, *Mental Life* (New Hyde Park, NY: University Books, 1962), 104–10; Sandro Bruschi, "The Survival of Mozambican, Pre-colonial Architecture," in *Traditional Informal Settlements in Mozambique: From Lichinga to Maputo*, trans. Carola Cuoco (Maputo: FAPF, 2004), 47.

64. See the description by artist Malangatana Ngwenya, "Prefácio," in *Com o mundo na cabeça: Homenagem às mulheres de Moçambique*, by Carlos Dominguez (Lisbon: Associação do Centro Cultural de Matalana, 1997), 6.

241

65. Clerc [with Mondlane], *Chitlangou, Son of a Chief*, 38. This passage was suggested to the author by Maria de Lurdes Torcato, who translated the text into Portuguese for the Mozambican edition.

66. For a description of reed house construction in the subúrbios during the late colonial era, see Armando Guilundo, interview with author, May 10, 2011. See also Brandberg, "Constructions"; Zounkata Tuina, "Les materiaux de construction au Mozambique," in *The Malhangalene Survey: A Housing Study of an Unplanned Settlement in Maputo, Mozambique, 1976, pt. 2* (Göteborg: Chalmers Tekniska Högskola, Arkitektur, 1977), 1–71.

67. Rita-Ferreira, "Os africanos de Lourenço Marques," 165.

68. Rita-Ferreira, 165n. Even today, there are some caniço stands in Maputo located beside the Manhiça line. See Gonçalves Mambo et al., interview with author, February 12, 2011.

69. Bruschi argues that a painting from Livingstone's 1858 expedition may prove that the origins of the rectilinear reed house can be traced to nineteenth-century Tete, in west-central Mozambique. Bruschi, "Survival," 47.

70. Brandberg, "Constructions," 7.

71. Pereira de Lima, "Casas que fizeram Lourenço Marques," 12.

72. Rita-Ferreira, "Os africanos de Lourenço Marques," 167. The area surveyed was the 770-hectare zone where most of the suburban population was said to be concentrated.

73. The missionary-anthropologist H. A. Junod, writing in 1927, juxtaposed the "charming" conical roof of regional rural architecture with the metal-panel roofs in an African location in Pretoria to demonstrate what he considered the negative influence of civilization. Junod, *Life of a South African Tribe*, 111.

74. Gabinete de Urbanização e Habitação da Região de Lourenço Marques, "Estudo do 'Caniço,'" 19.

75. In 1968, there were a reported 146 residential fires in the subúrbios, compared to 18 in the City of Cement. Areosa Pena and Marcos Cuembelo, "Bairro do caniço: 90 mil casebres para demolir," *Tempo*, February 27, 1972, 19; Areosa Pena, "Fogo," *Tempo*, December 24, 1972.

76. Rita-Ferreira, "Os africanos de Lourenço Marques," 180.

77. Armando Guilundo interview.

78. Henrique António, "Crónica da semana: Palhotas no ar!" *O Brado Africano*, October 3, 1959, 3.

79. Pereira de Lima, "Casas que fizeram Lourenço Marques," 34–47.

80. Pereira de Lima, 36; Gerhard-Mark van der Waal, *From Mining Camp to Metropolis: The Buildings of Johannesburg, 1886–1940* (Johannesburg: Chris van Rensburg and HSRC, 1987).

81. Daniel R. Headrick, *The Tools of Empire: Technology and European Imperialism in the Nineteenth Century* (New York: Oxford University Press, 1981); Anthony D. King, *The Bungalow: The Production of a Global Culture* (London: Routledge and Kegan Paul, 1984), 193–223.

82. King, *Bungalow*, 209–14. For a brief discussion of the role of housing technology in early European perceptions of African societies, see Michael Adas, *Machines as the Measure of Men: Science, Technology, and Ideologies of Western Dominance* (Ithaca, NY: Cornell University Press, 1989), 6, 36.

83. Pereira de Lima, "Casas que fizeram Lourenço Marques," 36; Gilbert Herbert, *Pioneers of Prefabrication: The British Contribution in the Nineteenth Century* (Baltimore: Johns Hopkins University Press, 1978), 144.

84. Honwana, "A velha casa."

85. The prohibition and its contravention are the subject of chapter 3.

86. Those interviewed whose parents or grandparents built such houses in the 1940s and 1950s include Elizabeth Eurica Cumbana and Gabriel Chiau, both of whom were still living in these houses.

87. Those interviewed whose parents or grandparents built such distinguished houses include Castigo Guambe, Isaac Araújo, and Luís Hunguana—all houses built before 1940.

88. Sociedade de Estudos de Moçambique, "Relato da Sessão de Matemática e Engenharia realizada no dia 8 de Setembro de 1947, de manhã," in *Primeiro Congresso da Sociedade de Estudos da Colónia de Moçambique*, vol. 4 (Lourenço Marques: Minerva Central, 1947), 100.

89. To be precise, he used the phrase "neighborhoods of tin in capitalist cities." Perhaps this was a hint of the Salazarist corporatist conservatism of the time, which was contemptuous of unconstrained, materialist capitalism. What was it, then, that produced the neighborhoods of tin 2 kilometers away? Manuel Pimentel dos Santos, "Alguns problemas do Município de Lourenço Marques," *Boletim da Sociedade de Estudos de Moçambique*, no. 64 (1950): 69.

90. Frates, "Memory of Place," 199.

91. The following account of Jochua Guambe's life is based on information provided by his son: see Castigo Guambe interviews. I stayed in the house for three weeks in June 2011.

92. Rita-Ferreira, "Os africanos de Lourenço Marques," 183–84.

93. Elizabeth Eurica Cumbana, interview with author, May 5, 2011.

94. Honwana, "A velha casa," 28–29.

95. Mendes de Oliveira, "Xitique," *Tempo*, June 25, 1972, 17–21; Jeanne Marie Penvenne, "Seeking the Factory for Women: Mozambican Urbanization in the Late Colonial Era," *Journal of Urban History* 23, no. 3 (1997): 368–69; Sheldon, *Pounders of Grain*, 58–69.

96. The following account of Salvador Simão Hunguana is based on information provided by his son: see Luís Hunguana, interviews with author, July 13, 17, and 22, 2009.

97. Honwana, "A velha casa," 25; Gabinete de Urbanização e Habitação da Região de Lourenço Marques, "Estudo do 'Caniço'—Habitat," Plano Director de urbanização de Lourenço Marques, no. 46, 1969, MITADER.

98. The following account of José da Costa and Glória da Conceição Nhambirre is based on information provided by their son Sérgio and a Portuguese who

243

was employed in their cantina as a teenager in the mid-1960s: see Sérgio da Costa, interviews with author, April 16 and 28, 2011, and Dinis Marques, interviews with author, October 10 and 17, 2010.

99. Rita-Ferreira, "Os africanos de Lourenço Marques," 313–14; Penvenne, *African Workers*, 40–43.

100. José Capela, *O vinho para o preto: Notas e textos sobre a exportação do vinho para África* (Porto: Edições Afrontamento, 1973); Penvenne, *African Workers*, 40–43.

101. The cantinas from the 1930s often have the date of construction inscribed in the pediment.

102. Penvenne, *African Workers*, 42.

103. See the series of articles on the subject in the November and December 1955 issues of *O Brado Africano*. Also see Paulo Negrão, "A cantina do china, pt. 1," *O Brado Africano*, October 1, 1960.

104. Dinis Marques interviews.

105. Paulo Negrão, "A cantina do china, pt. 3," *O Brado Africano*, October 15, 1960, 4.

106. Those with native status could not legally own formal businesses, and for people with assimilado status, the obstacles to owning a business were enormous. In the Beira-Mar area of Chamanculo, residents speak of the man who was once the single black owner of a cantina there. In the 1960s, when the municipality decided to pave the main roads through the neighborhood, most of this cantina was demolished because it was in the way, putting the black cantineiro out of business. Residents remember the demolition as a gratuitous act—noting that the paved road curved off its natural track to justify it—and they assert that it was intended as a favor to local Portuguese cantineiros.

107. Penvenne, *African Workers*, 40.

108. For analogous naming practices in rural Rhodesia, see Dennis Masaka, "Reflections on Black Indigenous People's Nicknaming of Colonial White Farmers in Zimbabwe," *Journal of Black Studies* 43, no. 5 (2012): 479–504.

109. Aldino Muianga, *Caderno de memórias*, vol. 2 (Maputo: CIEDIMA, 2015), 7; Honwana, "A velha casa," 30.

110. The following account of António Araújo is based on information provided by his son: see Isaac Araújo, interviews with author, June 8 and 15, 2011.

111. A semifictional account of Twist Bar and the compound appears in Muianga, *Caderno de memórias*, 2:47–49.

112. Pena and Cuembelo, "Bairro do caniço," 19; "Compound, n.2," *OED Online* (Oxford University Press, December 2013), http://www.oed.com/view/Entry/37832.

113. Zamparoni, "Entre *narros* e *mulungos*," 314–17; Penvenne, "History of African Labor," 269–76.

114. Penvenne, *African Workers*, 49, 53–54.

115. It was similar in significant ways to the "slum yard" in 1930s Johannesburg famously described by Ellen Hellman. Hellmann, *Rooiyard: A Sociological*

Survey of an Urban Native Slum Yard (Cape Town: Oxford University Press, for Rhodes-Livingston Institute, 1948).

116. Pena and Cuembelo, "Bairro do caniço," 19.

117. Sheldon, *Pounders of Grain*, 60.

118. Sebastião Chitombe, interviews with author, May 4, 9, and 16, 2011. Chitombe lived in a Chamanculo compound as a teenager, after migrating to the city in the mid-1960s.

119. Pena and Cuembelo, "Bairro do caniço," 14–15, 19.

120. Pena and Cuembelo, 19.

121. Penvenne, *African Workers*, 70–71.

122. Zamparoni, "Entre *narros* e *mulungos*," 320; Penvenne, *African Workers*, 72.

123. Albino Magaia, "Bairro da Munhuana de 1935 a 1973," *Tempo*, February 18, 1973; Magaia, "Carta aos habitantes do Bairro da Munhuana," *Tempo*, December 22, 1974. When a miner died before the end of the contract (or "disappeared"), the mining companies had agreed to indemnify the Portuguese government (rather than the deceased miner's family) for the sum remaining on the contract. It remains unclear whether the indemnification funds sat unused because of the negligence of the mining companies or Portuguese administrators or both.

124. Governo-Geral da Província de Moçambique, Diploma Legislativo No. 616.

125. Penvenne, *African Workers*, 72–73.

126. One hundred and ninety "huts" needed to be relocated to make way for the project, though surely some of the so-called huts were actually houses of wood and zinc, such as the childhood home of Lúcia da Silveira. Lúcia Joaquim da Silveira, interview with author, April 11, 2011; Câmara Municipal de Lourenço Marques, "Acta no. 15," March 28, 1940, 6. I thank António Sopa for forwarding to me the transcribed *actas* regarding the Bairro Indígena.

127. João Augusto Ornelas, Director (interino), Direcção dos Serviços de Saúde, Colónia de Moçambique, "Parecer: 1) Bairro indígena modelar da Munhana, 2) Bairros indígenas do Infulene e da Mahota," March 6, 1939, AHM/DSNI/cx. 528.

128. Ornelas, "Parecer," 2.

129. João Augusto Ornelas, Director (interino), Direcção dos Serviços de Saúde, Colónia de Moçambique, "Parecer No. 2: Implantação do primeiro bairro indígena modelar—tipo—'Bairro da Munhuana'—segundo projecto apresentado pela Câmara Municipal," April 18, 1939, n.p., AHM/DSNI/cx. 528.

130. Paulo Augusto do Rêgo, Presidente da Comissão de Construção de Pousadas ou Bairros Indígenas, Governador (interino) da Província do Sul do Save, "Informação," April 28, 1939, Repartição Central dos Negócias Indígenas, Colónia de Moçambique, AHM/DSNI/cx. 528.

131. "Informação," April 2, 1940, 1, Repartição Provincial de Obras Públicas do Sul do Save, filed in Câmara Municipal de Lourenço Marques, "Projecto para a construcção do Novo Bairro Indígena," 1940 [original cataloging data: proc. 3, cap. 2, cx. 104, vol. 2], MITADER.

132. Helena Alberto Macuacua, "Um breve historial sobre o Bairro Indígena" (manuscript, n.d.), 1.

133. Adelino José Macedo, "Relatório anual referente ao ano de 1946," January 31, 1947, 5, Administração do Concelho de Lourenço Marques, AHM/GDLM/cx. 352.

134. Macedo, "Relatório anual," 5.

135. A. A. Montanha, "Informação No. 9: Projecto de Diploma Legislativo respeitante às 'Vilas Indígenas,'" April 3, 1951, 3, AHM/DSNI/cx. 528.

136. Montanha, "Informação," 4.

137. Frates, "Memory of Place," 158–60.

138. Rosa Candla, interview with author, July 27, 2009.

139. Until well into the twentieth century, many women in Portugal carried loads on their heads as well, and the romanticized image of such humble workers is frequently depicted on the wall tiles for which Lisbon and Porto are famous. As in Mozambique, wheelbarrows and other conveyances were monopolized by men.

140. Sebastião Chitombe interviews; Adriano Matate, interview with author, November 18, 2011; Carlos Muchanga, interview with author, October 25, 2012. See also Penvenne, *African Workers*, 150–52.

141. Luís Polanah, "O moleque Salomone, pt. 12," *O Brado Africano*, January 23, 1960. Students at mission schools frequently worked in the fields in exchange for room and board and in lieu of paying school fees.

142. Luís Polanah, "O moleque Salomone, pt. 7," *O Brado Africano*, December 5, 1959, 5.

143. Polanah, "O moleque Salomone, pt. 12," 1.

144. Luís Polanah, "O moleque Salomone, pt. 16," *O Brado Africano*, February 20, 1960, 10. Former servants spoke in recent interviews of the ease with which they found work.

145. Penvenne, *African Workers*, 148–50.

146. Such a beating, after a woman alleges that her servants have stolen her gold watch, is portrayed in Momplé, "Caniço," 36.

147. Adriano Matate interview.

148. In 1950, Portugal's colonial ministry requested six thousand laborers from Mozambique's governor-general, and the quota was filled with "vagrants," "undesirables," and convicts. Zachary Kagan Guthrie, "Repression and Migration: Forced Labor Exile of Mozambicans to São Tomé, 1948–1955," *Journal of Southern African Studies* 37, no. 3 (2011): 449–62. For years, "São Tomé" served as shorthand for the worst punishment you could receive at the hands of police if you were not sufficiently cautious.

149. Filipe Mata, *N'lhomulo* (Maputo: Associação dos Escritores Moçambicanos, 1985), 26. Also see Muianga, *Caderno de memórias*, 2:9–12.

150. Frederick Cooper, "Urban Space, Industrial Time, and Wage Labor in Africa," in *Struggle for the City: Migrant Labor, Capital, and the State in Urban Africa*, ed. Frederick Cooper (Beverly Hills, CA: Sage, 1983), 36; Louis Wirth, "Urbanism as a Way of Life," *American Journal of Sociology* 44, no. 1 (1938): 1–24.

151. David B. Coplan, *In Township Tonight! South Africa's Black City Music and Theatre* (London: Longman, 1985); Phyllis Martin, *Leisure and Society in Colonial Brazzaville* (Cambridge: Cambridge University Press, 1995); Laura Fair, *Pastimes and Politics: Culture, Community, and Identity in Post-abolition Zanzibar, 1890–1945* (Athens: Ohio University Press, 2001); Marissa J. Moorman, *Intonations: A Social History of Music and Nation in Luanda, Angola, from 1945 to Recent Times* (Athens: Ohio University Press, 2008); Nate Plageman, *Highlife Saturday Night: Popular Music and Social Change in Urban Ghana* (Bloomington: Indiana University Press, 2013).

152. Frederick Cooper, *On the African Waterfront: Urban Disorder and the Transformation of Work in Colonial Mombasa* (New Haven, CT: Yale University Press, 1987).

153. Luise White, *The Comforts of Home: Prostitution in Colonial Nairobi* (Chicago: University of Chicago Press, 1990); Teresa Barnes, *"We Women Worked So Hard": Gender, Urbanization, and Social Reproduction in Colonial Harare, Zimbabwe, 1930–1956* (Portsmouth, NH: Heinemann, 1999).

154. Jeanne Marie Penvenne, *Women, Migration and the Cashew Economy in Southern Mozambique, 1945–1975* (Woodbridge, UK: James Currey, 2015); Eléusio dos Prazeres Viegas Filipe, "'Where Are the Mozambican Musicians?': Music, Marrabenta, and National Identity in Lourenço Marques, Mozambique, 1950s–1975" (PhD diss., University of Minnesota, 2012); António Sopa, *A alegria é uma coisa rara: Subsídios para a história da música popular urbana em Lourenço Marques (1920–1975)* (Maputo: Marimbique, 2014); Domingos, *Football and Colonialism*.

155. Garth Myers, *African Cities: Alternate Visions of Urban Theory and Practice* (London: Zed Books, 2011), 54–55.

156. On racial proximities, and intimacies, see also Alan Morris, *Bleakness & Light: Inner-City Transition in Hillbrow, Johannesburg* (Johannesburg: Witwatersrand University Press, 1999); Ginsburg, *At Home with Apartheid*; Busani Mpofu, "'Undesirable' Indians, Residential Segregation and the Ill-Fated Rise of the White 'Housing Covenanters' in Bulawayo, Colonial Zimbabwe, 1930–1973," *South African Historical Journal* 63, no. 4 (2011): 553–80; Christopher J. Lee, *Unreasonable Histories: Nativism, Multiracial Lives, and the Genealogical Imagination in British Africa* (Durham, NC: Duke University Press, 2014); Carina E. Ray, *Crossing the Color Line: Race, Sex, and the Contested Politics of Colonialism in Ghana* (Athens: Ohio University Press, 2015); Heidi Gengenbach, "'What My Heart Wanted': Gendered Stories of Early Colonial Encounters in Southern Mozambique," in *Women in African Colonial Histories*, ed. Jean Allman, Susan Geiger, and Nakanyike Musisi (Bloomington: Indiana University Press, 2002), 19–47.

Chapter 2: The Politics of Visibility

1. Dlamini, *Native Nostalgia*, 44; Spiro Kostof, "The City Shaped: The Grid," in *Gridded Worlds: An Urban Anthology*, ed. Reuben Rose-Redwood and Liora Bigon

(Cham, Switz.: Springer International Publishing, 2018), 55–73; Jill L. Grant, "The Dark Side of the Grid Revisited: Power and Urban Design," in *Gridded Worlds: An Urban Anthology*, ed. Reuben Rose-Redwood and Liora Bigon (Cham, Switz.: Springer International Publishing, 2018), 75–99; Eric Ross, "The Grid Plan in the History of Senegalese Urban Design," in *Urban Planning in Sub-Saharan Africa: Colonial and Post-colonial Planning Cultures*, ed. Carlos Nunes Silva (Abingdon, UK: Routledge, 2015), 110–28.

2. Mark Hinchman, "The Grid of Saint-Louis du Sénégal," in *Colonial Architecture and Urbanism in Africa: Intertwined and Contested Histories*, ed. Fassil Demissie (Farnham, UK: Ashgate, 2012), 307.

3. Soares-Zilhão, "Lourenço Marques," 16; José de Oliveira Boléo, "Geografia das cidades: Lourenço Marques," *Boletim da Sociedade de Geografia de Lisboa* 63, no. 5–6 (1945): 223.

4. Boléo, "Geografia," 223.

5. Pimentel dos Santos, "Alguns problemas," 60.

6. See Penvenne's comments on Hilary Flegg Mitchell's observations on order in the caniço: Penvenne, "Two Tales of a City," 261.

7. Myers, "Sticks and Stones," 259.

8. Soares-Zilhão, "Lourenço Marques," 16.

9. "Propriedade horizontal," *Tempo*, December 3, 1972; "A acção do Montepio de Moçambique," *Tempo*, June 17, 1973.

10. Cabaço, *Moçambique*, 247.

11. Penvenne, "Fotografando Lourenço Marques."

12. Ernesto Matos, *Calçada portuguesa no mundo: Stellis undis contactis* (Lisbon: Sessenta e Nove Manuscritos, 2016).

13. Scholars of Latin American cities have been at the forefront in establishing how a city and its "slums" constitute the same political and economic ecosystem. See Janice E. Perlman, *The Myth of Marginality: Urban Poverty and Politics in Rio de Janeiro* (Berkeley: University of California Press, 1976); James Holston, *The Modernist City: An Anthropological Critique of Brasília* (Chicago: University of Chicago Press, 1989); Fischer, *A Poverty of Rights*.

14. The chart of parcels for city and subúrbios can be found as an insert in Rita-Ferreira, "Os africanos de Lourenço Marques."

15. Macedo, "Relatório anual," 5. Also cited in Penvenne, "Two Tales of a City," 259.

16. Rita-Ferreira, "Os africanos de Lourenço Marques," 181. Only 100 hectares (13 percent) of the 770 hectares of suburban land were held by the municipality or the state.

17. For a list of the régulo jurisdictions in 1967, see Rita-Ferreira, 158–59.

18. M. D., "Nos bairros periféricos: Ocupação de terrenos com palhotas," *A Tribuna*, November 28, 1962.

19. See Carlos Muchanga, interviews with author, October 25, 2012, and January 30, 2013.

20. Since the late 1990s, there has been much greater diversity in concrete-block construction. Luís Lage, "The Building of Informal Dwellings: Case Study of Maputo," in *Traditional Informal Settlements in Mozambique: From Lichinga to Maputo*, trans. Carola Cuoco (Maputo: FAPF, 2004), 75–91; Andersen, Sollien, and Ouis, "Built Environment Study."

21. Ilídio Rocha, "Matsui," *A Tribuna*, November 21, 1962; Artur Raul da Silva Marques, "Cidade do caniço," *A Tribuna*, December 30, 1962; Presidéncia do Conselho, *III Plano de fomento para 1968–1973, Moçambique* (Lisbon: Imprensa Nacional de Lisboa, 1968), 29.

22. Rita-Ferreira, "Os africanos de Lourenço Marques," 185–212.

23. Rita-Ferreira, 183–85; Penvenne, "History of African Labor," 255–67.

24. The system was a vestige of the one that, earlier in the century, had served most of Lourenço Marques. Penvenne, *African Workers*, 52–54.

25. Ana Magaia, interview with author, February 9, 2011.

26. Carlos Carvalho, interviews with author, May 23 and 30, 2011.

27. On the deep significance of keeping one's land swept clean, see Nielsen, "In the Vicinity of the State," 133–35.

28. Carvalho interview, May 30, 2011.

29. On the idea of modernization in late colonial Mozambique, see Michael Mahoney, "Estado Novo, Homem Novo (New State, New Man): Colonial and Anti-colonial Development Ideologies in Mozambique, 1930–1977," in *Staging Growth: Modernization, Development, and the Global Cold War*, ed. David C. Engerman et al. (Amherst: University of Massachusetts Press, 2003), 165–97; Isaacman and Isaacman, *Dams, Displacement, and the Delusion of Development*.

30. Domingos, *Football and Colonialism*, 67.

31. See note 31 in the introduction regarding the different stylings of the name.

32. Rita-Ferreira, "Os africanos de Lourenço Marques," 330; Alexandrino José, "O operariado moçambicano e a sua história: Problemas e perspectivas," *Arquivo*, no. 2 (1987): 161. According to José, strikers were arrested and one was killed.

33. Moreover, as Penvenne has argued, historians' accounts of labor mobilization in Lourenço Marques in the 1940s and 1950s are thin on evidence and likely overstated. Penvenne, "A Luta Continua!" 117–22.

34. Records of the PIDE/DGS housed at its Lourenço Marques headquarters were destroyed in 1974, but I discovered in the archives of the governor-general a "burn after reading" report from the PIDE office, dated 1963. A number of case files were opened on people simply because they were overheard complaining about discriminatory treatment. SCCIM, "4° trimestre resenha de informações, nos. 38 — 50," 1963, AHM/GDLM/cx. 351. See also *Tortura na Colónia de Moçambique, 1963–1974: Depoimentos de presos políticos* (Porto: Edições Afrontamento, 1977); Albino Magaia, *Yô Mabalane!* 2nd ed. (Maputo: Cadernos Tempo, 1988); Dalila Cabrita Mateus, *A PIDE/DGS na guerra colonial (1961–1974)* (Lisbon: Terramar, 2004).

249

35. Bartolomeu Tembe, interview with author, June 18, 2012. Tembe, a retired carpenter in his eighties, traced his lineage to the original Mpfumu clan of the immediate Lourenço Marques area. In contemporary Maputo, the régulo is largely a ceremonial position, though elsewhere in Mozambique traditional leaders have been restored some of the governing authority that was lost at independence.

36. "Nos bairros periféricos"; "Um bairro de palhotas e casas clandestinas e os problemas levantados à roda do seu parcelamento," *A Tribuna*, November 24, 1962.

37. Bridget O'Laughlin, "Class and the Customary: The Ambiguous Legacy of the Indigenato in Mozambique," *African Affairs* 99, no. 394 (2000): 5–42.

38. Ana Laura Cumba interview. Cumba, Frederico's youngest child, passed away in 2012. She was interviewed at what had been her father's house in Chamanculo. All older residents of Chamanculo recalled Frederico, but a particularly informative perspective was offered in numerous conversations with Margarida Ferreira, daughter of one of Frederico's counselors: see Margarida Ferreira interviews.

39. Macedo, "Relatório anual," 13.

40. Hilário Matusse, "Chamanculo: Memórias de um bairro," *Tempo*, November 6, 1983.

41. Technically speaking, Frederico was not the régulo. There were only four régulos in the subúrbios of Lourenço Marques, and according to administrative diagrams, Frederico was subordinated to one of them. On paper, the leader of Chamanculo was the "head of the village grouping." Yet if his rank was officially below that of régulo and his presence in political ceremonies less visible, his duties were substantially the same. The people of Chamanculo called him régulo.

42. José Gabriel Taveira Pereira, "Relatório da inspecção ordinária ao Segundo Bairro do Concelho de Lourenço Marques," 1972, 132, Inspecção dos Serviços Administrativos, AHM/ISANI/cx. 3.

43. Augusto Vaz Spencer, "Relatório da inspecção ordinária ao Concelho de Lourenço Marques e Circunscrições de Marracuene e Maputo," 1950, 204, Inspecção dos Serviços Administrativos e dos Negócios Indígenas, Colónia de Moçambique, AHM/ISANI/cx 1. A similar recommendation was made by another official four years later. Abílio Mendes Gil, "Relatório da inspecção ordinária ao Concelho de Lourenço Marques e Circunscrições do Maputo e Marracuene," 1954, 218, Inspecção dos Serviços Administrativos e dos Negócios Indígenas, Província de Moçambique, AHM/ISANI/cx. 2.

44. "Divisão administrativa—autoridades tradicionais—população (1969)," AHM/GDLM/cx. 162.

45. As Domingos points out, the vacuum in governance led many to resort to supernatural remedies to resolve their disputes. Domingos, *Football and Colonialism*, 66–67.

46. Lúcia Joaquim da Silveira interview.

47. Rita-Ferreira, "Os africanos de Lourenço Marques," 159.

48. Rita-Ferreira, 257–60. Nor would the civil courts have had the capacity to handle even a fraction of the complaints if they had been brought to the court-house. Rita-Ferreira made a comparison with the criminal courts, where only a quarter of criminal cases ended in a judgment between 1961 and 1968. One criminal investigator he knew of was responsible for fifteen hundred cases.

49. Pereira, "Relatório da inspecção ordinária ao Segundo Bairro," 5–8.

50. Rita-Ferreira, "Os africanos de Lourenço Marques," 159, 163.

51. Numerous (if randomly organized) examples of these work logs can be found in AHM/GDLM/cx. 358, among other places.

52. The word people use for the trunk—*mala*—is also used for a suitcase. For a discussion of "tin-trunk texts," see Karin Barber, ed., *Africa's Hidden Histories: Everyday Literacy and Making the Self* (Bloomington: Indiana University Press, 2006). For a discussion of the importance of bureaucratic ephemera to residents of informal settlements, see Matthew S. Hull, *Government of Paper: The Materiality of Bureaucracy in Urban Pakistan* (Berkeley: University of California Press, 2012).

53. See Lorena Rizzo, "Visual Aperture: Bureaucratic Systems of Identification, Photography and Personhood in Colonial Southern Africa," *History of Photography* 37, no. 3 (2013): 263–82.

54. Armando Guilundo, interview with author, May 7, 2011. The landlord was a cantineiro, and it appears he issued the same receipts for rental payments that he used for transactions at the cantina.

55. The cases were found in AHM/DSNI/cx. 152. Other cases may exist, but those encountered in the archive suggest that housing cases were rare.

56. Processo 4773/A/43, AHM/DSNI/cx. 152.

57. Rita-Ferreira, "Os africanos de Lourenço Marques," 184.

58. Castigo Guambe interviews.

59. Manghezi, *O meu coração*, 163–210; Teresa Cruz e Silva, *Protestant Churches and the Formation of Political Consciousness in Southern Mozambique (1930–1974)* (Basel: P. Schlettwein, 2001), 123–24; José Manuel Duarte de Jesus, *Eduardo Mondlane: Um homem a abater* (Coimbra, Port.: Ediçoes Almedina, 2010), 95–105; Robert N. Faris, *Liberating Mission in Mozambique: Faith and Revolution in the Life of Eduardo Mondlane* (Eugene, OR: Pickwick Publications, 2014), 140–45.

60. Mondlane, *Struggle for Mozambique*, 68–69. Significant portions of Mondlane's book, a sweeping indictment of Portuguese rule published soon after his assassination in 1969, were based on his 1961 trip.

61. Faris, *Liberating Mission*, 140–43.

62. James Aggrey's parable also served as the basis of the final chapter of the 1950 book that Mondlane's mentor, missionary André-Daniel Clerc, had authored based on Mondlane's descriptions of his rural childhood. Clerc [and Mondlane], *Chitlangou*, 203–6; Cruz e Silva, *Protestant Churches*, 124; Vincent Dodoo, "Kwame Nkrumah's Mission and Vision for Africa and the World," *Journal of Pan African Studies* 4, no. 10 (2012): 82; Faris, *Liberating Mission*, 143–45.

63. Alfredo Nhanale, interview with author, June 6, 2011.

64. Filipe Ribeiro de Meneses, *Salazar: A Political Biography* (New York: Enigma Books, 2009), 504–12; Duarte de Jesus, *Eduardo Mondlane*, 95–105.

65. Meneses, *Salazar*, 460–509; Adriano Moreira, *Política ultramarina*, 3rd ed., Estudos de ciências políticas e sociais 1 (Lisbon: Junta de Investigações do Ultramar, Centro de Estudos Políticos e Sociais, 1960).

66. "Negro ou autóctone?" A *Tribuna*, November 7, 1962.

67. Castelo, *O modo português*.

68. Rita-Ferreira, "Os africanos de Lourenço Marques," 201–2.

69. Adriano Moreira, "Política de integração" *Estudos Ultramarinos*, no. 4 (1961): 7–22.

70. Mário de Oliveira, *Problemas essenciais do urbanismo no Ultramar: Estruturas urbanas de integração e convivência* (Lisbon: Agência-Geral do Ultramar, 1962); Ana Vaz Milheiro, *Nos trópicos sem Le Corbusier: Arquitectura luso-africana no Estado Novo* (Lisbon: Relógio D'Água, 2012), 348–54.

71. Oliveira, *Problemas essenciais*, 15.

72. Oliveira, 20.

73. Mário de Oliveira, "O 'habitat' nas zonas suburbanas de Quelimane: Um caso positivo de formação de sociedades multiraciais," *Geographica: Revista da Sociedade de Geografia de Lisboa*, no. 3 (1965): 67–75; Oliveira, "Relatório do arquitecto Mário de Oliveira da comissão eventual de serviço a Moçambique," March 3, 1966, Direcção dos Serviços de Urbanismo e Habitação, Direcção-Geral de Obras Públicas e Comunicações, Ministério do Ultramar, IPAD/no. 14419. See also Domingos, *Football and Colonialism*, 74–75.

74. Oliveira, "Relatório do arquitecto," 20.

75. Oliveira, *Problemas essenciais*, 13.

76. *Cafre*, the Portuguese equivalent of the slur *kaffir* (though without the same violent power), denoted something or someone not just essentially African but also inferior or savage as a result. There were many slurs that expressed a similar sentiment. The word nonetheless remains in use in some Mozambican expressions today, often with no greater sting than the word *native*. See Jochen S. Arndt, "What's in a Word? Historicising the Term 'Caffre' in European Discourses about Southern Africa between 1500 and 1800," *Journal of Southern African Studies* 44, no. 1 (2018): 59–75; Zamparoni, "Entre *narros* e *mulungos*," 398; Antoinette Errante, "White Skin, Many Masks: Colonial Schooling, Race, and National Consciousness among White Settler Children in Mozambique, 1934–1974," *International Journal of African Historical Studies* 36, no. 1 (2003): 22–24; Castelo, *Passagens para África*, 250–51; Cabaço, *Moçambique*, 185.

77. When residents of the Bairro da Munhuana (Bairro Indígena) were surveyed in 1963 by social workers about their housing preferences, the only ones to bring up the question of race or the possibility of multiracial communities were the social workers themselves. Residents were preoccupied with the terrible conditions

of their current housing, as will be discussed further. Centro de Estudos de Serviço Social e de Desenvolvimento Comunitário, *Inquérito habitacional realizado no Bairro da Munhuana*, Estudos de ciências políticas e sociais 72 (Lisbon: Junto do Instituto Superior de Ciências Sociais e Política Ultramarina, 1964).

78. Oliveira, "O 'habitat.'"

79. Penvenne, "Two Tales of a City," 259–60; Nuno Domingos, "A desigualdade como legado da cidade colonial: Racismo e reprodução de mão-de-obra em Lourenço Marques," in *Cidade e império: Dinâmicas coloniais e reconfigurações pós-coloniais*, ed. Nuno Domingos and Elsa Peralta (Lisbon: Edições 70, 2013), 68–75.

80. Rita-Ferreira, "Os africanos de Lourenço Marques."

81. The study was based on questionnaires distributed in the subúrbios by other researchers. João Pereira Neto, "Estudo sociológico do 'caniço,'" Plano Director de urbanização de Lourenço Marques, no. 48, Gabinete de Urbanização e Habitação da Região de Lourenço Marques, MITADER; João Pereira Neto, interview with author, November 26, 2010.

82. António Sopa, "Alguns aspectos do regime de censura prévia em Moçambique (1933–1975)," in *140 anos de imprensa em Moçambique*, ed. Fátima Ribeiro and António Sopa (Maputo: Associação Moçambicana da Língua Portuguesa, 1996), 95–97; Teresa de Sá Nogueira, "Uma mulher na informação moçambicana," in *140 anos de imprensa em Moçambique*, ed. Fátima Ribeiro and António Sopa (Maputo: Associação Moçambicana da Língua Portuguesa, 1996), 125–29; Fernando Magalhães, "Gouvêa Lemos: O homem que queria ser jornalista," in *140 anos de imprensa em Moçambique*, ed. Fátima Ribeiro and António Sopa (Maputo: Associação Moçambicana da Língua Portuguesa, 1996), 131–34; Ilídio Rocha, *A imprensa de Moçambique: História e catálogo* (Lisbon: Livros do Brasil, 2000), 193–98; Fátima Mendonça, "Dos confrontos ideológicos na imprensa em Moçambique," in *Os outros da colonização: Ensaios sobre o colonialismo tardio em Moçambique*, ed. Cláudia Castelo et al. (Lisbon: Imprensa de Ciências Sociais, 2012), 209–11; Drew A. Thompson, "Aim, Focus, Shoot: Photographic Narratives of War, Independence, and Imagination in Mozambique, 1950 to 1993" (PhD diss., University of Minnesota, 2013), 71–181.

83. Gouvêa Lemos, "Carta aos vereadores: LM = igual a 1/4 de cidade," *A Tribuna*, October 24, 1962.

84. Gouvêa Lemos, "Cartas aos vereadores," 3.

85. Ricardo Rangel, "Os primeiros passos de um fotojornalista famoso," in *140 anos de imprensa em Moçambique*, ed. Fátima Ribeiro and António Sopa (Maputo: Associação Moçambicana da Língua Portuguesa, 1996), 121–23; Thompson, "Aim, Focus, Shoot," 71–181.

86. "Falam os habitantes da 'cidade do caniço,'" *A Tribuna*, January 17, 1963, 2.

87. Albino Sive, "Escreve um leitor da cidade do caniço," *A Tribuna*, January 17, 1963, 3.

253

88. Pena, "Fogo."

89. "Falam os habitantes da 'cidade do caniço,'" A Tribuna, January 14, 1963, 2. *Promiscuidade* was frequently used to describe the perceived disorder and confusion of suburban life. As in English, the word also carries the connotation of sexual immorality. But the English *promiscuity* usually lacks the connotation of disorder.

90. It took him two attempts to get there. Colin Darch, "Armando Emílio Guebuza," in *Historical Dictionary of Mozambique* (Lanham, MD: Rowman and Littlefield, 2018), 180–81.

91. J. C., "Gente dos becos de caniço," A Tribuna, February 15, 1963.

92. Pancho Guedes, "A cidade doente," in *Manifestos, ensaios, falas, publicações* (Lisbon: Ordem dos Arquitectos, 2007), 30–33. See also Penvenne, "Two Tales of a City," 267–68; Domingos, *Football and Colonialism*, 73.

93. Miguel Santiago, *Pancho Guedes: Metamorfoses espaciais* (Casal de Cambra, Port.: Caleidoscópio, 2007); Pedro Guedes, ed., *Pancho Guedes: Vitruvius mozambicanus* (Lisbon: Museu Colecção Berardo, 2009); Guedes, ed., *As Áfricas de Pancho Guedes*.

94. Luís Bernardo Honwana, "Pancho Miranda Guedes," in *A velha casa de madeira e zinco*, 2nd ed. (Maputo: Alcance, 2017), 47–50; Honwana, "Comentário a 'Mecenas Desviante,'" in *A velha casa de madeira e zinco*, 2nd ed. (Maputo: Alcance, 2017), 51–52. See also Valente Matsinhe, interview with author, July 7, 2009; Matsinhe was with the Igreja Presbyteriana de Moçambique (formerly the Swiss Mission) and worked closely with Guedes on several projects.

95. Guedes, "Caniços of Mozambique." See also Pancho Guedes, interview with author, October 30, 2010.

96. Guedes, "A cidade doente," 30.

97. Guedes, 31.

98. Neves, [Ricardo] Rangel, and [Teresa de] Sá Nogueira, "Forja dos homens de amanhã," A Tribuna, August 3, 1963, 6–7; Sá Nogueira, "Uma mulher na informação moçambicana," 128.

99. Sopa, "Alguns aspectos"; José Capela, "A imprensa de Moçambique até a independência," in *140 anos de imprensa em Moçambique*, ed. Fátima Ribeiro and António Sopa (Maputo: Associação Moçambicana da Língua Portuguesa, 1996), 9–27; Mendonça, "Dos confrontos ideológicos."

100. Rocha, *A imprensa*, 268–69.

101. Teresa de Sá Nogueira and Ricardo Rangel, "O bairro das Lagoas," A Tribuna, September 22, 1963, 7.

102. Teresa Cruz e Silva, "A 'IV Região' da FRELIMO no sul de Moçambique: Lourenço Marques, 1964–1965," *Estudos moçambicanos*, no.8 (1990): 125–41; Mateus, A PIDE/DGS, 195; Matias Mboa, *Memórias da luta clandestina* (Maputo: Marimbique, 2009). Thanks to Colin Darch, all issues of *Estudos moçambicanos* are available online at www.mozambiquehistory.net.

103. Manuel Faria de Almeida, *Catembe*, film (Produções Cunha Telles, 1965), Arquivo Nacional das Imagens em Movimento (ANIM), Cinemateca Portuguesa, Bucelas, Portugal.

104. Mário Lopes, "A vida a preto e branco em Lourenço Marques que a censura não deixou ver," *Público*, January 16, 2013.

105. Only eleven minutes of censored material from the film survives, viewable at ANIM.

106. "Bairro residencial abandonado: No meio da desolação o capim é rei," *A Tribuna*, January 17, 1963.

107. Centro de Estudos de Serviço Social e de Desenvolvimento Comunitário, *Inquérito habitacional*, 11.

108. "Bairro residencial abandonado," 3.

109. Alvaro Chovane, "A extinção da cidade do caniço," *A Tribuna*, October 27, 1963; A. Samuel, "Rescaldo de um debate: 'Extinção da cidade do caniço,'" *A Tribuna*, October 28, 1963; Grupo Central de Trabalhos para o Problema Habitacional dos Económicamente Débeis, "O problema habitacional dos económicamente débeis," January 1964, ANTT/SCCIM/no. 84. See also Rita-Ferreira, "Os africanos de Lourenço Marques," 222; Domingos, *Football and Colonialism*, 74.

110. Chovane, "A extinção," 8.

111. For a fictional but vivid portrayal of how white *padrinhos* represented African *afilhados* (godchildren) in important matters, see João Paulo Borges Coelho, *As visitas do Dr. Valdez*, 3rd ed. (Maputo: Ndjira, 2010), 20. See also Penvenne, *African Workers*, 127.

112. Grupo Central de Trabalhos para o Problema Habitacional dos Económicamente Débeis, "O problema habitacional," 12–19.

113. Grupo Central de Trabalhos para o Problema Habitacional dos Económicamente Débeis, 15.

114. Mário de Azevedo, "O Plano Director de urbanização de Lourenço Marques (1969)," *Boletim Municipal da Câmara Municipal de Lourenço Marques*, no. 7 (December 31, 1969): 17–54.

115. Centro de Estudos de Serviço Social e de Desenvolvimento Comunitário, *Inquérito habitacional*.

116. Centro de Estudos de Serviço Social e de Desenvolvimento Comunitário, 11, 23.

117. Centro de Estudos de Serviço Social e de Desenvolvimento Comunitário, 111.

118. Centro de Estudos de Serviço Social e de Desenvolvimento Comunitário, 111.

119. Centro de Estudos de Serviço Social e de Desenvolvimento Comunitário, 118.

120. Centro de Estudos de Serviço Social e de Desenvolvimento Comunitário, 94.

121. Centro de Estudos de Serviço Social e de Desenvolvimento Comunitário, 95.

122. Centro de Estudos de Serviço Social e de Desenvolvimento Comunitário, 109.

123. Centro de Estudos de Serviço Social e de Desenvolvimento Comunitário, 112n11.

124. Centro de Estudos de Serviço Social e de Desenvolvimento Comunitário, 119–20.

125. Lília Maria Clara Carriére Momplé, "Relatório síntese do sector social," 1966, Junta dos Bairros e Casas Populares, MITADER.

126. Momplé, "Relatório síntese," 16.

127. Momplé, 7.

128. Momplé, 7. Momplé reported that the man later relaxed his stance and responded to the survey "after getting to know us better."

129. Momplé, 7.

130. Momplé, 11.

131. FRELIMO Departamento da Informação, "O Bairro Indígena," *Boletim de Informação*, February 1964, 7.

132. Momplé, "Relatório síntese," 11.

133. Momplé, 17.

134. Duffy, *Portugal in Africa*; C. R. Boxer, *Race Relations in the Portuguese Colonial Empire, 1415–1825* (Oxford: Clarendon Press, 1963); Mondlane, *Struggle for Mozambique*; Bender, *Angola under the Portuguese*; Isaacman, *Cotton Is the Mother of Poverty*; Cabaço, *Moçambique*.

135. W. G. Clarence-Smith, *The Third Portuguese Empire, 1825–1975: A Study in Economic Imperialism* (Manchester, UK: Manchester University Press, 1985), 192–221.

136. Frederick Cooper, *Decolonization and African Society: The Labor Question in French and British Africa* (Cambridge: Cambridge University Press, 1996); Cooper, *Africa since 1940: The Past of the Present* (New York: Cambridge University Press, 2002).

137. Cooper, *Decolonization*; Frederick Cooper, *Citizenship between Empire and Nation* (Princeton, NJ: Princeton University Press, 2014).

138. Scholars of Lusophone Africa have only recently begun to examine late colonialism beyond questions of oppression and nationalist mobilization. Todd Cleveland, *Following the Ball: The Migration of African Soccer Players across the Portuguese Colonial Empire, 1949–1975* (Athens: Ohio University Press, 2017); Cleveland, *Diamonds in the Rough: Corporate Paternalism and African Professionalism on the Mines of Colonial Angola, 1917–1975* (Athens: Ohio University Press, 2015); Havstad, "Multiracial Women and the African Press"; Domingos, *Football and Colonialism*.

139. See João Pereira Neto interview. In the early 1960s, Neto was one of the top officials at the Ministry of the Ultramar.

140. Penvenne, "Two Tales of a City," 265. The study, according to Penvenne, surveyed two hundred households in the neighborhood of Josefa.

Chapter 3: The Politics of Proximity

1. José Craveirinha, "Inclandestinidade," in *Cela 1* (Lisbon: Edições 70, 1980), 85.

2. The following account is based on photographs of the party kept in Daniel Malé's personal archives and information provided by Malé and Adelina Cossa

and by stonemason José Cossa: see Daniel Malé and Adelina Cossa, interviews with author, June 4 and 7, 2011, and José Inácio Cossa, interview with author, June 14, 2011.

3. The handwritten speech was kept for fifty years in the same envelope as Daniel Malé's photographs.

4. Governo-Geral da Província de Moçambique, Diploma Legislativo No. 616, arts. 5 and 6; Governo-Geral de Moçambique, Diploma Legislativo No. 1976, May 10, 1960, published in *Boletim Oficial de Moçambique (Suplemento)*, series 1, no. 19 (May 10, 1960): 497–511.

5. The most recent plan for Lourenço Marques had been produced in the 1950s by the colonial urbanization office, in Lisbon. João Aguiar, "Plano Geral de Urbanização de Lourenço Marques, vol. 1, Inquérito," 1955, IPAD/no. 13082; Aguiar, "Plano Geral de Urbanização de Lourenço Marques, vol. 2, Memória descritiva e justificativa," 1955, IPAD/no. 13083.

6. Registries for the obras clandestinas (clandestine constructions) files, which provide data for homeowner name, parcel, and lot, are located in the Departamento de Urbanização e Construção of the Conselho Municipal da Cidade de Maputo. If registries exist from before 1961 and from after mid-1971 until independence, I could not locate them. I sampled approximately 150 of the files themselves. They are archived at the municipal headquarters building, but staffers could only retrieve a handful of files at a time, and often none could be retrieved at all; thus, more files were not reviewed for this book. Case files will be cited by the colonial-era institution that created them—the Câmara Municipal de Lourenço Marques, Departamento de Serviços de Urbanização e Obras (CMLM-DSUO)—and by that department's coding system: [Case number]/ OC [obras clandestinas]/ [Year].

7. On slum clearance more generally, see Mayne, *Slums*, 89–191.

8. Rita-Ferreira, "Os africanos de Lourenço Marques," 192–95.

9. See also Ferguson, *Global Shadows*, 18–19, from which I quote in note 28 of the introduction.

10. Fourchard, "Between World History and State Formation."

11. Jeanne Marie Penvenne, "Mozambique: A Tapestry of Conflict," in *History of Central Africa: The Contemporary Years since 1960*, ed. David Birmingham and Phyllis Martin (London: Longman, 1998), 243–46; Penvenne, "Two Tales of a City," 256–57; Clarence-Smith, *Third Portuguese Empire, 1825–1975*, 192–223; Malyn Newitt, "The Late Colonial State in Portuguese Africa," *Itinerario* 23, no. 3–4 (1999): 110–22; Amorim Remigio Manuel Pery, "A evolução da economia moçambicana e a promoção do bem-estar socioeconómico (1960–2001)" (undergraduate thesis, Universidade Eduardo Mondlane, 2004); Victor Pereira, "A economia do império e os planos de fomento," in *O império colonial em questão (séculos XIX–XX): Poderes, saberes e instituições*, ed. Miguel Bandeira Jerónimo (Lisbon: Edições 70, 2012), 251–85; Kagan Guthrie, "'This Was Being Done Only to Help.'"

257

12. Jeanne Marie Penvenne, "Settling against the Tide: The Layered Contradictions of Twentieth-Century Portuguese Settlement in Mozambique," in *Settler Colonialism in the Twentieth Century: Projects, Practices, Legacies*, ed. Caroline Elkins and Susan Pedersen (New York: Taylor and Francis, 2005), 79–94; Castelo, *Passagens para África*, 107–61.

13. The figures are for legal permanent construction by private entities in the city and its subúrbios: 7,877 household units from 1959 through 1967 versus 7,610 units from the nineteenth century through 1958. Câmara Municipal de Lourenço Marques, Direcção dos Serviços de Urbanização e Obras, "Número total de edifícios particulares de alvenaria existentes na cidade de Lourenço Marques e subúrbios, até 31 de Dezembro de 1969," folder entitled "Diários de Serviço 1968–1971," AHM/GDLM/cx. 361.

14. Luís Filipe Ranito Catalão, "Providências tendentes a desenvolver a industrialização da construção de edifícios de habitação e a aumentar a sua produtividade," in *Primeiras jornadas de engenharia de Moçambique: 25 a 30 de Abril de 1965—Comunicações* (Lourenço Marques, 1965), 350–57.

15. Rita-Ferreira, "Os africanos de Lourenço Marques," 157.

16. Rita-Ferreira, 342.

17. Penvenne, "Two Tales of a City," 262–63.

18. Women were recruited for work in cashew-processing facilities, for instance, because they were considered easier to exploit. Penvenne, "Seeking the Factory for Women," 356–57; Penvenne, *Women, Migration and the Cashew Economy*.

19. "Africanos!" [advertisement], *A Tribuna*, August 4, 1963, 21.

20. Albino Magaia, "Bairro do Triunfo: O gato não quer mostrar o rabo," *Tempo*, August 5, 1973.

21. Rita-Ferreira, "Os africanos de Lourenço Marques," 211–22.

22. See Lage, "Building of Informal Dwellings"; Ana Magaia interview, February 18, 2011.

23. Lage emphasized the practicality of "fan"-patterned roof inclines. (From above, the roof looks like a fan.) Such a plan accommodates room-by-room incremental construction.

24. Ana Magaia interview.

25. José Inácio Cossa interview.

26. The account that follows is based on information provided by Tembe: see Jaime Tembe, interviews with author, April 30, May 9, and May 11, 2011.

27. The cousin was Bartolomeu Tembe, who appears in this book several times in several different roles.

28. Penvenne, "Seeking the Factory for Women," 368.

29. This information was provided by Maduela and her daughter: see Josefa Alfonso Maduela and Isabel de Conceição Maduela, interview with author, June 4, 2016.

30. *Xicolone* is a Ronga version of *colono*, a catch-all term for Portuguese settlers.

31. Penvenne, *African Workers*, 127.

32. Nielsen, "In the Vicinity of the State," 157.

33. As noted in the book's introduction, however, people in reed houses sometimes painted their doors and wood trim in colorful patterns.

34. Rita Chaves, "José Craveirinha, da Mafalala, de Moçambique, do mundo," *Via Atlântica*, no. 3 (1999): 140–68; Nataniel Ngomane, "José Craveirinha: Nota biobibliográfica," *Via Atlântica*, no. 5 (2002): 14–18.

35. José Craveirinha, "Ao meu belo pai ex-emigrante," in *Karingana ua karingana* (Maputo: Instituto Nacional do Livro e do Disco, 1982), 107–10. The poem was written in 1958. See also "Na morte do meu Tio António segunda elegia a meu pai," in *Karingana ua karingana*, 76–77.

36. José Craveirinha, "A população dos subúrbios, a habitação e a higiene," *O Brado Africano*, February 5, 1955, 1. See also Craveirinha, "Uma presença que é necessario olhar com simpatia," *O Brado Africano*, February 19, 1955.

37. Craveirinha, "Uma presença," 2.

38. "Crianças na sucata," *A Tribuna*, October 16, 1962, sec. 2.

39. J. C., "Gente dos becos de caniço," 2.

40. Cabaço, *Moçambique*, 212.

41. Penvenne, "Fotografando Lourenço Marques," 182.

42. Errante, "White Skin, Many Masks"; Castelo, *Passagens para África*, 263–66.

43. Castelo, *Passagens para África*, 285.

44. Castelo, 287–88.

45. Quoted in Castelo, 287.

46. Errante uses the term *artificial homogenization*. Errante, "White Skin, Many Masks," 14.

47. Cabaço, *Moçambique*, 211–12.

48. Castelo, *Passagens para África*, 352; Cabaço, *Moçambique*, 220.

49. Afonso Ramos, "Angola 1961, o horror das imagens," in *O império da visão: Fotografia no contexto colonial (1860–1960)*, ed. Filipa Lowndes Vicente (Lisbon: Edições 70, 2014), 399–434.

50. Eugénio Lisboa, *Acta est fabula—Memórias*, vol. 3, *Lourenço Marques Revisited, 1955–1976* (Guimarães, Port.: Opera Omnia, 2013), 129. Lisboa's memoirs record his own shock at the gruesomeness of the guerrilla attacks, but he registers no reaction to the reprisals that followed. White civilian militias and Portuguese forces killed tens of thousands of Angolans that year.

51. Castelo, *Passagens para África*, 274–75; Cabaço, *Moçambique*, 163.

52. Castelo, *Passagens para África*, 359–61.

53. Cabaço, *Moçambique*, 220.

54. "Os habitantes do bairro clandestino do aeroporto defendem o seu direito a um tecto," *A Tribuna*, November 21, 1967; "Bairro do Aeroporto: A mais definitiva das situações precárias," *Tempo*, May 9, 1971.

55. Lindo Nhlongo, interview with author, May 3, 2013.

56. Moreira, "Política de integração."

57. Governo-Geral de Mozambique, Diploma Legislativo no. 1976.

58. Morais, *Maputo*, 156.

59. J. M., "Edilidade, progresso, clandestinidades, terrenos, etc.," *A Tribuna*, March 24, 1963. For a response, see António Manuel Ralha, "O bairro do Aeroporto continua a dar que falar . . . ," *A Tribuna*, May 3, 1963.

60. Tiago Castela, "A Liberal Space: A History of the Illegalized Working-Class Extensions of Lisbon" (PhD diss., University of California–Berkeley, 2011). See also Abílio S. Cardoso, *The Illegal Housing Sector in Portugal: Bairros Clandestinos*, Geographical Papers (Reading, UK: Department of Geography, University of Reading, 1983).

61. In Luanda in the early 1970s, there was a similar controversy involving clandestine construction by working-class whites. Moorman, *Intonations*, 42–43.

62. Morais, *Maputo*, 160–61.

63. On the "poor white problem" in other settler-colonial contexts see Anne Laura Stoler, "Rethinking Colonial Categories: European Communities and the Boundaries of Rule," *Comparative Studies in Society and History* 31, no. 1 (1989): 134–61; Will Jackson, "White Man's Country: Kenya Colony and the Making of a Myth," *Journal of East African Studies* 5, no. 2 (2011): 344–68. Gary Minkley discusses the threat that "in-between" spaces posed to white municipal officials in East London, South Africa. Minkley, "'Corpses behind Screens': Native Space in the City," in *Blank: Architecture, Apartheid, and After*, ed. Hilton Judin and Ivan Vladislavić (Rotterdam: NAi Publishers, 1999), 202–19.

64. "Pensamentos. . . . O bairro clandestino," *O Brado Africano*, May 9, 1964.

65. Cruz e Silva, "A 'IV Região' da FRELIMO."

66. On legibility-illegibility relative to state power, see James C. Scott, *Seeing Like a State: How Certain Schemes to Improve the Human Condition Have Failed* (New Haven, CT: Yale University Press, 1998), 9–83.

67. CMLM-DSUO 10/OC/63, "Joaquim da Costa."

68. Perhaps this was comparable to the reproach directed at those "who feed only themselves," an idiom used in northern Mozambique. Harry G. West, *Kupilikula: Governance and the Invisible Realm in Mozambique* (Chicago: University of Chicago Press, 2005), 35–39. I thank Jeanne Penvenne for the reference. Morten Nielsen has described how newly built houses in contemporary Maputo allow their builders to "hide their heads" in a way that reeds, because they are more permeable, cannot. By shielding one's personal affairs from neighbors, one can avoid making them envious about what one has, and thus safeguard oneself against potential witchcraft reprisals. Decades ago, however, building a masonry house was not so common, and building one would have provoked jealousies, not hidden potential sources of it. Nielsen, "In the Vicinity of the State," 129.

69. "Candonga de fósforos," *Tempo*, July 29, 1973; "Mercado negro de moeda estrangeira em Moçambique," *Tempo*, August 19, 1973; Mário Lindolfo, "Escape livre no contrabando de automóveis," *Tempo*, September 16, 1973; Calane da Silva,

"Vinho clandestino: Candongueiros em guerra aberta," *Tempo*, April 22, 1973; Albino Magaia, "Ilegalidade e a ineficiência prejudicam o turismo," *Tempo*, May 6, 1973; Calane da Silva, "Motoristas e taxeiros piratas em pé de guerra," *Tempo*, June 24, 1973; "Contrabando nas boutiques," *Tempo*, March 18, 1973; Ribeiro Pacheco, "O mundo fechado do pano verde," *Tempo*, October 14, 1973.

70. Areosa Pena, "Construtores civis em luta pela legalidade," *Tempo*, February 25, 1973.

71. Rui Cartaxana, "A 'lei' do chapéu na mão," *Tempo*, September 16, 1973, 80.

72. For the aspirational, work-in-progress nature of colonial states, see Comaroff, "Reflections on the Colonial State."

73. Domingos Ozias, interview with author, September 13, 2012. Ozias worked for the municipality in the late colonial era, including a year's stint in the building inspection office.

74. Lúcia Joaquim da Silveira interview.

75. CMLM-DSUO 163/OC/63, "Ricardo Niquisse."

76. CMLM-DSUO 243/OC/66, "António Almone."

77. CMLM-DSUO 36/OC/65, "Alice Malendya."

78. For the meanings of *cafreal* and *cafrealização*, see note 76 in chapter 2.

79. CMLM-DSUO 75/OC/64, "António Samora Sebanhana."

80. CMLM-DSUO 164/OC/63, "Inácio Manjate 'Mazino.'"

81. CMLM-DSUO 283/OC/68, "Daniel Malé."

82. Handwritten speech provided by Malé.

83. That was the fourth class, a level few black Mozambicans were given an opportunity to achieve. CMLM-DSUO 96/OC/64, "Bernardo Ernesto Mário."

84. CMLM-DSUO 272/OC/66, "Essau Ezequia Maninguane."

85. Moreira, "Política de integração."

86. CMLM-DSUO 250/OC/66, "Jossias Filimão Pondeca."

87. CMLM-DSUO 93/OC/65, "Fernando Andreas Miglietti"; CMLM-DSUO 23/OC/68, "Felisberto Elías Pondeca."

88. Rita-Ferreira, "Os africanos de Lourenço Marques," 187.

89. Rita-Ferreira, 167–69, 187.

90. Câmara Municipal de Lourenço Marques, Edital 3/65, April 13, 1965, a legal alteration that appeared in local newspapers. The wording of the Edital also appeared in the case files themselves (which is where I consulted it).

91. Rita-Ferreira, "Os africanos de Lourenço Marques," 192; Pereira, "Relatório da inspecção ordinária ao Segundo Bairro," 137.

92. Cabaço, *Moçambique*, 221.

93. João Pereira Neto interview.

94. Castelo, *Passagens para África*, 284.

95. Areosa Pena, "Não reservado o direito de admissão," *Tempo*, April 18, 1971.

96. "Balanço de 4 anos: Que fizeram (ou puderam fazer) os 'homens-bons' de Lourenço Marques," *Tempo*, October 8, 1972.

97. "Vereação: Quatro anos ou pouco tempo para fazer muito," *Tempo*, October 22, 1972, 19.

98. Marcelo Rebelo de Sousa, *Baltazar Rebelo de Sousa: Fotobiografia*, 2nd ed. (Venda Nova, Port.: Bertrand Editora, 1999), 182–277; Amélia Neves de Souto, *Caetano e o ocaso do "Império": Administração e guerra colonial em Moçambique durante o Marcelismo (1968–1974)* (Porto: Edições Afrontamento, 2007), 120–22; Lisboa, *Acta est fabula*, 3: 398–400.

99. The governor set an example for his friend Marcelo Caetano, who succeeded Salazar as prime minister shortly after Rebelo de Sousa's posting to Mozambique and who sought a limited opening of the regime to opposition voices. Hard-liners ensured that the "Marcelista Spring" did not last long.

100. Notations in the "clandestine constructions" files indicate that the Office of the Caniço, officially the Gabinete de Urbanização e Habitação da Região de Lourenço Marques (GUHRLM), began taking a role in the regularization of clandestine construction in the early 1970s, perhaps explaining why the municipal registries of clandestine works halt in 1971. City officials told reporters in 1972 that GUHRLM was now solely responsible for the subúrbios, so perhaps later files are stored at MITADER, which houses the GUHRLM archives. Unfortunately, these archives are not well organized, and I could not find such files there. Mendes de Oliveira, "O presidente da C.M.L.M. presta contas aos munícipes," *Tempo*, July 23, 1972, 68.

101. CMLM-DSUO 341/OC/66, "Malangatana Valente Ngwenya." It appears the house was only regularized in 1982, well after independence.

102. Rebelo de Sousa, *Baltazar Rebelo de Sousa*, 215.

103. Santiago, *Pancho Guedes*, 109–10; Pancho Guedes interview.

104. Honwana, *Life History of Raúl Honwana*, 96.

105. Alfredo Manjate, interview with author, February 15, 2011.

106. Commercial establishments were legally required to build in concrete, but to avoid the time-consuming approvals process, many merchants in the subúrbios built their shops, illegally, in a single weekend—and afterward paid the requisite fine. Alfredo Nhanale, interview with author, June 6, 2011.

107. Gastrow, "Cement Citizens," 233.

108. Ingemar Sävfors, *Maxaquene: A Comprehensive Account of the First Urban Upgrading Experience in the New Mozambique* (UNESCO, 1986), 10.

109. Sävfors, *Maxaquene*, 17.

110. Mário Ângelo, "A indústria de cimento no contexto de transição moçambicana, c. 1960–1994, com referência especial à Fábrica de Cimentos da Matola" (undergraduate thesis, Universidade Eduardo Mondlane, 2005).

Chapter 4: An Immovable Legacy

1. Sebastião Chitombe, interviews with author, May 4, 9, and 16 and September 17, 2011.

2. By early 1975, 80,000 Europeans had left out of what had been a total population of between 120,000 and 160,000 (figures vary). Margaret Hall and Tom Young, *Confronting Leviathan: Mozambique since Independence* (London: C. Hurst, 1997), 45; António Rita-Ferreira, "Moçambique post–25 de Abril: Causas do êxodo da população de origem europeia e asiática," in *Moçambique: Cultura e história de um país*, Publicações do Centro de Estudos Africanos 8 (Coimbra, Port.: Universidade de Coimbra, 1988), 122.

3. Machel, "Independência implica benefícios," 69.

4. The Maputo River flows into what is now called the Bay of Maputo but not through the capital itself; nor is the former chiefdom that gave the river its name particularly close to the capital. However, the phrase "from the Rovuma to the Maputo," evoking a Mozambique united from its northernmost river to its southernmost river, was a Frelimo slogan during the war and featured in Mozambique's national anthem.

5. Otto Greger, "Angola," in *Housing Policies in the Socialist Third World*, ed. Kosta Mathéy (Munich: Profil, 1990), 129–45; Djaffar Lesbet, "Algeria," in *Housing Policies in the Socialist Third World*, ed. Kosta Mathéy (Munich: Profil, 1990), 249–73. These cities are notable for the scale and abruptness of white emigration, but comparisons could also be made to the larger cities of Zimbabwe, the Republic of the Congo-Léopoldville (today's Democratic Republic of the Congo), and Kenya, among others.

6. Extrapolated from the 1970 census data published in Serviços de Centralização e Coordenação de Informações de Moçambique, *Moçambique na actualidade*, 39.

7. Hall and Young, *Confronting Leviathan*, 50.

8. Madani Safar Zitoun, "Les stratégies résidentielles des acteurs sociaux dans un contexte de modernisation bloquée: Alger 1962–1998," in *La ville et l'urbain dans le monde arabe et en Europe: Acteurs, organisations et territoires*, ed. Pierre Robert Baduel (Tunis: Institut de Recherche sur le Maghreb Contemporain, 2009), 109–33; Brennan, *Taifa*, 189–94.

9. Gastrow, "Negotiated Settlements," 58–60.

10. Elias Yitbarek Alemayehu, "Revisiting 'Slums,' Revealing Responses: Urban Upgrading in Tenant-Dominated Inner-City Settlements, in Addis Ababa, Ethiopia" (PhD diss., Norwegian University of Science and Technology, 2008), 83–84.

11. Júlio Carrilho, interviews with author, July 29, 2009, and June 5, 2012 (Carrilho was minister of public works and housing in the first independence-era cabinet). For a later period, see João Paulo Borges Coelho, "Antigos soldados, novos cidadãos: A reintegração dos desmobilizados de Maputo," *Estudos moçambicanos*, no. 20 (2002): 168n20.

12. Nightingale, *Segregation*, 402–9. For somewhat different approaches to the issue, see also Cristina Udelsmann Rodrigues, "Angolan Cities: Urban (Re)Segregation?" in *African Cities: Competing Claims on Urban Spaces*, ed. Francesca

263

264

Locatelli and Paul Nugent (Leiden: Brill, 2009), 37–54; Freek Colombijn, *Under Construction: The Politics of Urban Space and Housing during the Decolonization of Indonesia, 1930–1960* (Leiden: KITLV Press, 2010).

13. A housing preference survey in 1967 registered similar concerns by suburban residents. Rita-Ferreira, "Os africanos de Lourenço Marques," 169–77.

14. Significant contributions include (but are not limited to): Barry Munslow, *Mozambique: The Revolution and Its Origins* (London: Longman, 1983); Alan Isaacman and Barbara Isaacman, *Mozambique: From Colonialism to Revolution, 1900–1982* (Boulder, CO: Westview Press, 1983); Joseph Hanlon, *Mozambique: The Revolution under Fire* (London: Zed Books, 1984); John S. Saul, ed., *A Difficult Road: The Transition to Socialism in Mozambique* (New York: Monthly Review Press, 1985); Michel Cahen, *Mozambique, la revolution implosée: Études sur 12 ans d'indépendance, 1975–1987* (Paris: L'Harmattan, 1987); Christian Geffray, *A causa das armas: Antropologia da guerra contemporânea em Moçambique*, trans. Adelaide Odete Ferreira (Porto: Edições Afrontamento, 1991); Hall and Young, *Confronting Leviathan*; M. Anne Pitcher, *Transforming Mozambique: The Politics of Privatization, 1975–2000* (Cambridge: Cambridge University Press, 2002); Yussuf Adam, *Escapar aos dentes do crocodile e cair na boca do leopardo: Trajectória de Moçambique pós-colonial (1975–1990)* (Maputo: Promédia, 2006); Alice Dinerman, *Revolution, Counter-revolution, and Revisionism in Postcolonial Africa: The Case of Mozambique, 1975–1994* (London: Routledge, 2006).

15. State structures were hard to distinguish from party structures. When I refer to Frelimo I will be talking about both state and party, making the distinction when necessary between the regime's Central Committee and the state bureaucracy.

16. This is not to say that in rural areas people were not also interpreting Frelimo policies for themselves. They undoubtedly were. Pitcher, *Transforming Mozambique*, 97.

17. António de Almeida Santos, *Quinze meses no governo ao serviço da descolonização* (Porto: Ediçoes ASA, 1975); Rita-Ferreira, "Moçambique post–25 de Abril," 125–32; Norrie Macqueen, *The Decolonization of Portuguese Africa: Metropolitan Revolution and the Dissolution of Empire* (London: Longman, 1997), 124–57; Fernando Amado Couto, *Moçambique 1974: O fim do império e o nascimento da nação* (Maputo: Texto Editores, 2011), 314–18.

18. Couto, *Moçambique 1974*, 321–24; Isabella Oliveira, M. & U., *Companhia Ilimitada* (Porto: Edições Afrontamento, 1999); Dinis Marques interviews.

19. Cruz e Silva, "A 'IV Região' da FRELIMO."

20. Clothilde Mesquitela, *Sete de Setembro: Memórias da revolução* (Lisbon: A Rua, 1977); Rita-Ferreira, "Moçambique post–25 de Abril," 132–34; Couto, *Moçambique 1974*, 425–43; Ribeiro Cardoso, *O fim do império: Memória de um soldado português—O 7 de Setembro de 1974 em Lourenço Marques*, 2nd ed. (Alfragide, Port.: Caminho, 2014); Aurélio Le Bon, *Mafalala 1974: Memórias do 7 de Setembro—A grande operação* (Maputo: Movimento Editora, 2015); Benedito Machava,

"Galo amanheceu em Lourenço Marques: O 7 de Setembro e o verso da descolonização de Moçambique," *Revista Crítica de Ciências Sociais* 106 (2015): 53–84. There is some question as to how premeditated the revolt was. It appears to have been planned, but planned very badly.

21. Sérgio José da Costa interviews. The Xibinhana cantina, perhaps the only one in Chamanculo dating from the colonial era still under the same family ownership today, is described in chapter 1.

22. Frederico's rule is discussed at length in chapter 2. The following account is based on information provided by his daughter: see Ana Laura Cumba interview.

23. Matusse, "Chamanculo."

24. As one might expect, estimates of the number killed vary widely. The official number of fatalities was 82, but most accounts suggest the toll was much higher. Reporters at the time put it between 1,500 and 3,000. Victor Crespo, who arrived in Mozambique just after the revolt as Portugal's high commissioner, later suggested to journalist Ribeiro Cardoso that it was "many hundreds." Rita-Ferreira, "Moçambique post–25 de Abril," 134; Cardoso, *O fim*, 303; Le Bon, *Mafalala 1974*, 110–12.

25. Carlos Camilo, "Moçambique. Os acontecimentos de 7 de Setembro e 21 de Outubro de 1974," in *Seminário "25 de Abril 10 anos depois"* (Lisbon: Associação 25 de Abril, 1985), 341–43; Rita-Ferreira, "Moçambique post–25 de Abril," 136–38; Macqueen, *The Decolonization of Portuguese Africa*, 151; Couto, *Moçambique 1974*, 451–52.

26. Sérgio Vieira, *Participei, por isso testemunho* (Maputo: Ndjira, 2011), 671.

27. People had been leaving in numbers for some years already. As Thomaz and Nascimento pointed out, net migration to the province was negative in 1971 for the first time in years. Also, thousands of members of the local Ismaili community began leaving in 1973, following an order by the Aga Khan. Whether it was fear of a Frelimo victory that motivated the order is unclear, but that year, Idi Amin had expelled Uganda's ethnic South Asians, two years after Tanzania had dispossessed many of its own South Asian citizens. In Mozambique itself, Portugal detained and then expelled "British Indians" in 1961 in retaliation for India's annexation of Goa. Omar Ribeiro Thomaz and Sebastião Nascimento, "Nem Rodésia, nem Congo: Moçambique e os dias do fim das comunidades de origem europeia e asiática," in *Os outros da colonização: Ensaios sobre o colonialismo tardio em Moçambique*, ed. Cláudia Castelo et al. (Lisbon: Imprensa de Ciências Sociais, 2012), 323–26.

28. Rita-Ferreira, "Moçambique post–25 de Abril," 127–28.

29. Benedito Luís Machava, "The Morality of Revolution: Urban Cleanup Campaigns, Reeducation Camps, and Citizenship in Socialist Mozambique (1974–1988)" (PhD diss., University of Michigan, 2018).

30. Rita-Ferreira, 141–45. For a more in-depth take on Machel's weeks-long journey, see Colin Darch and David Hedges, "Political Rhetoric in the Transition to Mozambican Independence: Samora Machel in Beira, June 1975," *Kronos* 39

(2013): 32–65. The authors offered an incredibly nuanced reading of one of the speeches he made during the trip, in Mozambique's second-largest city.

31. Amélia Neves de Souto, "Moçambique, descolonização e transição para independência: Herança e memória," in *O adeus ao império: 40 anos de descolonização portuguesa*, ed. Fernando Rosas, Mário Machaqueiro, and Pedro Aires Oliveira (Lisbon: Vega, 2015), 150.

32. Frelimo also spoke of the "national bourgeoisie," meaning mestiços and assmilados.

33. Having one child adopt Mozambican nationality was a strategy for departing families who hoped to maintain a foothold in the country as they waited to see how events played out, as Colin Darch mentioned to me in correspondence.

34. Alfredo Manjate, interview with author, September 17, 2011.

35. Mendes da Oliveira, "Manter os 'escritos' ou baixar as rendas," *Tempo*, December 15, 1974.

36. Oliveira, "Manter os 'escritos,'" 41.

37. On squatting and the "right to the city," see Alexander Vasudevan, *The Autonomous City: A History of Urban Squatting* (London: Verso, 2017).

38. Gillian Walt, "The Evolution of Health Policy," in *Mozambique: Towards a People's Health Service*, ed. Gillian Walt and Angela Melamed (London: Zed Books, 1984), 2.

39. Darch and Hedges, "Political Rhetoric," 50–56.

40. Hall and Young, *Confronting Leviathan*, 49–50.

41. Carol Barker, "Bringing Health Care to the People," in *A Difficult Road: The Transition to Socialism in Mozambique*, ed. John S. Saul (New York: Monthly Review Press, 1985), 323.

42. Samora Machel, "A nossa luta é uma revolução," in *A nossa luta é uma revolução: Nacionalizações—Moçambique* (Lisbon: CIDA-C, 1976), 7–32; Rita-Ferreira, "Moçambique post–25 de Abril," 145–48; Hanlon, *Mozambique*, 46–47.

43. The nationalizations occurred one hundred years to the day after the Bay of Lourenço Marques was definitively declared in international arbitration to be a Portuguese possession, a date important enough in city history that one of the city's principal avenues was named for it. When the colonial era names of Maputo's streets were changed to reflect new heroes, such as Vladimir Lenin, Karl Marx, Mao Tse-tung, and Eduardo Mondlane, Avenida 24 de Julho kept its name, but marble slabs were installed beside sidewalks that explained its new meaning as the "Day of the Nationalizations." The Day of the Nationalizations was celebrated annually in the first decade or so after independence, and though the nationalizations of rental properties occurred on a much later date, for the sake of official commemoration it was bundled in official memory with the Frelimo "achievements" of July 24, 1975, as if it had been planned from the beginning. The Portuguese word meaning "achievement," *conquista*, can also be translated as "conquest."

44. Hélder Martins, interview with author, June 18, 2016. Martins was the minister of health in 1975 when funeral services became part of his portfolio.

45. On what Anne Pitcher calls Frelimo's "tactical transition," see Pitcher, *Transforming Mozambique*, 37–43.

46. Machava, "The Morality of Revolution"; Machava, "State Discourse on Internal Security and the Politics of Punishment in Post-independence Mozambique (1975–1983)," *Journal of Southern African Studies* 37, no. 3 (2011), 593–609.

47. See chapter 1.

48. "Agrava-se no país problema das cheias," *Notícias*, January 30, 1976; "Redobremos esforço colectivo na produção e planeamento," *Notícias*, February 1, 1976; "Presidente Samora Machel contacta populações afectadas," *Notícias*, February 3, 1976.

49. The trio consisted of the minister of public works and housing, the minister of justice, and the minister of finance. Much of the following narrative derives from interviews with the former longtime minister of public works and housing: see Carrilho interviews.

50. Article 2 of Mozambique's first constitution dedicated the state to the "construction of a new society, free from the exploitation of man by man." Constituição da República Popular de Moçambique, which appears in *Principal legislação promulgada pelo governo da República Popular de Moçambique*, vol. 3 (Maputo: Imprensa Nacional de Moçambique, 1976), 3.

51. The order was published as Decreto-Lei No. 5/76, February 5, 1976, which appears in *Principal legislação promulgada pelo governo*, vol. 3, 125–30. The measure led even more people to leave the country, but according to Rita-Ferreira it was not the decisive factor that many take it to be, given how few major property owners there were. The average building owner in cities of cement had a single apartment block of perhaps only four units; many such buildings belonged to retirees (who lived in one of the units) for whom rental income served as a kind of pension. The legislation ensured that those who relied on rental income in this way were entitled to a monthly indemnification that, given the costs of running a building, was roughly comparable to the lost income. (Not to mention that the buildings were generally highly mortgaged, and thus owners did not stand to lose much equity.) A fierce critic of Frelimo, Rita-Ferreira nonetheless described the housing nationalizations as an "inevitable" measure. "No sovereign state that prizes its economic independence could permit that its cities continue to belong to a minority of foreigners, most of them absent from the country." The Marxist scholar Michel Cahen argued that the housing nationalizations were a "typical means" of weakening a local "petite bourgeoisie"—he highlighted landlords of South Asian descent remaining in Mozambique—who might rival the regime for power. Rita-Ferreira, "Moçambique post–25 de Abril," 153; Cahen, "Check on Socialism in Mozambique: What Check? What Socialism?," *Review of the African Political Economy* 57 (1993): 51.

267

52. Machel, "Independência implica benefícios," 60.

53. Cahen criticized Frelimo for never having been socialist at all, but rather a power-hungry cabal of urban elites who merely spoke the language of Marxism. Cahen, "Check on Socialism."

54. Maria Clara Mendes, "Les répercussions de l'indépendance sur la ville de Maputo," in *Bourgs et villes en Afrique lusophone*, ed. Michel Cahen (Paris: Editions L'Harmattan, 1989), 281–96; J. D. Sidaway and M. Power, "Sociospatial Transformations in the 'Postsocialist' Periphery: The Case of Maputo, Mozambique," *Environment and Planning* A 27, no. 9 (1995): 1472–75.

55. Officials considered the progressive rent structure the equivalent of an income tax. Direcção-Geral, APIE, "Fundamentação, Semanário Nacional sobre Novas Rendas," November 21, 1987, MITADER.

56. By 1980, there were twenty-four thousand unfulfilled requests for housing in Maputo, and APIE was only able to furnish thirty units per month. Luís David, "Mais de onze mil inquilinos não pagam renda de casa," *Tempo*, December 7, 1980, 14.

57. The figure actually measured the percentage of working-class households with electricity and running water. Most people living with such amenities resided in one of the country's cities of cement. Júlio Carrilho, "Ajustar as rendas ao valor das casas," *Tempo*, October 4, 1987, 27.

58. "Iniciadas medidas de emergência para socorrer populações atingidas," *Notícias*, February 7, 1977. Within the week, more than fourteen hundred of the families were reportedly given shelter in the City of Cement.

59. One is left to wonder whether there were officials telling people that furniture was required to live in buildings.

60. Helena Macuacua, interviews with author, July 2 and 6, 2009.

61. Benjamim Benfica, interview with author, September 30, 2011.

62. The law permitted a second house if it was located in the countryside or at the beach.

63. Júlio Carrilho interviews.

64. Munslow, *Mozambique: The Revolution*, 151–53; Isaacman and Isaacman, *Mozambique: From Colonialism to Revolution*, 116–21; Barry Pinsky, "Territorial Dilemmas: Changing Urban Life," in *A Difficult Road: The Transition to Socialism in Mozambique*, ed. John S. Saul (New York: Monthly Review Press, 1985), 288–306; Bertil Egerö, *Mozambique: The Dream Undone—The Political Economy of Democracy* (Uppsala: Nordiska Afrikainstitutet, 1987), 65–72; Jeremy Grest, "Urban Management, Local Government Reform, and the Democratisation Process in Mozambique: Maputo City 1975–1990," *Journal of Southern African Studies* 21, no. 1 (1995): 147–64. Six former GD members were interviewed for this book: Benjamim Benfica, September 30, 2011, and June 14, 2012, Adriano Matate, November 18 and 21 and December 5, 2011, and Gabriel Chiau, June 21, 2011 (all in Chamanculo); Augusto Duvane and Salomão Manjate, March 23, 2013 (in

Maxaquene C); Lídia Massinge, March 25, 2013 (in Polana Caniço A). (Massinge served as the mandatory representative in her GD of the Mozambican women's organization, the OMM.)

65. "Comités e grupos dinamizadores: Da crítica à autocrítica a prática forja o militante," *Tempo*, March 2, 1975, 62.

66. Events confirmed by Maputo's onetime APIE chief (and later government minister) José Chichava: "Devemos defender nossas conquistas alcançadas com a independencia—exorta José Chichava," *Notícias*, July 23, 2011.

67. Zitoun, "Stratégies résidentielles"; Gastrow, "Negotiated Settlements," 58–60; Brennan, *Taifa*, 189–95.

68. Brennan, *Taifa*, 191.

69. Alemayehu, "Revisiting 'Slums,'" 83–84.

70. In Portuguese, the State Real Estate Administration. The figure for nationalized units is from Paul Jenkins, "Mozambique," in *Housing Policies in the Socialist Third World*, ed. Kosta Mathéy (Munich: Profil, 1990), 168.

71. "Cidade do caniço: Realidades novas no reino da miséria," *Tempo*, February 22, 1976, 29.

72. Albertina Amaral, interview with author, July 21, 2009.

73. Benjamim Benfica interview, September 30, 2011.

74. Castigo Guambe interviews. See also chapters 1 and 2.

75. The following information was provided by his son: see Isaac Araújo interviews.

76. See also chapter 1 for a description of the compound.

77. Conselho dos Ministros da Republica Popular de Moçambique, Regulamentação do Decreto-Lei no. 5/76, February 14, 1976, which appears in "Cidade do caniço: Realidades novas," 29. The clarification essentialy extended to certain suburban residents the parts of the law intended to indemnify Portuguese retirees.

78. Albertina Amaral interview.

79. Fernando Manuel, "Reparação de casas: APIE reembolsa . . . mas ninguém sabe," *Tempo*, February 7, 1982.

80. José Forjaz, interview with author, April 15, 2013 (Forjaz was the former national housing and planning director); conversation with José Luís Cabaço, former minister of communications and transport, April 25, 2013.

81. Júlio Carrilho interview, July 29, 2009.

82. Munslow, *Mozambique: The Revolution*, 153; Hanlon, *The Revolution under Fire*, 50, 190; Egerö, *Mozambique: The Dream Undone*, 67–71.

83. The key intervention reminding scholars that the revolution took place in a real-life context, not an idealized one, is Aquino de Bragança and Jacques Depelchin, "Da idealização da Frelimo à compreensão da história de Moçambique," *Estudos moçambicanos*, no. 5–6 (1986): 29–52.

84. On GDs being at times more radical than the Frelimo hierarchy, see Pitcher, *Transforming Mozambique*, 48–49.

85. For the nearly contemporaneous version of antiurbanism in Tanzania, see Callaci, *Street Archives and City Life*, 18–58.

86. Machel, "Independência implica benefícios," 52. For other searing anti-urban rhetoric, see Machel, "We Are Declaring War on the Enemy Within," in *Samora Machel: An African Revolutionary: Selected Speeches and Writings*, ed. Barry Munslow, trans. Michael Wolfers (London: Zed Books, 1985), 86–103.

87. FRELIMO, *Xiconhoca, o inimigo* (Maputo: FRELIMO Departamento de Trabalho Ideológico, 1979); Lars Buur, "Xiconhoca: Mozambique's Ubiquitous Post-independence Traitor," in *Traitors: Suspicion, Intimacy, and the Ethics of State-Building*, ed. Sharika Thiranagama and Tobias Kelly (Philadelphia: University of Pennsylvania Press, 2010), 24–47.

88. Machel, "We Are Declaring War," 98–99.

89. "Combate à corrupção na APIE," *Notícias*, October 15, 1977; "Está ocupada," *Notícias*, January 30, 1978; Rui Zunguza, "Doença da APIE: Financeira não . . . de gestão talvez!" *Tempo*, August 19, 1984.

90. On the launch of the offensives, see Machel, "We Are Declaring War."

91. "Detidos cinco responsáveis por desvirtuamento das orientações," *Notícias*, January 25, 1980.

92. "Novas irregularidades detectadas na APIE," *Notícias*, January 26, 1980; "Proseguiu ofensiva presidencial contra a incompetência e o desleixo," *Notícias*, January 30, 1980.

93. David, "Mais de onze mil," 17.

94. Alfredo Tembe, "Materiais de construção: Quem não tem divisas fica 'a ver navios,'" *Tempo*, September 20, 1987.

95. In 1980, APIE reported that almost twelve thousand repair requests had been made at its Maputo offices in the four years since the nationalizations, and only about two thousand had been addressed (which is not to say addressed satisfactorily). "Na APIE a melhoria ainda vem a passo de tartaruga," *Notícias*, March 18, 1981.

96. "Parque imobilário do estado: Serviços de manutenção em reorganização no Maputo," *Notícias*, September 8, 1979.

97. Arnaldo Henrique, "Quando irá acabar 'alpinismo' forçado?" *Tempo*, August 30, 1987.

98. "Quem controla os guardas dos prédios?" *Tempo*, March 23, 1980; Filipe Mata, "Roubos nos prédios: Qual a responsabilidade dos guardas?" *Tempo*, January 17, 1982.

99. "Nacionalizações," *Notícias*, July 24, 1977.

100. "Nacionalizações"; David, "Mais de onze mil," 14.

101. "Inquilinos assumirão parte activa na valorização dos imoveis do estado," *Notícias*, August 14, 1979, 6.

102. Narciso Castanheira, "APIE: Limpar a própria casa," *Tempo*, May 22, 1983, 21.

103. "Quem controla os guardas dos prédios?" 13.

104. Rui Zunguza, "APIE reclama estatuto jurídico," *Tempo*, July 29, 1984, 8.

105. Tabo Motema, "APIE: Que função social?" *Tempo*, May 22, 1983; Fernando Manuel, "Habitação: Para preservar o património," *Tempo*, March 31, 1985; "Consolidar política habitacional," *Tempo*, June 23, 1985.

106. The "housing hygiene" series appeared in numerous editions of *Notícias*, the national daily newspaper, in the late 1970s.

107. "O insólito: Fazer uma vida normal ao lado de fezes," *Notícias*, May 31, 1980.

108. Machel, "Independência implica benefícios," 53. There was some ambiguity to his words, as he was speaking in the context of communal villages, the "cities of the countryside." He may have meant that *all* cities, including the new ones, would benefit from an infusion of rural values.

109. Mahoney, "Estado Novo, Homem Novo"; Hall and Young, *Confronting Leviathan*, 84; João Titterington Gomes Cravinho, "Modernizing Mozambique: Frelimo Ideology and the Frelimo State" (PhD diss., University of Oxford, 1995), 108–9.

110. Cravinho, "Modernizing Mozambique," 109n58.

111. Marcelo Panguana, "Na hora da mudança," in *As vozes que falam de verdade* (Maputo: Associação dos Escritores Moçambicanos, 1987); Ungulani Ba Ka Khosa, "Morte inesperada," in *Orgia dos loucos*, 2nd ed. (Maputo: Imprensa Universitária, 1990), 61–70; Lília Momplé, *Neighbours* (Maputo: Associação dos Escritores Moçambicanos, 1995); João Paulo Borges Coelho, *Crónica da Rua 513.2* (Lisbon: Caminho, 2006); Momplé, "Stress" and "Um canto para morrer," both in *Os olhos da cobra verde* (Maputo: CIEDIMA, 2008), 5–18 and 45–66; Luís Savele, "Tsendzeleni," in *Teatro moçambicano: Três peças num só palco* (Maputo: FUNDAC, 2011), 3–84.

112. Ba Ka Khosa, "Morte inesperada."

113. On Renamo, see Alex Vines, *Renamo: Terrorism in Mozambique* (London: James Currey, 1991); William Minter, *Apartheid's Contras: An Inquiry into the Roots of War in Angola and Mozambique* (London: Zed Books, 1994). Initially, the group was referred to as MNR and then RENAMO. Today, as a political party, the name is styled in lower case, and for the sake of readability this is how it will appear in this book.

114. Jeanne Vivet, *Os deslocados de guerra em Maputo: Percursos migratórios, "citadinização" e transformações urbanas da capital moçambicana (1976–2010)* (Maputo: Alcance, 2015), 111.

115. In 1985, the public works ministry conducted surveys in a handful of buildings in the City of Cement to evaluate the state of building degradation (which was extensive in all cases). The reports also listed the professions of the heads of households as well as the number of people living in each unit. The surveys, though not organized, are stored at the MITADER library.

116. Filipe Ribas, "Não há gás, não há carvão, não há lenha," *Tempo*, November 20, 1983.

117. Savele, "Tsendzeleni." The title (in Changana) means something to the effect of "I wander, naked to the elements." It is repeated as the first line of the play's chorus, followed by the lines (in Changana and in Portuguese) "I keep living, naked to the elements / Though they hate me, I keep living, naked to the elements."

Chapter 5: Planning in the Subúrbios, 1977–92

1. Azevedo, "O Plano Director." See also Clara Mendes, interview with author, January 12, 2010; Morais, *Maputo*, 171–87; Domingos, *Football and Colonialism*, 75–76. The full set of the plan's volumes is stored in the library at MITADER, which is the former complex of the Office of the Caniço.

2. Aguiar, "Plano Geral de urbanização," vol. 1; Aguiar, "Plano Geral de Urbanização," vol. 2.

3. In late 1974, in fact, one architect blasted the plan for keeping much of the caniço intact and seeking only to legalize housing there—evidence, he said, of the "apartheid" thinking of colonial era planning. Catorze, "'Apartheid' na habitação."

4. Gabinete de Urbanização e Habitação da Região de Lourenço Marques (GUHRLM), as noted in chapter 3.

5. António Barata Feyo, interview with author, November 30, 2010 (Feyo was an architect who worked on the 1969 plan); José Bruschy, interview with author, January 13, 2010 (Bruschy was the chief architect for the the city's urbanization office who also worked on the plan).

6. For a brief summary of late colonial housing interventions, see Jenkins, "Mozambique," 151–52.

7. Rebelo de Sousa returned to Portugal in 1970, and by 1971–72, "the impetus would be lost, totally," wrote his son (who, as I write, is president of Portugal). Rebelo de Sousa, *Baltazar Rebelo de Sousa*, 215. See also Mendes, *Maputo antes da independência*, 419; António Matos Veloso and António Gomes Ribeiro, interview with author, November 3, 2010 (both were architects who worked in Lorenço Marques at the time).

8. República Popular de Moçambique, "Cidade de Maputo Plano de Estrutura" (Maputo: Instituto Nacional do Planeamento Físico, 1985), appendix 4, FAPF/no. 558a. See also the map of Lourenço Marques schools and their 1973 student populations (with racial breakdowns) in Mendes, *Maputo antes da independência*, 217.

9. This is according to Castigo Guambe, whose family has lived across the lane for ninety years and who until recently was the school's chairperson.

10. For the challenges facing the National Housing Directorate at its founding, see Pinsky, "Territorial Dilemmas," 293–94; Jenkins, "Mozambique"; Paul Jenkins, "The Role of Civil Society in Shelter at the Periphery: The Experience of Peri-urban Communities in Maputo, Mozambique," in *Urban Development and Civil Society: The Role of Communities in Sustainable Cities*, ed. Michael Carley, Paul Jenkins, and Harry Smith (London: Earthscan, 2001), 33–50.

11. See, among many others: Jane Jacobs, *The Death and Life of Great American Cities* (New York: Random House, 1961); Marshall Berman, *All That Is Solid Melts into Air: The Experience of Modernity* (New York: Penguin Books, 1988); and Scott, *Seeing Like a State.*

12. Scott, *Seeing Like a State.*

13. Scott, 4. For the applicability of Scott to African contexts, see Erik Bähre and Baz Lecocq, "The Drama of Development: The Skirmishes behind High Modernist Schemes in Africa," *African Studies* 66, no. 1 (2007): 1–8.

14. Many have addressed Frelimo's economic program of the 1970s and 1980s; the following discussion of high modernism in Mozambique owes much to Pitcher, *Transforming Mozambique*, 67–100.

15. When villagization proved slow going and after agriculture failed to take off, Frelimo sympathizers pointed to catastrophic flooding and drought, the sacrifices made to maintain the UN sanctions on neighboring Rhodesia, and the attacks on Mozambique by Rhodesia and Renamo; the problem was not with Frelimo's agricultural policy itself. Pitcher argues that Frelimo policy, like any good policy, ought to have accounted for such "exogenous" factors. Moreover, she points out, until 1983 not even Frelimo cited war as a reason for declining agricultural output. Pitcher, *Transforming Mozambique*, 68–69; 90–91.

16. For housing and planning interventions through the 1980s, see Jenkins, "Mozambique." For latrine-building programs, see "Latrinas nas zonas suburbanas eliminam sistema de baldes," *Notícias*, March 26, 1978; António Sopa and Bartolomeu Rungo, *Maputo: Roteiro histórico iconográfico da cidade* (Maputo: Centro de Estudos Brasileiros da Embaixada do Brasil, 2006), 55.

17. See chapter 4.

18. Pitcher argues that people in the countryside were not "prostrate," as Scott described the typical victims of state economic planning to be, which reminds us of Fanon's comments on the supposedly "prostrate" residents of colonial slums, cited in the introduction. I am making the case for Lourenço Marques/Maputo that Pitcher makes for the countryside: that people did not just passively submit to state power. Yet the dynamic I describe here and in the previous chapter involved a much more welcoming approach to the state than the oppositional or transactional response to state power that Pitcher describes: "over time, those affected also shaped and eventually undermined villagization, cooperative, and state farm production as they did in Tanzania, or they protested government neglect. In some parts of the country, producers, traders, and even some private companies took the form of engaging with the state, taking advantage of state incapacity to strike compromises with state officials." Pitcher, *Transforming Mozambique*, 97. For dynamics similar to those Pitcher observes, see Lal, *African Socialism in Postcolonial Tanzania.*

19. República Popular de Moçambique, "Cidade de Maputo Plano de Estrutura."

20. This account of the Maxaquene Project is a synthesis of the published and unpublished reports of project participants, primarily Saevfors, *Maxaquene,*

273

and also Barry Pinsky, "Notes on the Maxaquene Urbanization Experience" (Toronto, November 1980), FAPF; Pinsky, "Análise do projecto de Maxaquene/Polana Caniço e da situação do projecto de PNUD/DNH," June 18, 1979, BP; Pinsky, "Territorial Dilemmas," 279–315; Diego Robles Rivas, "Barrio Maxaquene monografia" (Direcção Nacional de Habitação, República Popular de Moçambique and UNDP-Habitat, 1981), MITADER/no. D-6481. It is also based on interviews with a number of people involved in the project: see Ingemar Sävfors and Eva Sävfors, interview with author, March 10, 2013; Ingemar Sävfors, interviews with author, September 19, 2012, and March 11–12, 2013; Barry Pinsky, interviews with author, November 5, 2012, and January 15, 2013; Patrice Comiche Mussenge and Carlos Macave, interview with author, October 18, 2012; Augusto Duvane and Salomão Manjate interview; Lídia Massinge interview; José Forjaz interview; Daniel Nhambaga, interview with author, April 21, 2013; Antastásia Titos Mahumane, Antonietta Titos Mahumane, Ana Vasco Machaieie, et al., interview with author, May 4, 2013; and Prafulta Jaiantilal, interview with author, May 13, 2013. More clearly individualized points of view will be specifically cited. Paul Jenkins addressed the Maxaquene Project in his "Role of Civil Society," 39–40.

21. Sumila Gulyani and Ellen M. Bassett, "Retrieving the Baby from the Bathwater: Slum Upgrading in Sub-Saharan Africa," *Environment and Planning C: Government and Policy* 25 (2007): 486–515; Paul Jenkins, Harry Smith, and Ya Ping Wang, *Planning and Housing in the Rapidly Urbanising World* (London: Routledge, 2006).

22. See the discussion of Lusaka's site-and-service schemes in Hansen, *Keeping House in Lusaka*, 51–67.

23. John F. C. Turner, "Housing as a Verb," in *Freedom to Build: Dweller Control of the Housing Process*, ed. John F. C. Turner and Robert Fichter (New York: Macmillan, 1972), 148–75; Turner, *Housing by People: Towards Autonomy in Building Environments* (London: Marion Boyars, 1976). Turner worked in Peru.

24. It appears that the project might have been the one followed up by architect Antoni Folkers and others in the 1980s. Folkers, *Modern Architecture in Africa* (Amsterdam: Sun, 2010), 97–138.

25. Krisno Nimpuno et al., *The Malhangalene Survey: A Housing Study of an Unplanned Settlement in Maputo, Mozambique, 1976*, 2 vols. (Göteborg: Chalmers Tekniska Högskola, Arkitektur, 1977). Much of the area called Malhangalene at the time of the survey was later identified as Maxaquene when neighborhood boundaries were given greater definition.

26. For the origins of the GDs, see chapter 4.

27. Duvane and Manjate interview.

28. For that matter, even the street grid of the City of Cement was not perfectly rectilinear. See chapter 2.

29. Jaiantilal interview.

30. Saevfors, *Maxaquene*, 35.

31. *Manual de parcelamento* (Maputo: Direcção Nacional de Habitação, 1978), BP.

32. Narciso Castanheira, "Em todo o país: Em marcha o ordenamento das zonas suburbanas," *Tempo*, April 2, 1978, 32.

33. Callaci, *Street Archives and City Life*, 8.

34. Jaiantilal interview.

35. Roberto Cordeiro, "Jornais de parede," *Tempo*, December 22, 1974.

36. Massinge interview; Hanlon, *Mozambique: The Revolution under Fire*, 152.

37. Sheldon, *Pounders of Grain*, 129–43; Isabel Maria Casimiro, "*Paz na terra, guerra na casa*": *Feminismo e organizações de mulheres em Moçambique* (Maputo: Promédia, 2004), 183–93.

38. OMM statute cited in Sheldon, *Pounders of Grain*, 132.

39. Massinge interview.

40. Anastásia Titos Mahumane, Antonietta Titos Mahumane, Ana Vasco Machaieie, et al. interview. See also Sheldon, *Pounders of Grain*, 157.

41. Gerhard Seibert, "Auto-organização e entreajuda das populações nos bairros peri-urbanos de Maputo e Luanda," in *Subúrbios de Luanda e Maputo*, ed. Jochen Oppenheimer and Isabel Raposo (Lisbon: Edições Calibri, 2007), 163–74. Many of these were eventually joined by men.

42. República Popular de Moçambique, *Documentos da II Conferência da Organização da Mulher Moçambicana, realizada em Maputo 10 a 17 de Novembro de 1976* (Maputo: Imprensa Nacional de Moçambique, 1977), 55–56.

43. República Popular de Moçambique, *Documentos*, 102.

44. República Popular de Moçambique, 102.

45. Sävfors has many Super-8 short films of the project in his personal archive in Stockholm. Ten of them were recorded for this study.

46. Pinsky, "Notes on the Maxaquene Urbanization Experience," 15.

47. Guilherme da Silva Pereira, "Bairro do COOP: A peregrinação semanal," *Tempo*, June 20, 1971.

48. On water provision as a mediator of relationships between citizens and state, see Anand, *Hydraulic City*. See also Brian Larkin, "The Politics and Poetics of Infrastructure," *Annual Review of Anthropology* 42 (2013): 327–43.

49. Saevfors, *Maxaquene*, 49. See also Ingemar Sävfors, interview, March 12, 2013.

50. Sävfors and Sävfors interview.

51. Internal memo, "Implicações urbanísticas das intervenções no caniço," Bárbara Lopes and Filipe Lopes, October 23, 1978, Direcção Nacional de Habitação, República Popular de Moçambique, 2–3, IS.

52. Internal memo, 3.

53. Internal memo.

54. Bartolomeu Tomé, "Ordenamento dos subúrbios: Porque pararam os trabalhos em Maputo," *Tempo*, November 16, 1980.

55. Forjaz interview.

56. Barry Pinsky wrote in a 1980 report that the officials at the municipality, charging 5,000 meticais per request, were "profiting from *burocratismo* to exploit people who only want to build very simple 2 to 4 room houses in any case!" Pinsky, "Notes on the Maxaquene Urbanization Experience," 10.

57. Tomé, "Ordenamento dos subúrbios."

58. Architect and planning scholar Paul Jenkins, who in the 1980s worked for the Maputo municipality, told me that the budget at the time would not support even the barest planning initiatives, let alone the Maxaquene Project with its need for heavy machinery and water infrastructure. When Jenkins wanted to survey plots in a distant neighborhood, for instance, he could not get approval to purchase cement for marker beacons. Instead, workers put sticks in the soil. Some eventually grew into trees. Jenkins, conversation with author, October 23, 2018.

59. República Popular de Moçambique, *Primeira Reunião sobre Cidades e Bairros Comunais: Resolução geral* (Maputo: Imprensa Nacional de Moçambique, 1979), FAPF/no. 13767.

60. Pinsky, "Territorial Dilemmas," 300; Jenkins, "Role of Civil Society," 39.

61. República Popular de Moçambique, *I Recenseamento geral da população* (Maputo: Conselho Coordenador de Recenseamento, 1983).

62. Oscar Monteiro, "Construir a vida nova nas cidades," *Tempo*, March 4, 1979, 19.

63. Victor Igreja, "Frelimo's Political Ruling through Violence and Memory in Postcolonial Mozambique," *Journal of Southern African Studies* 36, no. 4 (2010): 781–99; Machava, "State Discourse."

64. Monteiro, "Construir a vida nova nas cidades," 18.

65. Each bairro was to be divided, in turn, into "communal units" of no more than 2,000 people, and each unit was to be broken down into "blocks" of no more than 250 people. República Popular de Moçambique, *Primeira Reunião*, 19.

66. Adriano Matate interview, December 5, 2011.

67. Augusto Casimiro, "Drenagem de Maputo: Afogar as inundações," *Tempo*, January 27, 1985.

68. Darch, "Drainage," in *Historical Dictionary of Mozambique*, 137.

69. República Popular de Moçambique, "Plano de Estrutura," appendix 4, 1–4, FAPF/no. 558a.

70. António Elias, "Hulene: Experiência-piloto em risco de desaparecer?" *Tempo*, March 30, 1986; Alexandre Luís, "Bairro George Dimitrov: Entre dificuldades e auto-suficiência," *Tempo*, November 15, 1987; Luís, "Mahlazine: Bairro que se ergue do esforço popular," *Tempo*, December 20, 1987.

71. "Zonas verdes para as cidades," *Tempo*, March 25, 1979; Hilário Matusse, "Zonas verdes: Produzir comida nos quintais," *Tempo*, May 30, 1982; Matusse, "Zonas verdes: Combate à fome começa nos nossos quintais," *Tempo*, June 6, 1982.

72. "Zonas verdes para as cidades"; Paul Jenkins, "Image of the City in Mozambique: Civilization, Parasite, Engine of Growth or Place of Opportunity?" in

African Urban Economies: Viability, Vitality, or Vitiation? ed. Deborah Fahy Bryceson and Deborah Potts (New York: Palgrave Macmillan, 2006), 107–30.

73. Albino Magaia, "No Hulene: Uma vida nova para um bairro," *Tempo*, July 1, 1979, 24; Magaia, "Hulene: Kanimambo Frelimo!" *Tempo*, July 1, 1979.

74. "Benfica" had been painted on a prominent water tower during a 1960s visit by the team to Lourenço Marques.

75. One resident compared it to the common practice of naming children with an eye to a future patron. Luís, "Bairro George Dimitrov," 26.

76. Hanlon, *Mozambique: The Revolution under Fire*, 252–54.

77. Narciso Castanheira, "Operação Produção: Primeiros voluntários avançam," *Tempo*, July 10, 1983; Castanheira, "Operação Produção: De casa em casa," *Tempo*, August 14, 1983; Albano Naroromele, "Operação Produção: Uma missão histórica," *Tempo*, August 14, 1983; Hanlon, *Mozambique: The Revolution under Fire*, 244–51; Machava, "The Morality of Revolution," 112–56; Carlos Domingos Quembo, *Poder do poder: Operação Produção e a invenção dos "improdutivos" urbanos no Moçambique socialista, 1983–1988* (Maputo: Alcance, 2017).

78. Bartolomeu Tembe, interview with author, May 17, 2013 (Tembe was head organizer of Operação Produção in Chamanculo). Also see Narciso Castanheira, "Operação Produção: Punir os desvios," *Tempo*, July 24, 1983.

79. Sheldon, *Pounders of Grain*, 155.

80. Hanlon, *Mozambique: The Revolution under Fire*, 246.

81. Vines, *Renamo*, 98, 100.

82. Vivet, *Os deslocados de guerra*.

83. The following account of the golf club is based primarily on information provided by two men who have been running it since independence, as well as a discussion with a longtime employee: Alfredo Dique Fumo and Samuel Languene, interview with author, November 9, 2012, and conversation with Dinis Nhaca, November 6, 2012. Before independence, Polana Caniço was known to its inhabitants as Ka-Polanah. Polana "Caniço" distinguished the neighborhood from Polana "Cimento," the exclusive neighborhood just to the south, in the City of Cement.

84. Using old, donated equipment, the caddies would get together on off-days at a course they made for themselves in the bush. Because there were only six holes, a proper thirty-six-hole championship required six tours of the "greens."

85. Barry Pinsky interview, January 15, 2013.

86. Alfredo Dique Fumo and Samuel Languene interview.

87. Timothy Mitchell, "The Limits of the State: Beyond Statist Approaches and Their Critics," *American Political Science Review* 85, no. 1 (1991): 77–96; Akhil Gupta, "Blurred Boundaries: The Discourse of Corruption, the Culture of Politics, and the Imagined State," *American Ethnologist* 22, no. 2 (1995): 375–402; Michael Taussig, *The Magic of the State* (New York: Routledge, 1997); George Steinmetz, "Introduction: Culture and the State," in *State/Culture: State-Formation after the Cultural Turn*, ed. George Steinmetz (Ithaca, NY: Cornell University Press, 1999),

277

278

1–49; Thomas Blom Hansen and Finn Stepputat, "Introduction: States of Imagination," in *States of Imagination: Ethnographic Explorations of the Postcolonial State*, ed. Thomas Blom Hansen and Finn Stepputat (Durham, NC: Duke University Press, 2001), 1–38; Crais, "Introduction," 1–25; Talal Asad, "Where Are the Margins of the State?" in *Anthropology in the Margins of the State*, ed. Veena Das and Deborah Poole (Santa Fe, NM: School of American Research Press, 2004), 279–88.

88. Finn Stepputat, "Urbanizing the Countryside: Armed Conflict, State Formation, and the Politics of Place in Contemporary Guatemala," in *States of Imagination: Ethnographic Explorations of the Postcolonial State*, ed. Thomas Blom Hansen and Finn Stepputat (Durham, NC: Duke University Press, 2001), 284–312; Stepputat, "Marching for Progress: Rituals of Citizenship, State and Belonging in a High Andes District," *Bulletin of Latin American Research* 23, no. 2 (2004): 244–59; Veena Das, "The Signature of the State: The Paradox of Illegibility," in *Anthropology in the Margins of the State*, ed. Veena Das and Deborah Poole (Santa Fe, NM: School of American Research Press, 2004), 225–52; Monique Nuijten and David Lorenzo, "Ritual and Rule in the Periphery: State Violence and Local Governance in a Peruvian Comunidad," in *Rules of Law and Laws of Ruling*, ed. Franz von Benda-Beckmann, Keebet von Benda-Beckmann, and Julia Eckert (Farnham, UK: Ashgate, 2009), 101–23.

89. Morten Nielsen, "Filling in the Blanks: The Potency of Fragmented Imageries of the State," *Review of African Political Economy* 34, no. 114 (2007): 695–708; Nielsen, "In the Vicinity of the State"; Nielsen, "Mimesis of the State"; Nielsen, "Inverse Governmentality: The Paradoxical Production of Peri-urban Planning in Maputo, Mozambique," *Critique of Anthropology* 31, no. 4 (2011): 329–58; Jørgen Eskemose Andersen, Paul Jenkins, and Morten Nielsen, "Who Plans the African City? A Case Study of Maputo: Part 2—Agency in Action," *International Development Planning Review* 37, no. 4 (2015): 423–43.

Conclusion: Multiple Trajectories

1. Pitcher, *Transforming Mozambique*, 101–78; Iraê Baptista Lundin, "Negotiating Transformation: Urban Livelihoods in Maputo Adapting to Thirty Years of Political and Economic Changes" (PhD diss., Göteborg University, 2007).

2. Views summarized in John S. Saul, "Afterword: Nkomati and After," in *A Difficult Road: The Transition to Socialism in Mozambique*, ed. John S. Saul (New York: Monthly Review Press, 1985), 391–418.

3. Carrilho, "Ajustar as rendas ao valor das casas"; Brigitte Lachartre, *Enjeux urbains au Mozambique: De Lourenço Marques à Maputo* (Paris: Karthala, 2000), 254–56.

4. Joseph Hanlon, "Mozambique: Under New Management," *Soundings*, no. 7 (1997): 184–94.

5. Fredrik Söderbaum and Ian Taylor, "Transmission Belt for Transnational Capital or Facilitator for Development? Problematising the Role of the State in

the Maputo Development Corridor," *Journal of Modern African Studies* 39, no. 4 (2001): 675–95; Lachartre, *Enjeux urbains au Mozambique*, 266–73.

6. Joshua Kirshner and Marcus Power, "Mining and Extractive Urbanism: Post-development in a Mozambican Boomtown," *Geoforum* 61 (2015): 67–78.

7. Johan Lagerkvist, "As China Retuns: Perceptions of Land Grabbing and Spatial Power Relations in Mozambique," *Journal of Asian and African Studies* 49, no. 3 (2014): 251–66; Morten Axel Pedersen and Morten Nielsen, "Trans-temporal Hinges: Reflections on an Ethnographic Study of Chinese Infrastructural Projects in Mozambique and Mongolia," *Social Analysis* 57, no. 1 (2013): 122–42; Howard W. French, *China's Second Continent: How a Million Migrants Are Building a New Empire in Africa* (New York: Vintage, 2015), 11–41.

8. Andersen, Sollien, and Ouis, "Built Environment Study."

9. Reuters, "Mozambique Files Case against Credit Suisse in London's High Court," *New York Times*, February 28, 2019, https://www.nytimes.com/reuters/2019/02/28/business/28reuters-mozambique-credit-suisse-lawsuit.html.

10. Lundin, "Negotiating Transformation."

11. Jochen Oppenheimer and Isabel Raposo, *Pobreza em Maputo* (Lisbon: Ministério do Trabalho e da Solidariedade, Departamento de Cooperação, 2002); Bénard da Costa, *O preço da sombra*; Lundin, "Negotiating Transformation"; Rowan Moore Gerety, *Go Tell the Crocodiles: Chasing Prosperity in Mozambique* (New York: Basic Books, 2018).

12. See also Nielsen, "Futures Within"; Archambault, "'One Beer, One Block.'"

13. "Bairro do Aeroporto: Persistem ligações eléctricas clandestinas e conflitos de terra," *Verdade*, December 18, 2014, http://www.verdade.co.mz/nacional/50919.

14. Anastásia Titos Mahumane, Antonietta Titos Mahumane, Ana Vasco Machaieie, et al. interview.

15. Conversation with Albano Goda, April 17, 2013.

16. See chapter 4.

17. Conversation with Benjamim Benfica, January 22, 2013.

18. On modernization and modernization theory, see Ferguson, *Expectations of Modernity*; Stephan F. Miescher, "Building the City of the Future: Visions and Experiences of Modernity in Ghana's Akosombo Township," *Journal of African History* 53, no. 3 (2012): 367–90; Peter J. Bloom, Stephan F. Miescher, and Takyiwaa Manuh, eds., *Modernization as Spectacle in Africa* (Bloomington: Indiana University Press, 2014); Frederick Cooper, "Modernity," in *Colonialism in Question: Theory, Knowledge, History* (Berkeley: University of California Press, 2005), 113–49.

SOURCES

Maputo Area

Helena Macuacua. July 2, 6, and 27, 2009.
Luciana Nhmavila. July 2, 2009.
Afonso Carlos Mapelane. July 3 and 7, 2009.
Valente Matsinhe. July 7, August 14, 2009.
Calane da Silva. July 8, 2009.
Orray Muianga. July 9, 2009.
Luís Hunguana. July 13, 17, and 22, 2009.
Albertina Amaral. July 21, 2009.
Gabriel da Cunha Amaral. July 21, 2009.
Gertrude Vitoriano. July 27, 2009.
Rosa Joaquina Candla. July 27, 2009.
Júlio Carrilho. July 29, 2009; June 5, 2012.
Dinis Singulane. January 27, 2011.
Alfredo Manjate. February 8 and 15, September 17, 2011.
Ana Magaia. February 9 and 18, 2011.
Luís Marques. February 11, 2011.
Gonçalves Mambo et al. February 12, 2011.
Alberto Batu. February 20, 2011.
Filipe Muhale. February 24, 2011.
Filipe Muhale and Lídia Fazenda Manhiça Muhale. March 22, 2011.
Maria Esperança Tavares and José Gonçalves Tavares. April 5, 7, and 18, 2011.
Maria Júlia Mandlate. April 10, 2011.
Rute Chaguala. April 10, 2011.
Lúcia Joaquim da Silveira. April 11, 2011.

282   Margarida Fernanda Ferreira Neves. April 11 and 13, September 28, 2011; June 13, 2012.
Carolina Adelaide Inguane. April 13, May 13, 16, 20, and 27, June 6, 2011.
Margarida Manuel Botão. April 13, 2011.
Castigo Jochua Guambe. April 14 and 26, May 17, 2011.
Sérgio José da Costa. April 16 and 28, 2011.
Faustino Vilankulo. April 18, 2011.
Francisco Machava and Feliciano Banze. April 27, 2011.
Ana Laura Cumba. April 29, 2011.
Jaime Tembe. April 30, May 9 and 11, 2011; May 17, 2013.
Gilmar Ferreira. May 3, 2011.
Sebastião Alfredo Chitombe. May 4, 9, and 16, September 17, 2011.
Elizabeth Eurica Cumbana. May 5 and 12, 2011.
Armando Guilundo. May 7 and 10, 2011.
Carlos Carvalho. May 23 and 30, 2011.
João Ernesto Mbanguine. May 26, 2011.
Daniel Malé and Adelina Cossa. June 4 and 7, 2011.
Alfredo Nhanale. June 5, November 6, 2011.
Isabel Bila. June 6, 2011.
Elídio Sanduane and Olga Zucula. June 7, 2011.
Isaac Araújo. June 8 and 15, 2011.
João Madeira. June 8, 2011; January 12, 2012.
Eugénio Rafael. June 11, 2011.
Celeste da Conceção. June 12, 2011.
José Inácio Cossa. June 14, 2011.
Aporino Massinga. June 15, 2011.
Armando Grachane. June 16, 2011.
Gabriel Chiau. June 21, 2011.
Benjamim Benfica. September 30, 2011; June 14, 2012.
Félix Vaz. November 1 and 8, 2011.
Maria da Graça Ferreira. November 2, 2011; May 7, 2013.
Bartolomeu Tembe. November 11, 2011; June 18, 2012; May 17, 2013.
Adriano Matate. November 18 and 21, December 5, 2011.
José Wetela Missanga. November 21, 2011.
Zubaida Ussein Vazirna. January 10, 2012.
Zacarias Rafael Mazive. January 12, April 9, 2012.
André Ernesto Charidze. April 19, 2012.
Madalena João Tivane. June 13 and 22, 2012.
Domingos Ozias. September 13, 2012.
Manuel Gonçalves. September 18, 2012.
Björn Brandberg. September 20, 2012.
Amélia Mbeve. October 17, 2012.
Patrício Comege Mussenge and Carlos Macave. October 18, 2012.

Armando Cossa. October 25, 2012.

Carlos Muchanga. October 25, 2012; January 30, 2013.

Regina Massinga. November 6, 2012.

Alfredo Dique Fumo and Samuel Languene. November 9, 2012.

Augusto Duvane and Salomão Manjate. March 23, 2013.

Lídia Massinge. March 25, 2013.

José Forjaz. April 15, 2013.

António Maqueto Ndeve. April 17, 2013.

Daniel Nhambaga. April 21, 2013.

Lindo Nhlongo. May 3, 2013.

Anastásia Titos Mahumane, Antonietta Titos Mahumane, Ana Vasco Machaieie, et al. May 4, 2013.

Prafulta Jaiantilal. May 13, 2013.

Josefa Alfonso Maduela and Isabel da Conceição Maduela. June 4, 2016.

Rui Gonçalves (by Skype). August 23, 2018.

Portugal

Isabel Raposo. January 11, 2010.

Clara Mendes. January 12, 2010.

José Bruschy. January 13, 2010.

Dinis Marques. October 10 and 17, 2010.

Daniel Pedrosa. October 12, 2010.

Pancho Guedes. October 30, 2010.

António Matos Veloso and António Gomes Ribeiro. November 3, 2010.

João Pereira Neto. November 26, 2010.

Nicolau Brandão and José Capela. November 26, 2010.

Ducílio Sapinho. November 27, 2010.

António Barata Feyo. November 30, 2010.

Elsewhere

Ingemar Sävfors, Stockholm. September 19, 2012 (by Skype); March 11–12, 2013.

Barry Pinsky, Toronto. November 5, 2012 (by Skype); January 15, 2013 (by Skype).

Ingemar Sävfors and Eva Sävfors, Stockholm. March 10, 2013.

ARCHIVES AND COLLECTIONS

Mozambique (all in Maputo)

Biblioteca Nacional de Moçambique

Centro de Documentação e Formacão Fotográfica (CDFF)

Conselho Municipal da Cidade de Maputo
   Biblioteca do Conselho Municipal

284

Departamento de Urbanização e Construção
 Arquivo de Obras Clandestinas (CMLM-DSUO)
Ministério da Terra, Ambiente e Desenvolvimento Rural (MITADER)
Notícias archive
Universidade Eduardo Mondlane
 Arquivo Histórico de Moçambique (AHM)
  Fundo da Administração do Concelho de Lourenço Marques (ACLM)
  Fundo da Direcção dos Serviços de Administração Civil (DSAC)
  Fundo da Direcção dos Serviços dos Negócios Indígenas (DSNI)
  Fundo do Gabinete do Distrito de Lourenço Marques (GDLM)
  Fundo da Inspecção dos Serviços Administrativos e dos Negócios
   Indígenas (ISANI)
  Iconoteca
 Biblioteca da Faculdade de Arquitectura e Planeamento Físico (FAPF)
 Biblioteca do Centro de Estudos Africanos

 Portugal (all in or around Lisbon)

Arquivo Nacional da Torre do Tombo (ANTT)
 Arquivo PIDE/DGS
  Fundo dos Serviços de Centralização e Coordinação de Informações de
   Moçambique (SCCIM)
Arquivo Nacional das Imagens em Movimento, Cinemateca Portuguesa (ANIM)
Biblioteca Municipal de Lisboa
 Hemeroteca
Biblioteca Nacional de Portugal
Instituto de Investigação Científica Tropical
 Arquivo Histórico Ultramarino (AHU)
 Centro de Documentação e Informação
Ministério dos Negócios Estrangeiros de Portugal
 Arquivo do Instituto Português de Apoio ao Desenvolvimento (IPAD)
Sociedade de Geografia de Lisboa

 Elsewhere

Barry Pinsky, personal archive, Toronto (BP)
Ingemar Sävfors, personal archive, Stockholm (IS)

PERIODICALS

 (All in Lourenço Marques/Maputo)

Boletim da República de Moçambique
Boletim Municipal: Edição da Câmara Municipal de Lourenço Marques
Boletim Oficial de Moçambique
O Brado Africano

Notícias
Tempo
A Tribuna

SELECTED PUBLISHED WORKS

(A complete bibliography can be accessed at https://www.ohioswallow.com/ book/Age+of+Concrete.)

Abu-Lughod, Janet L. *Rabat: Urban Apartheid in Morocco.* Princeton, NJ: Princeton University Press, 1980.

Adam, Yussuf. *Escapar aos dentes do crocodilo e cair na boca do leopardo: Trajectória de Moçambique pós-colonial (1975–1990).* Maputo: Promédia, 2006.

Ahlman, Jeffrey S. *Living with Nkrumahism: Nation, State, and Pan-Africanism in Ghana.* Athens: Ohio University Press, 2017.

Allina, Eric. *Slavery by Any Other Name: African Life under Company Rule in Colonial Mozambique.* Charlottesville: University of Virginia Press, 2012.

AlSayyad, Nezar, ed. *Forms of Dominance: On the Architecture and Urbanism of the Colonial Enterprise.* Aldershot, UK: Avebury, 1992.

Anand, Nikhil. *Hydraulic City: Water and the Infrastructures of Citizenship in Mumbai.* Durham, NC: Duke University Press, 2017.

Andersen, Jørgen Eskemose, Paul Jenkins, and Morten Nielsen. "Who Plans the African City? A Case Study of Maputo: Part 1—The Structural Context." *International Development Planning Review* 37, no. 3 (2015): 329–50.

———. "Who Plans the African City? A Case Study of Maputo: Part 2—Agency in Action." *International Development Planning Review* 37, no. 4 (2015): 423–43.

Andersen, Jørgen Eskemose, Silje Erøy Sollien, and Khadidja Ouis. "Built Environment Study." In *Home Space Maputo,* 2012. http://www.homespace.dk /tl_files/uploads/publications/Full%20reports/HomeSpace_Built_Environment _Study.pdf.

Araújo, Manuel G. Mendes de. "Cidade de Maputo: Espaços constrastantes—Do urbano ao rural." *Finisterra* 34, no. 67–68 (1999): 175–90.

Archambault, Julie Soleil. "'One Beer, One Block': Concrete Aspiration and the Stuff of Transformation in a Mozambican Suburb." *Journal of the Royal Anthropological Institute* 24, no. 4 (2018): 692–708.

Bähre, Erik, and Baz Lecocq. "The Drama of Development: The Skirmishes behind High Modernist Schemes in Africa." *African Studies* 66, no. 1 (2007): 1–8.

Ba Ka Khosa, Ungulani. *Orgia dos loucos.* 2nd ed. Maputo: Imprensa Universitária, 1990.

Bank, Leslie J. "City Slums, Rural Homesteads: Migrant Culture, Displaced Urbanism and the Citizenship of the Serviced House." *Journal of Southern African Studies* 41, no. 5 (2015): 1067–81.

——. *Home Spaces, Street Styles: Contesting Power and Identity in a South African City.* New York: Pluto Press, 2011.

Baptista, Idalina. "How Portugal Became an 'Unplanned Country': A Critique of Scholarship on Portuguese Urban Development and Planning." *International Journal of Urban and Regional Research* 36, no. 5 (2012): 1076–92.

Barnes, Teresa. "*We Women Worked So Hard*": Gender, Urbanization, and Social Reproduction in Colonial Harare, Zimbabwe, 1930–1956. Portsmouth, NH: Heinemann, 1999.

Bauböck, Rainer. "Reinventing Urban Citizenship." *Citizenship Studies* 7, no. 2 (2003): 139–60.

Becker, Felicitas, and Joel Cabrita. "Introduction: Performing Citizenship and Enacting Exclusion on Africa's Indian Ocean Littoral." *Journal of African History* 55, no. 2 (2014): 161–71.

Bekker, Simon, and Laurent Fourchard, eds. *Governing Cities in Africa: Politics and Policies.* Cape Town: HSRC Press, 2013.

Bénard da Costa, Ana. *O preço da sombra: Sobrevivência e reprodução social entre famílias de Maputo.* Lisbon: Livros Horizonte, 2007.

Benda-Beckmann, Franz von, Keebet von Benda-Beckmann, and Julia Eckert, eds. *Rules of Law and Laws of Ruling.* Farnham, UK: Ashgate, 2009.

Benda-Beckmann, Keebet von, and Fernanda Pirie, eds. *Order and Disorder: Anthropological Perspectives.* New York: Berghahn Books, 2007.

Bender, Gerald J. *Angola under the Portuguese: The Myth and the Reality.* Berkeley: University of California Press, 1978.

Berman, Marshall. *All That Is Solid Melts into Air: The Experience of Modernity.* New York: Penguin Books, 1988.

Bertelsen, Bjørn Enge, Inge Tvedten, and Sandra Roque. "Engaging, Transcending, and Subverting Dichotomies: Discursive Dynamics of Maputo's Urban Space." *Urban Studies* 51, no. 13 (2014): 2752–69.

Bissell, William Cunningham. *Urban Design, Chaos, and Colonial Power in Zanzibar.* Bloomington: Indiana University Press, 2011.

Bloom, Peter J., Stephan F. Miescher, and Takyiwaa Manuh, eds. *Modernization as Spectacle in Africa.* Bloomington: Indiana University Press, 2014.

Borges Coelho, João Paulo. "Antigos soldados, novos cidadãos: A reintegração dos desmobilizados de Maputo." *Estudos moçambicanos,* no. 20 (2002): 141–236.

——. *Crónica da Rua 513.2.* Lisbon: Caminho, 2006.

Bozzoli, Belinda. *Theatres of Struggle and the End of Apartheid.* Athens: Ohio University Press, 2004.

Bragança, Aquino de, and Jacques Depelchin. "Da idealização da Frelimo à compreensão da história de Moçambique." *Estudos moçambicanos,* no. 5–6 (1986): 29–52.

Brennan, James R. *Taifa: Making Race and Nation in Urban Tanzania.* Athens: Ohio University Press, 2012.

Bruschi, Sandro, Júlio Carrilho, and Luís Lage. *Era uma vez uma palhota: História da casa moçambicana*. Maputo: Edições FAPF, 2005.

Cabaço, José Luís. *Moçambique: Identidades, colonialismo e libertação*. Maputo: Marimbique, 2010.

Cahen, Michel. "Check on Socialism in Mozambique: What Check? What Socialism?" *Review of African Political Economy*, no. 57 (1993): 46–59.

———. *Mozambique, la révolution implosée: Études sur 12 ans d'indépendance, 1975–1987*. Paris: L'Harmattan, 1987.

Callaci, Emily. *Street Archives and City Life: Popular Intellectuals in Postcolonial Tanzania*. Durham, NC: Duke University Press, 2017.

Cardoso, Ribeiro. *O fim do império: Memória de um soldado português—O 7 de setembro de 1974 em Lourenço Marques*. 2nd ed. Alfragide, Port.: Caminho, 2014.

Carrilho, Júlio, Sandro Bruschi, Carlos Menezes, and Luís Lage. *Traditional Informal Settlements in Mozambique: From Lichinga to Maputo*. Translated by Carola Cuoco. Maputo: FAPF, 2004.

Casimiro, Isabel Maria. *"Paz na terra, guerra na casa": Feminismo e organizações de mulheres em Moçambique*. Maputo: Promédia, 2004.

Castelo, Cláudia. *O modo português de estar no mundo: O luso-tropicalismo e a ideologia colonial portuguesa (1933–1961)*. Porto: Afrontamento, 2001.

———. *Passagens para África: O povoamento de Angola e Moçambique com naturais da Metrópole (1920–1974)*. Porto: Edições Afrontamento, 2007.

Castelo, Cláudia, Omar Ribeiro Thomaz, Sebastião Nascimento, and Teresa Cruz e Silva, eds. *Os outros da colonização: Ensaios sobre o colonialismo tardio em Moçambique*. Lisbon: Imprensa de Ciências Sociais, 2012.

Çelik, Zeynep. *Urban Forms and Colonial Confrontations: Algiers under French Rule*. Berkeley: University of California Press, 1997.

Chilundo, Arlindo, Aurélio Rocha, David Hedges, Eduardo Medeiros, and Gerhard Liesegang. *História de Moçambique*, vol. 2, *1930–1961*. Edited by David Hedges. 2nd ed. Maputo: Livraria Universitária, 1999.

Cleveland, Todd. *Following the Ball: The Migration of African Soccer Players across the Portuguese Colonial Empire, 1949–1975*. Athens: Ohio University Press, 2017.

Colombijn, Freek. *Under Construction: The Politics of Urban Space and Housing during the Decolonization of Indonesia, 1930–1960*. Leiden: KITLV Press, 2010.

Comaroff, John L. "Reflections on the Colonial State, in South Africa and Elsewhere: Factions, Fragments, Facts, and Fictions." *Social Identities* 4, no. 3 (1998): 321–61.

Cooper, Frederick. *Africa since 1940: The Past of the Present*. New York: Cambridge University Press, 2002.

———. *Citizenship between Empire and Nation*. Princeton, NJ: Princeton University Press, 2014.

———. *Colonialism in Question: Theory, Knowledge, History*. Berkeley: University of California Press, 2005.

288

——. *Decolonization and African Society: The Labor Question in French and British Africa.* Cambridge: Cambridge University Press, 1996.

——. *On the African Waterfront: Urban Disorder and the Transformation of Work in Colonial Mombasa.* New Haven, CT: Yale University Press, 1987.

——. "Possibility and Constraint: African Independence in Historical Perspective." *Journal of African History* 49, no. 2 (2008): 167–96.

——, ed. *Struggle for the City: Migrant Labor, Capital, and the State in Urban Africa.* Beverly Hills, CA: Sage Publications, 1983.

Coquery-Vidrovitch, Catherine. "African Urban Spaces: History and Culture." In *African Urban Spaces in Historical Perspective*, edited by Steven J. Salm and Toyin Falola, xv–xl. Rochester, NY: University of Rochester Press, 2005.

——. "From Residential Segregation to African Urban Centres: City Planning and the Modalities of Change in Africa South of the Sahara." *Journal of Contemporary African Studies* 32, no. 1 (2014): 1–12.

Couto, Fernando Amado. *Moçambique 1974: O fim do império e o nascimento da nação.* Maputo: Texto Editores, 2011.

Crais, Clifton C., ed. *The Culture of Power in Southern Africa: Essays on State Formation and the Political Imagination.* Portsmouth, NH: Heinemann, 2003.

Craveirinha, José. *Cela 1.* Lisbon: Edições 70, 1980.

——. *Karingana ua karingana.* Maputo: Instituto Nacional do Livro e do Disco, 1982.

Cruz e Silva, Teresa. "A 'IV Região' da FRELIMO no sul de Moçambique: Lourenço Marques, 1964–1965." *Estudos moçambicanos*, no.8 (1990): 125–41.

——. *Protestant Churches and the Formation of Political Consciousness in Southern Mozambique (1930–1974).* Basel: P. Schlettwein, 2001.

Darch, Colin. *Historical Dictionary of Mozambique.* Lanham, MD: Rowman and Littlefield, 2018.

Darch, Colin, and David Hedges. "Political Rhetoric in the Transition to Mozambican Independence: Samora Machel in Beira, June 1975." *Kronos* 39 (2013): 32–65.

Das, Veena, and Deborah Poole, eds. *Anthropology in the Margins of the State.* Santa Fe, NM: School of American Research Press, 2004.

Demissie, Fassil, ed. *Colonial Architecture and Urbanism in Africa: Intertwined and Contested Histories.* Farnham, UK: Ashgate, 2012.

Dinerman, Alice. *Revolution, Counter-revolution and Revisionism in Post-colonial Africa: The Case of Mozambique, 1975–1994.* London: Routledge, 2006.

Dlamini, Jacob. *Native Nostalgia.* Johannesburg: Jacana Media, 2009.

Domingos, Nuno. "A desigualdade como legado da cidade colonial: Racismo e reprodução de mão-de-obra em Lourenço Marques." In *Cidade e império: Dinâmicas coloniais e reconfigurações pós-coloniais*, edited by Nuno Domingos and Elsa Peralta, 59–112. Lisbon: Edições 70, 2013.

——. "Colonial Architectures, Urban Planning and the Representation of Portuguese Imperial History." *Portuguese Journal of Social Science* 14, no. 3 (2015): 235–55.

———. *Football and Colonialism: Body and Popular Culture in Urban Mozambique*. Athens: Ohio University Press, 2017.

Donham, Donald L. *Marxist Modern: An Ethnographic History of the Ethiopian Revolution*. Berkeley: University of California Press, 1999.

Duffy, James. *Portugal in Africa*. Baltimore: Penguin Books, 1962.

Elleh, Nnamdi. *Architecture and Power in Africa*. Westport, CT: Praeger, 2002.

Egerö, Bertil. *Mozambique: The Dream Undone—The Political Economy of Democracy*. Uppsala: Nordiska Afrikainstitutet, 1987.

Enwezor, Okwui, ed. *Under Siege: Four African Cities—Freetown, Johannesburg, Kinshasa, Lagos*. Ostfildern-Ruit, Ger.: Hatje Cantz, 2002.

Errante, Antoinette. "White Skin, Many Masks: Colonial Schooling, Race, and National Consciousness among White Settler Children in Mozambique, 1934–1974." *International Journal of African Historical Studies* 36, no. 1 (2003): 7–33.

Fair, Laura. *Pastimes and Politics: Culture, Community, and Identity in Post-abolition Zanzibar, 1890–1945*. Athens: Ohio University Press, 2001.

Fanon, Frantz. *The Wretched of the Earth*. Translated by Richard Philcox. New York: Grove Press, 2004.

Ferguson, James. *Expectations of Modernity: Myths and Meanings of Urban Life on the Zambian Copperbelt*. Berkeley: University of California Press, 1999.

———. *Global Shadows: Africa in the Neoliberal World Order*. Durham, NC: Duke University Press, 2006.

Fernandes, José Manuel, Maria de Lurdes Janeiro, and Olga Iglésias Neves. *Moçambique 1875/1975: Cidades, território e arquitecturas*. Lisbon: Maisimagem, 2006.

Fischer, Brodwyn. *A Poverty of Rights: Citizenship and Inequality in Twentieth-Century Rio de Janeiro*. Stanford, CA: Stanford University Press, 2008.

Folkers, Antoni. *Modern Architecture in Africa*. Amsterdam: Sun, 2010.

Forty, Adrian. *Concrete and Culture: A Material History*. London: Reaktion Books, 2012.

Fourchard, Laurent. "Between World History and State Formation: New Perspectives on Africa's Cities." *Journal of African History* 52, no. 2 (2011): 223–48.

Freund, Bill. *The African City: A History*. New York: Cambridge University Press, 2007.

Freyre, Gilberto. *Um brasileiro em terras portuguêsas*. Rio de Janeiro: J. Olympio, 1953.

Fuller, Mia. *Moderns Abroad: Architecture, Cities, and Italian Imperialism*. London: Routledge, 2007.

Gastrow, Claudia. "Cement Citizens: Housing, Demolition and Political Belonging in Luanda, Angola." *Citizenship Studies* 21, no. 2 (2017): 224–39.

Gengenbach, Heidi. "'What My Heart Wanted': Gendered Stories of Early Colonial Encounters in Southern Mozambique." In *Women in African Colonial*

Histories, edited by Jean Allman, Susan Geiger, and Nakanyike Musisi, 19–47. Bloomington: Indiana University Press, 2002.

Gerety, Rowan Moore. *Go Tell the Crocodiles: Chasing Prosperity in Mozambique*. New York: Basic Books, 2018.

Ginsburg, Rebecca. *At Home with Apartheid: The Hidden Landscapes of Domestic Service in Johannesburg*. Charlottesville: University of Virginia Press, 2011.

———. "'Now I Stay in a House': Renovating the Matchbox in Apartheid-Era Soweto." *African Studies* 55, no. 2 (1996): 127–39.

Goerg, Odile. "From Hill Station (Freetown) to Downtown Conakry (First Ward): Comparing French and British Approaches to Segregation in Colonial Cities at the Beginning of the Twentieth Century." *Canadian Journal of African Studies* 32, no. 1 (1998): 1–31.

Gonçalves, Euclides. "*Orientações superiores*: Time and Bureaucratic Authority in Mozambique." *African Affairs* 112, no. 449 (2013): 602–22.

Grest, Jeremy. "Urban Management, Local Government Reform, and the Democratisation Process in Mozambique: Maputo City 1975–1990." *Journal of Southern African Studies* 21, no. 1 (1995): 147–64.

Gruffydd Jones, Branwen. "Civilizing African Cities: International Housing and Urban Policy from Colonial to Neoliberal Times." *Journal of Intervention and Statebuilding* 6, no. 1 (2012): 23–40.

Guedes, Amâncio d'Alpoim [Pancho]. "The Caniços of Mozambique." In *Shelter in Africa*, edited by Paul Oliver, 200–209. London: Barrie and Jenkins, 1971.

———. *Manifestos, ensaios, falas, publicações*. Lisbon: Ordem dos Arquitectos, 2007.

Guedes, Pedro, ed. *As Áfricas de Pancho Guedes*. Lisbon: Sextante Editora, 2010.

———, ed. *Pancho Guedes: Vitruvius mozambicanus*. Lisbon: Museu Colecção Berardo, 2009.

Gulyani, Sumila, and Ellen M. Bassett. "Retrieving the Baby from the Bathwater: Slum Upgrading in Sub-Saharan Africa." *Environment and Planning C: Government and Policy* 25 (2007): 486–515.

Gupta, Akhil. "Blurred Boundaries: The Discourse of Corruption, the Culture of Politics, and the Imagined State." *American Ethnologist* 22, no. 2 (1995): 375–402.

Guyer, Jane I. "Household and Community in African Studies." *African Studies Review* 24, no. 2–3 (1981): 87–137.

Hall, Margaret, and Tom Young. *Confronting Leviathan: Mozambique since Independence*. London: C. Hurst, 1997.

Hanlon, Joseph. *Mozambique: The Revolution under Fire*. London: Zed Books, 1984.

Hansen, Karen Tranberg, ed. *African Encounters with Domesticity*. New Brunswick, NJ: Rutgers University Press, 1992.

———. *Keeping House in Lusaka*. New York: Columbia University Press, 1997.

Hansen, Karen Tranberg, and Mariken Vaa, eds. *Reconsidering Informality: Perspectives from Urban Africa*. Uppsala: Nordiska Afrikainstitutet, 2004.

Hansen, Thomas Blom, and Finn Stepputat. *States of Imagination: Ethnographic Explorations of the Postcolonial State*. Durham, NC: Duke University Press, 2001.

Havstad, Lilly. "Multiracial Women and the African Press in Post–World War II Lourenço Marques, Mozambique." *South African Historical Journal* 68, no. 3 (2016): 390–414.

Headrick, Daniel R. *The Tools of Empire: Technology and European Imperialism in the Nineteenth Century*. New York: Oxford University Press, 1981.

Healy-Clancy, Meghan, and Jason Hickel, eds. *Ekhaya: The Politics of Home in KwaZulu-Natal*. Pietermaritzburg, South Africa: University of KwaZulu-Natal Press, 2014.

Henriques, Cristina Delgado. *Maputo: Cinco décadas de mudança territorial*. Lisbon: IPAD, 2008.

Holston, James. *Insurgent Citizenship: Disjunctions of Democracy and Modernity in Brazil*. Princeton, NJ: Princeton University Press, 2008.

———. *The Modernist City: An Anthropological Critique of Brasília*. Chicago: University of Chicago Press, 1989.

Home, Robert. *Of Planting and Planning: The Making of British Colonial Cities*. 2nd ed. New York: Routledge, 2013.

Honwana, Luís Bernardo. *A velha casa de madeira e zinco*. 2nd ed. Maputo: Alcance, 2017.

Honwana, Raúl Bernardo Manuel. *The Life History of Raúl Honwana: An Inside View of Mozambique from Colonialism to Independence, 1905–1975*. Edited by Allen F. Isaacman. Translated by Tamara L. Bender. Boulder, CO: Lynne Rienner, 1988.

Igreja, Victor. "Frelimo's Political Ruling through Violence and Memory in Postcolonial Mozambique." *Journal of Southern African Studies* 36, no. 4 (2010): 781–99.

Isaacman, Allen F., and Barbara Isaacman. *Dams, Displacement, and the Delusion of Development: Cahora Bassa and Its Legacies in Mozambique, 1965–2007*. Athens: Ohio University Press, 2013.

———. *Mozambique: From Colonialism to Revolution, 1900–1982*. Boulder, CO: Westview Press, 1983.

———. *The Tradition of Resistance in Mozambique: The Zambesi Valley, 1850–1921*. Berkeley: University of California Press, 1976.

Isaacman, Allen F., and David Morton. "Harnessing the Zambezi: How Mozambique's Planned Mphanda Nkuwa Dam Perpetuates the Colonial Past." *International Journal of African Historical Studies* 45, no. 2 (2012): 157–90.

Jackson, Kenneth T. *Crabgrass Frontier: The Suburbanization of the United States*. New York: Oxford University Press, 1985.

SELECTED PUBLISHED WORKS

Jacobs, Jane. *The Death and Life of Great American Cities*. New York: Random House, 1961.

Jenkins, Paul. "Image of the City in Mozambique: Civilization, Parasite, Engine of Growth or Place of Opportunity?" In *African Urban Economies: Viability, Vitality, or Vitiation?*, edited by Deborah Fahy Bryceson and Deborah Potts, 107–30. New York: Palgrave Macmillan, 2006.

———. "Mozambique." In *Housing Policies in the Socialist Third World*, edited by Kosta Mathéy, 147–79. Munich: Profil, 1990.

———. "The Role of Civil Society in Shelter at the Periphery: The Experience of Peri-urban Communities in Maputo, Mozambique." In *Urban Development and Civil Society: The Role of Communities in Sustainable Cities*, edited by Michael Carley, Paul Jenkins, and Harry Smith, 33–50. London: Earthscan, 2001.

———. *Urbanization, Urbanism, and Urbanity in an African City: Home Spaces and House Cultures*. New York: Palgrave Macmillan, 2013.

Jenkins, Paul, Harry Smith, and Ya Ping Wang. *Planning and Housing in the Rapidly Urbanising World*. London: Routledge, 2006.

Jerónimo, Miguel Bandeira, ed. *O império colonial em questão (séculos XIX–XX): Poderes, saberes e instituições*. Lisbon: Edições 70, 2012.

Judin, Hilton, and Ivan Vladislavić, eds. *Blank: Architecture, Apartheid, and After*. Rotterdam: NAi Publishers, 1999.

Kagan Guthrie, Zachary. *Bound for Work: Labor, Mobility, and Colonial Rule in Central Mozambique, 1940–1965*. Charlottesville: University of Virginia Press, 2018.

———. "'This Was Being Done Only to Help': Development and Forced Labor in Barue, Mozambique, 1959–1965." *International Labor and Working-Class History* 92 (2017): 134–54.

Keese, Alexander. *Living with Ambiguity: Integrating an African Elite in French and Portuguese Africa, 1930–1961*. Stuttgart: Franz Steiner Verlag, 2007.

King, Anthony D. "The Social Production of Building Form: Theory and Research." *Environment and Planning Development: Society and Space* 2 (1984): 429–46.

Lachartre, Brigitte. *Enjeux urbains au Mozambique: De Lourenço Marques à Maputo*. Paris: Karthala, 2000.

Lal, Priya. *African Socialism in Postcolonial Tanzania: Between the Village and the World*. Cambridge: Cambridge University Press, 2015.

Larkin, Brian. "The Politics and Poetics of Infrastructure." *Annual Review of Anthropology* 42 (2013): 327–43.

Le Bon, Aurélio. *Mafalala 1974: Memórias do 7 de Setembro—A grande operação*. Maputo: Movimento Editora, 2015.

Lee, Rebekah. *African Women and Apartheid: Migration and Settlement in Urban South Africa*. London: Tauris Academic Studies, 2009.

Liesegang, Gerhard. "Lourenço Marques antes de 1895: Aspectos da história dos estados vizinhos, da interacção entre a povoação e aqueles estados e do comércio na baía e na povoação." *Arquivo: Boletim do Arquivo Histórico de Moçambique*, no. 2 (1987): 19–75.

Lobato, Alexandre. *Lourenço Marques, Xilunguíne: Biografia da cidade*. Lisbon: Agência-Geral do Ultramar, 1970.

Machava, Benedito Luís. "Galo amanheceu em Lourenço Marques: O 7 de Setembro e o verso da descolonização de Moçambique." *Revista Crítica de Ciências Sociais* 106 (2015): 53–84.

——. "State Discourse on Internal Security and the Politics of Punishment in Post-independence Mozambique (1975–1983)." *Journal of Southern African Studies* 37, no. 3 (2011): 593–609.

Machel, Samora. "Independência implica benefícios para as massas exploradas." In *A nossa luta é uma revolução: Nacionalizações—Moçambique*, 33–70. Lisbon: CIDA-C, 1976.

Macqueen, Norrie. *The Decolonization of Portuguese Africa: Metropolitan Revolution and the Dissolution of Empire*. London: Longman, 1997.

Mahoney, Michael. "Estado Novo, Homem Novo (New State, New Man): Colonial and Anti-colonial Development Ideologies in Mozambique, 1930–1977." In *Staging Growth: Modernization, Development, and the Global Cold War*, edited by David C. Engerman, Nils Gilman, Mark H. Haefele, and Michael E. Latham, 165–97. Amherst: University of Massachusetts Press, 2003.

Makhulu, Anne-Maria. *Making Freedom: Apartheid, Squatter Politics, and the Struggle for Home*. Durham, NC: Duke University Press, 2015.

Manghezi, Nadja. *O meu coração está nas maos de um negro: Uma história da vida de Janet Mondlane*. Maputo: Livraria Universitária, 1999.

Mateus, Dalila Cabrita. *A PIDE/DGS na guerra colonial (1961–1974)*. Lisbon: Terramar, 2004.

Mathéy, Kosta, ed. *Housing Policies in the Socialist Third World*. Munich: Profil, 1990.

Mayne, Alan. *Slums: The History of a Global Injustice*. London: Reaktion Books, 2017.

Melly, Caroline. *Bottleneck: Moving, Building, and Belonging in an African City*. Chicago: University of Chicago Press, 2017.

——. "Inside-Out Houses: Urban Belonging and Imagined Futures in Dakar, Senegal." *Comparative Studies in Society and History* 52, no. 1 (2010): 37–65.

Melo, Vanessa de Pacheco. "The Production of Urban Peripheries For and By Low-Income Populations at the Turn of the Millennium: Maputo, Luanda and Johannesburg." *Journal of Southern African Studies* 42, no. 4 (2016): 619–41.

Mendes, Maria Clara. *Maputo antes da independência: Geografia de uma cidade colonial*. Vol. 68. Memórias do Instituto de Investigação Científica Tropical. Lisbon: IICT, 1985.

293

294

Meneses, Filipe Ribeiro de. *Salazar: A Political Biography*. New York: Enigma Books, 2009.

Middlemas, Keith. "Twentieth Century White Society in Mozambique." *Tarikh* 6, no. 2 (1979): 30–45.

Miescher, Stephan F. "Building the City of the Future: Visions and Experiences of Modernity in Ghana's Akosombo Township." *Journal of African History* 53, no. 3 (2012): 367–90.

Milheiro, Ana Vaz. *Nos trópicos sem Le Corbusier: Arquitectura luso-africana no Estado Novo*. Lisbon: Relógio D'Água, 2012.

Minkley, Gary. "'Corpses behind Screens': Native Space in the City." In *Blank: Architecture, Apartheid, and After*, edited by Hilton Judin and Ivan Vladislavić, 202–19. Rotterdam: NAi Publishers, 1999.

Minter, William. *Apartheid's Contras: An Inquiry into the Roots of War in Angola and Mozambique*. London: Zed Books, 1994.

Mitchell, Hilary Flegg. *Aspects of Urbanisation and Age Structure in Lourenço Marques, 1957*. Lusaka: NECZAM and Institute for African Studies, University of Zambia, 1975.

Mitchell, Timothy. *Colonizing Egypt*. Berkeley: University of California Press, 1991.

———. "The Limits of the State: Beyond Statist Approaches and Their Critics." *American Political Science Review* 85, no. 1 (1991): 77–96.

———. *Rule of Experts: Egypt, Techno-politics, Modernity*. Berkeley: University of California Press, 2002.

Momplé, Lília. *Ninguém matou Suhura*. 4th ed. Maputo: CIEDIMA, 2008.

———. *Os olhos da cobra verde*. Maputo: CIEDIMA, 2008.

Mondlane, Eduardo. *The Struggle for Mozambique*. Baltimore: Penguin Books, 1969.

Moorman, Marissa J. *Intonations: A Social History of Music and Nation in Luanda, Angola, from 1945 to Recent Times*. Athens: Ohio University Press, 2008.

Morais, João Sousa. *Maputo: Património da estrutura e forma urbana, topologia do lugar*. Lisbon: Livros Horizonte, 2001.

Morton, David. "Chamanculo in Reeds, Wood, Zinc & Concrete." *S.L.U.M. Lab*, no. 9 (2014): 43–46.

———. "From Racial Discrimination to Class Segregation in Postcolonial Urban Mozambique." In *Geographies of Privilege*, edited by France Winddance Twine and Bradley Gardener, 231–62. New York: Routledge, 2013.

———. "A Voortrekker Memorial in Revolutionary Maputo." *Journal of Southern African Studies* 41, no. 2 (2015): 335–52.

Mosca, João. *A experiência "socialista" em Moçambique (1975–1986)*. Lisbon: Instituto Piaget, 1999.

Mpofu, Busani. "'Undesirable' Indians, Residential Segregation and the Ill-Fated Rise of the White 'Housing Covenanters' in Bulawayo, Colonial Zimbabwe, 1930–1973." *South African Historical Journal* 63, no. 4 (2011): 553–80.

Muianga, Aldino. *Caderno de memórias.* Vol. 1. Maputo: Alcance, 2014.

——. *Caderno de memórias.* Vol. 2. Maputo: CIEDIMA, 2015.

——. *Xitala mati.* Maputo: Associação dos Escritores Moçambicanos, 1987.

Munslow, Barry, ed. *Samora Machel: An African Revolutionary (Selected Speeches and Writings).* Translated by Michael Wolfers. London: Zed Books, 1985.

Murray, Martin J. *The Urbanism of Exception: The Dynamics of Global City Building in the Twenty-First Century.* Cambridge: Cambridge University Press, 2017.

Myers, Garth Andrew. *African Cities: Alternate Visions of Urban Theory and Practice.* London: Zed Books, 2011.

——. Political Ecology and Urbanization: Zanzibar's Construction Materials Industry." *Journal of Modern African Studies* 37, no. 1 (1999): 83–108.

——. "Sticks and Stones: Colonialism and Zanzibari Housing." *Africa* 67, no. 2 (1997): 252–72.

——. "The Unauthorized City: Late Colonial Lusaka and Postcolonial Geography." *Singapore Journal of Tropical Geography* 27, no. 3 (2006): 289–308.

——. *Verandahs of Power: Colonialism and Space in Urban Africa.* Syracuse, NY: Syracuse University Press, 2003.

Newitt, Malyn. *A History of Mozambique.* London: Hurst, 1995.

——. "The Late Colonial State in Portuguese Africa." *Itinerario* 23, no. 3–4 (1999): 110–22.

Nielsen, Morten. "Filling in the Blanks: The Potency of Fragmented Imageries of the State." *Review of African Political Economy* 34, no. 114 (2007): 695–708.

——. "Futures Within: Reversible Time and House-Building in Maputo, Mozambique." *Anthropological Theory* 11, no. 4 (2011): 397–423.

——. "Inverse Governmentality: The Paradoxical Production of Peri-urban Planning in Maputo, Mozambique." *Critique of Anthropology* 31, no. 4 (2011): 329–58.

——. "Mimesis of the State: From Natural Disaster to Urban Citizenship on the Outskirts of Maputo, Mozambique." *Social Analysis* 54, no. 3 (2010): 153–73.

Nightingale, Carl H. *Segregation: A Global History of Divided Cities.* Chicago: University of Chicago Press, 2012.

Nimpuno, Krisno, Ingemar Sävors, Lars Buur, Ruth Näslund, Nea Lavén, Björn Brandberg, Zounkata Tuina, and Hans Tollin. *The Malhangalene Survey: A Housing Study of an Unplanned Settlement in Maputo, Mozambique, 1976.* 2 vols. Göteborg: Chalmers Tekniska Högskola, Arkitektur, 1977.

Njoh, Ambe J. "Colonial Philosophies, Urban Space, and Racial Segregation in British and French Colonial Africa." *Journal of Black Studies* 38, no. 4 (2008): 579–99.

——. "The Experience and Legacy of French Colonial Urban Planning in Sub-Saharan Africa." *Planning Perspectives* 19, no. 4 (2004): 435–54.

Nuttall, Sarah, and Achille Mbembe, eds. *Johannesburg: The Elusive Metropolis.* Durham, NC: Duke University Press, 2008.

296

O'Laughlin, Bridget. "Class and the Customary: The Ambiguous Legacy of the Indigenato in Mozambique." *African Affairs* 99, no. 394 (2000): 5–42.

Oliveira, Mário de. "O 'habitat' nas zonas suburbanas de Quelimane: Um caso positivo de formação de sociedades multiraciais." *Geographica: Revista da Sociedade de Geografia de Lisboa*, no. 3 (1965): 67–75.

———. *Problemas essenciais do urbanismo no Ultramar: Estruturas urbanas de integração e convivência.* Lisbon: Agência-Geral do Ultramar, 1962.

Oppenheimer, Jochen, and Isabel Raposo. *Pobreza em Maputo.* Lisbon: Ministério do Trabalho e da Solidariedade, Departamento de Cooperação, 2002.

———. eds. *Subúrbios de Luanda e Maputo.* Lisbon: Edições Calibri, 2007.

Parnell, Stephen. "The Meanings of Concrete: Introduction." *Journal of Architecture* 20, no. 3 (2015): 371–75.

Pena, Areosa. *O cronista.* Edited by Sol Carvalho. Maputo: Cadernos Tempo, n.d.

Penvenne, Jeanne Marie. *African Workers and Colonial Racism: Mozambican Strategies and Struggles in Lourenço Marques, 1877–1962.* Portsmouth, NH: Heinemann, 1995.

———. "A Luta Continua! Recent Literature on Mozambique." *International Journal of African Historical Studies* 18, no. 1 (1985): 109–38.

———. "Fotografando Lourenço Marques: A cidade e os seus habitantes de 1960 a 1975." In *Os outros da colonização: Ensaios sobre o colonialismo tardio em Moçambique,* edited by Cláudia Castelo, Omar Ribeiro Thomaz, Sebastião Nascimento, and Teresa Cruz e Silva, 173–92. Lisbon: Imprensa de Ciências Sociais, 2012.

———. "'Here We All Walked with Fear': The Mozambican Labor System and the Workers of Lourenço Marques, 1945–1962." In *Struggle for the City: Migrant Labor, Capital, and the State in Urban Africa,* edited by Frederick Cooper, 131–66. Beverly Hills, CA: Sage Publications, 1983.

———. "Mozambique: A Tapestry of Conflict." In *History of Central Africa: The Contemporary Years since 1960,* edited by David Birmingham and Phyllis Martin, 243–46. London: Longman, 1998.

———. "Seeking the Factory for Women: Mozambican Urbanization in the Late Colonial Era." *Journal of Urban History* 23, no. 3 (1997): 368–69.

———. "Settling against the Tide: The Layered Contradictions of Twentieth-Century Portuguese Settlement in Mozambique." In *Settler Colonialism in the Twentieth Century: Projects, Practices, Legacies,* edited by Caroline Elkins and Susan Pedersen, 79–94. New York: Taylor and Francis, 2005.

———. "Two Tales of a City: Lourenço Marques, 1945–1975." *Portuguese Studies Review* 19, no. 1–2 (2011): 249–69.

———. "'We Are All Portuguese!' Challenging the Political Economy of Assimilation: Lourenço Marques, 1870–1933." In *The Creation of Tribalism in Southern Africa,* edited by Leroy Vail, 255–88. London: Currey, 1989.

———. *Women, Migration and the Cashew Economy in Southern Mozambique,*

1945–1975. Woodbridge, UK: James Currey, 2015.

Pereira de Lima, Alfredo. "Casas que fizeram Lourenço Marques." *Studia*, no. 24 (1968): 7–71.

——. *Pedras que já não falam*. Lourenço Marques: Tipografia Notícias, 1972.

Perlman, Janice E. *The Myth of Marginality: Urban Poverty and Politics in Rio de Janeiro*. Berkeley: University of California Press, 1976.

Pimenta, Fernando Tavares. "Decolonisation Postponed: The Failure of the Colonial Politics of Marcelo Caetano (1968–1974)." *Social Dynamics* 42, no. 1 (2016): 12–30.

Pine, Adam M. "The Performativity of Urban Citizenship." *Environment and Planning A* 42 (2010): 1103–20.

Pinsky, Barry. "Territorial Dilemmas: Changing Urban Life." In *A Difficult Road: The Transition to Socialism in Mozambique*, edited by John S. Saul, 279–315. New York: Monthly Review Press, 1985.

Pitcher, M. Anne. *Transforming Mozambique: The Politics of Privatization, 1975–2000*. Cambridge: Cambridge University Press, 2002.

Plageman, Nate. *Highlife Saturday Night: Popular Music and Social Change in Urban Ghana*. Bloomington: Indiana University Press, 2013.

Ponte, Bruno da, ed. *Gostar de ler: Selecção de crónicas apontamentos e comentários*. Maputo: Cadernos Tempo, 1981.

Prochaska, David. *Making Algeria French: Colonialism in Bône, 1870–1920*. Cambridge: Cambridge University Press, 1990.

Quayson, Ato. *Oxford Street, Accra: City Life and the Itineraries of Transnationalism*. Durham, NC: Duke University Press, 2014.

Quembo, Carlos Domingos. *Poder do poder: Operação Produção e a invenção dos "improdutivos" urbanos no Moçambique socialista, 1983–1988*. Maputo: Alcance, 2017.

Rangel, Ricardo. *Pão nosso de cada noite*. Maputo: Marimbique, 2004.

Ranger, Terence. *Bulawayo Burning: The Social History of a Southern African City, 1893–1960*. Woodbridge, UK: James Currey, 2010.

Rao, Vyjayanthi. "Slum as Theory: The South/Asian City and Globalization." *International Journal of Urban and Regional Research* 30, no. 1 (2006): 225–32.

Raposo, Isabel, and Cristina Salvador. "Há diferença: Ali é cidade, aqui é subúrbio—Urbanidade dos bairros, tipos e estratégias de habitação em Luanda e Maputo." In *Subúrbios de Luanda e Maputo*, edited by Jochen Oppenheimer and Isabel Raposo, 105–38. Lisbon: Edições Calibri, 2007.

Ray, Carina E. *Crossing the Color Line: Race, Sex, and the Contested Politics of Colonialism in Ghana*. Athens: Ohio University Press, 2015.

Rebelo de Sousa, Marcelo. *Baltazar Rebelo de Sousa: Fotobiografia*. 2nd ed. Venda Nova, Port.: Bertrand Editora, 1999.

Ribeiro, Fátima, and António Sopa, eds. *140 anos de imprensa em Moçambique*. Maputo: Associação Moçambicana da Língua Portuguesa, 1996.

Rita-Ferreira, António. "Moçambique post–25 de Abril: Causas do êxodo da população de origem europeia e asiática." In *Moçambique: Cultura e história de um país*, 119–69. Publicações do Centro de Estudos Africanos 8. Coimbra, Port.: Universidade de Coimbra, 1988.

———. "Os africanos de Lourenço Marques." *Memórias do Instituto Científica de Moçambique*, series C, 9 (1967–68): 95–491.

Robertson, Claire C. *Sharing the Same Bowl: A Socioeconomic History of Women and Class in Accra, Ghana*. Bloomington: Indiana University Press, 1984.

Robinson, Jennifer. "Johannesburg's 1936 Empire Exhibition: Interaction, Segregation and Modernity in a South African City." *Journal of Southern African Studies* 29, no. 3 (2003): 759–89.

———. *Ordinary Cities: Between Modernity and Development*. New York: Routledge, 2006.

Rocha, Ilídio. *A imprensa de Moçambique: História e catálogo*. Lisbon: Livros do Brasil, 2000.

Rodrigues, Cristina Udelsmann. "Angolan Cities: Urban (Re)Segregation?" In *African Cities: Competing Claims on Urban Spaces*, edited by Francesca Locatelli and Paul Nugent, 37–54. Leiden: Brill, 2009.

Roy, Ananya, and Nezar AlSayyad, eds. *Urban Informality: Transnational Perspectives from the Middle East, Latin America, and South Asia*. Lanham, MD: Lexington Books, 2004.

Saevfors, Ingemar. *Maxaquene: A Comprehensive Account of the First Urban Upgrading Experience in the New Mozambique*. UNESCO, 1986.

Santiago, Miguel. *Pancho Guedes: Metamorfoses espaciais*. Casal de Cambra, Port.: Caleidoscópio, 2007.

Santos, António de Almeida. *Quinze meses no governo ao serviço da descolonização*. Porto: Edições ASA, 1975.

Sapire, Hilary. "Township Histories, Insurrection and Liberation in Late Apartheid South Africa." *South African Historical Journal* 65, no. 2 (2013): 167–98.

Saul, John S., ed. *A Difficult Road: The Transition to Socialism in Mozambique*. New York: Monthly Review Press, 1985.

Savele, Luís. *Teatro moçambicano: Três peças num só palco*. Maputo: FUNDAC, 2011.

Scott, James C. *Seeing Like a State: How Certain Schemes to Improve the Human Condition Have Failed*. New Haven, CT: Yale University Press, 1998.

Serviços de Centralização e Coordenação de Informações de Moçambique. *Moçambique na actualidade*. Lourenço Marques: Imprensa Nacional de Moçambique, 1974.

Sheldon, Kathleen. *Pounders of Grain: A History of Women, Work, and Politics in Mozambique*. Portsmouth, NH: Heinemann, 2002.

Sidaway, James D. "Urban and Regional Planning in Post-independence Mozambique." *International Journal of Urban and Regional Research* 17, no. 2 (1993): 241–59.

Sidaway, J. D., and M. Power. "Sociospatial Transformations in the 'Postsocialist' Periphery: The Case of Maputo, Mozambique." *Environment and Planning A* 27, no. 9 (1995): 1463–91.

Silva, Calane da. *Dos meninos da Malanga.* Maputo: Cadernos Tempo, 1982.

Silva, Carlos Nunes, ed. *Urban Planning in Lusophone African Countries.* Abingdon, UK: Routledge, 2015.

———. ed. *Urban Planning in Sub-Saharan Africa: Colonial and Post-colonial Planning Cultures.* Abingdon, UK: Routledge, 2015.

Simone, AbdouMaliq. *City Life from Jakarta to Dakar: Movements at the Crossroads.* New York: Routledge, 2010.

———. *For the City Yet to Come: Changing African Life in Four Cities.* Durham, NC: Duke University Press, 2004.

Sopa, António, and Bartolomeu Rungo. *Maputo: Roteiro histórico iconográfico da cidade.* Maputo: Centro de Estudos Brasileiros da Embaixada do Brasil, 2006.

Souto, Amélia Neves de. *Caetano e o ocaso do "Império": Administração e guerra colonial em Moçambique durante o Marcelismo (1968–1974).* Porto: Edições Afrontamento, 2007.

———. "Moçambique no período da descolonização portuguesa (1973–1974): Que descolonização?" In *Moçambique: Relações históricas, regionais e com países da CPLP,* edited by Augusto Nascimento, Aurélio Rocha, and Eugénia Rodrigues, 183–226. Maputo: Alcance, 2011.

Stepputat, Finn. "Marching for Progress: Rituals of Citizenship, State and Belonging in a High Andes District." *Bulletin of Latin American Research* 23, no. 2 (2004): 244–59.

Stoler, Anne Laura. "Rethinking Colonial Categories: European Communities and the Boundaries of Rule." *Comparative Studies in Society and History* 31, no. 1 (1989): 134–61.

Turner, John F. C. "Barriers and Channels for Housing Development in Modernizing Countries." *Journal of the American Institute of Planners* 33, no. 3 (1967): 167–81.

———. *Housing by People: Towards Autonomy in Building Environments.* London: Marion Boyars, 1976.

Turner, John F. C., and Robert Fichter, eds. *Freedom to Build: Dweller Control of the Housing Process.* New York: Macmillan, 1972.

Van Onselen, Charles. *New Babylon, New Nineveh: Everyday Life on the Witwatersrand, 1886–1914.* Johannesburg: Jonathan Ball, 2001.

Vasudevan, Alexander. *The Autonomous City: A History of Urban Squatting.* London: Verso, 2017.

Veloso, Jacinto. *Memórias em voo rasante.* 3rd ed. Maputo: JVCI, 2007.

Vieira, Sérgio. *Participei, por isso testemunho.* 2nd ed. Maputo: Editorial Ndjira, 2011.

Vines, Alex. *Renamo: Terrorism in Mozambique.* London: James Currey, 1991.

Vivet, Jeanne. *Os deslocados de guerra em Maputo: Percursos migratórios, "citadinização" e transformações urbanas da capital moçambicana (1976–2010)*. Maputo: Alcance, 2015.

West, Harry G. *Kupilikula: Governance and the Invisible Realm in Mozambique*. Chicago: University of Chicago Press, 2005.

West, Michael O. *The Rise of an African Middle Class: Colonial Zimbabwe, 1898–1965*. Bloomington: Indiana University Press, 2002.

White, Luise. *The Comforts of Home: Prostitution in Colonial Nairobi*. Chicago: University of Chicago Press, 1990.

——. "Hodgepodge Historiography: Documents, Itineraries, and the Absence of Archives." *History in Africa* 42 (2015): 309–18.

Wright, Gwendolyn. *The Politics of Design in French Colonial Urbanism*. Chicago: University of Chicago Press, 1991.

Yeoh, Brenda S. A. *Contesting Space: Power Relations and the Urban Built Environment in Colonial Singapore*. Kuala Lumpur: Oxford University Press, 1996.

Zitoun, Madani Safar. "Les stratégies résidentielles des acteurs sociaux dans un contexte de modernisation bloquée: Alger 1962–1998." In *La ville et l'urbain dans le monde arabe et en Europe: Acteurs, organisations et territoires*, edited by Pierre Robert Baduel, 109–33. Tunis: Institut de Recherche sur le Maghreb Contemporain, 2009.

UNPUBLISHED WORKS AND THESES

Alemayehu, Elias Yitbarek. "Revisiting 'Slums,' Revealing Responses: Urban Upgrading in Tenant-Dominated Inner-City Settlements, in Addis Ababa, Ethiopia." PhD diss., Norwegian University of Science and Technology, 2008.

Ângelo, Mário. "A indústria de cimento no contexto de transição moçambicana, c. 1960–1994, com referência especial à Fábrica de Cimentos da Matola." Undergraduate thesis, Universidade Eduardo Mondlane, 2005.

Benson, Koni. "Crossroads Continues: Histories of Women Mobilizing against Forced Removals and for Housing in Cape Town, South Africa, 1975–2005." PhD diss., University of Minnesota, 2009.

Castela, Tiago. "A Liberal Space: A History of the Illegalized Working-Class Extensions of Lisbon." PhD diss., University of California–Berkeley, 2011.

Cravinho, João Titterington Gomes. "Modernizing Mozambique: Frelimo Ideology and the Frelimo State." PhD diss., University of Oxford, 1995.

Filipe, Eléusio dos Prazeres Viegas. "'Where Are the Mozambican Musicians?': Music, Marrabenta, and National Identity in Lourenço Marques, Mozambique, 1950s–1975." PhD diss., University of Minnesota, 2012.

Frates, L. Lloys. "Domestic Space and Gender Relations amongst the Swahili." Master's thesis, University of California–Los Angeles, 1994.

———. "Memory of Place, the Place of Memory: Women's Narrations of Late Colonial Lourenço Marques, Mozambique." PhD diss., University of California–Los Angeles, 2002.

Gastrow, Claudia. "Negotiated Settlements: Housing and the Aesthetics of Citizenship in Luanda, Angola." PhD diss., University of Chicago, 2014.

Gonçalves, Euclides. "Chronopolitics: Public Events and the Temporalities of State Power in Mozambique." PhD diss., University of the Witwatersrand, 2012.

Jorge, Sílvia Manuela Branco. "Lugares interditos: Os bairros pericentrais autoproduzidos de Maputo." PhD diss., Universidade de Lisboa, 2017.

Lundin, Iraê Baptista. "Negotiating Transformation: Urban Livelihoods in Maputo Adapting to Thirty Years of Political and Economic Changes." PhD diss., Göteborg University, 2007.

Machava, Benedito Luís. "The Morality of Revolution: Urban Cleanup Campaigns, Reeducation Camps, and Citizenship in Socialist Mozambique (1974-1988)." PhD diss., University of Michigan, 2018.

Macuacua, Helena Alberto. "Um breve historial sobre o Bairro Indígena." Manuscript, n.d.

Martins, Olga. "'Va ka Mpfumu,' Lourenço Marques, e Maputo: Uma inter-relação problemática." Undergraduate thesis, Universidade Eduardo Mondlane, 1995.

Myers, Garth Andrew. "Reconstructing Ng'ambo: Town Planning and Development on the Other Side of Zanzibar." PhD diss., University of California–Los Angeles, 1993.

Neto, Maria da Conceição. "In Town and Out of Town: A Social History of Huambo (Angola)." PhD diss., School of Oriental and African Studies, 2012.

Nielsen, Morten. "In the Vicinity of the State: House Construction, Personhood, and the State in Maputo, Mozambique." PhD diss., University of Copenhagen, 2008.

Penvenne, Jeanne Marie. "A History of African Labor in Lourenço Marques, Mozambique, 1877–1950." PhD diss., Boston University, 1982.

Pery, Amorim Remigio Manuel. "A evolução da economia moçambicana e a promoção do bem-estar socioeconómico (1960–2001)." Undergraduate thesis, Universidade Eduardo Mondlane, 2004.

Sumich, Jason Michael. "Elites and Modernity in Mozambique." PhD diss., London School of Economics, 2005.

Thompson, Drew A. "Aim, Focus, Shoot: Photographic Narratives of War, Independence, and Imagination in Mozambique, 1950 to 1993." PhD diss., University of Minnesota, 2013.

Tomás, António Andrade. "Refracted Governmentality: Space, Politics, and Social Structure in Contemporary Luanda." PhD diss., Columbia University, 2012.

Zamparoni, Valdemir Donizette. "Entre *narros* e *mulungos*: Colonialismo e paisagem social em Lourenço Marques, c. 1890–c. 1940." PhD diss., Universidade de São Paulo, 1998.

INDEX

Numbers in *italics* signify graphics.

INDEX

Machava, 65, 104–5, 106
Machava, Benedito, 161
Machel, Samora, 157, 175, 177, 209–10; on
cities as strongholds of evil, 174; on com-
munal neighborhoods, 209; death of,
220; housing nationalization announced
by, 27–28, 151–52, 163–64, 169
Macuacua, Helena, 166
Maduela, Josefa Alfonso, 122–23
Mafalala, 24, 30, 130, 137, 190, 211
Mahumane, Anastásia Titos, 223–24
Makhulu, Anne-Maria, 14
Malangatana (Ngwenya), 128, 143–44
Malé, Daniel, 113–16, 117, 134, 137–38
Malé, Rute, 112
Malendya, Alice, 136–37
Malhangalene, 56–57, 159, 274n25
Malhazine, 212
Maninguane, Essau Ezequia, 138
Manjate, Alfredo, 147, 148, 158, 160
Manjate, Inácio, 137
Maputo (formerly Lourenço Marques):
building culture in, 223; and decoloni-
zation, 153; economic revitalization of,
221; government as landlord in, 18, 155,
168, 169, 173, 183, 220; infrastructural
capacity of, 208; map of, 8; municipal
government of, 207; name change from
Lourenço Marques, 152, 263n4; population growth of, 12, 208, 233n16; port of,
221; refugee influx into, 154–55, 180–81.
See also City of Cement; Lourenço
Marques; subúrbios
Mário, Bernardo Ernesto, 138
market reforms, 219, 220–21
Marques, Dinis, 59
marrabenta, 72
Marxism-Leninism, 154, 219, 266n43
masonry house construction: of commercial establishments, 147, 262n106; demand for, 114, 118, 123–24; emergence of
suburban, 78; facing possible demolition,
9, 114–15, 138, 139–40; getting permits
for, 9, 198, 207; neighbors' jealousies
about, 195; number of, 138–39; postindependence expansion of, 149, 221–22;
and roofs, 118, 119, 140; sturdiness of,
140. See also cement; clandestine house
construction; concrete blocks
Matate, Adriano, 71, 209–11, 216

Matola, 119, 218; diversity of, 142; government-subsidized housing projects
in, 65, 104–5, 106, 118, 125, 186, 189; as
Lourenço Marques satellite city, 86, 117;
population growth in, 12, 233n16; postindependence government as landlord in,
220; site-and-service project in, 189–90
Mavalane, 36
Maxaquene Project, 188–91; administration
of, 207; and awakening of expectations,
195–98; critics of, 206–7; funding of, 207,
276n58; and grid layout, 200, 216; and
mobilization of neighbors, 198, 202–7;
photos of, *192, 193, 201, 217*; and plot
dimensions, 197–98; and straight roads,
194, 195; surveying for, 196; symbolic
value of, 208; and tenure recognition,
196, 198; and water access, 188, 204–5;
women's involvement in, 204
migration to cities, 43, 62, 69–70, 129
miners' indemnification, 64, 245n123
Ministry of Public Works and Housing,
205–6
Ministry of the Ultramar, 96, 99, 142, 230
Momplé, Lília, 28, 108–9
Mondlane, Eduardo, 46, 95, 102
Mondlane, Janet, 20–21
Monteiro, Oscar, 208–9
Moreira, Adriano, 96–98
Morocco, 237–38n7
Mozambique constitution, 160–61, 267n50
Mozambique economy: growth of, 221–22;
neoliberal and market reforms of,
219–20, 222, 223; and shortages, 149,
175, 181
Muhale, Lídia Manhiça, 73
Myers, Garth, 14, 76

Näslund, Ruth, *49, 141*
National Housing Directorate, 186, 190,
205–6
nationalization, housing, 151–83; and
neighbor relations, 172–73; in Angola,
Algeria, and Tanzania, 169–70; from
below, 168–74, 187; and Chamanculo,
158, 166, 171–72, 221; and City of Cement, 27, 163, 178–79, 183; decree for,
163–64, 267n51; government as landlord
following, 18, 155, 168, 169, 173, 183,
220; as improvisation, 154, 168;